The Fate of Family Farming

# The Fate of

# FAMILY FARMING

## Variations on an American Idea

*Ronald Jager*

University Press of New England

Hanover and London

Published by University Press of New England,
One Court Street, Lebanon, NH 03766
www.upne.com
© 2004 by Ronald Jager
Printed in the United States of America
5 4 3 2 1

Library of Congress Cataloging-in-Publication Data

Jager, Ronald.
    The fate of family farming : variations on an American idea / Ronald
Jager.
        p.    cm.
    ISBN 1–58465–026–5 (cloth : alk. paper)
    1. Agriculture—United States.   2. Family farms—United States.
3. Agricultural productivity—United States.   I. Title.
    S441.J27 2004
    338.1'6'0973—dc22                                    2003025293

*For Grace—again*

In contrast with the long-term trend of declining farm numbers, the 1990s saw relative stability in the number of farms and even modest increases since 1996.

—UNITED STATES DEPARTMENT OF AGRICULTURE,
*Food and Agriculture Policy: Taking Stock for the New Century* (2001), p. 24

Every improvement in husbandry should be gratefully received and peculiarly fostered in this Country, not only as promoting the interests and lessening the labour of the farmer, but as advancing our respectability in a national point of view; for in the present State of America, our welfare and prosperity depend upon the cultivation of our lands.

—GEORGE WASHINGTON, letter to Samuel Chamberlain, April 3, 1788

# Contents

## Part III.  Prospects

# *Preface*

*The family farm*: it is way up there next to God and country, close to baseball and motherhood.

Perhaps other nations too have regarded their family farm tradition as central to their national life, but we Americans have been especially blatant about it. For us it is not only a matter of food and livelihood, not just pride and tradition; it has to do with our national origins, our history, our literary culture, and our perceived character as well. Family farming belongs to our secular theology.

From seventeenth-century American beginnings, livelihood and even survival itself depended almost wholly upon agriculture; and from the beginning, too, our idea and ideal of community was firmly shaped by rural experience. In the eighteenth century, so it was said, a collection of raw yeomen wrested independence from a nation of shopkeepers—or was it an empire? American rural character and agrarian culture were proudly celebrated by its earliest spokesmen, such as Thomas Jefferson and Hector St. John de Crèvecoeur. Jefferson affirmed that "our governments will remain virtuous for many centuries; as long as they are chiefly agricultural." And somehow this original self-congratulatory attitude has remained in the American air ever since.

By the nineteenth century the American family farm, dividing and multiplying itself by hundreds of thousands across the flat and fertile plains of the Midwest and eventually trickling down the Pacific Coast, had become a kind of national icon, despite the fact that by that time it had also become, as an image, blurred or disfigured in countless ways, including the dust and roar of the Industrial Revolution. How could *family farm* be sustained as a national defining image in full view of the southern slave plantation, the wide-open western prairies, the northern factory city, or, for that matter, the bleak and abandoned family farms in the Northeast?

Yet it was. By the beginning of the twentieth century we still chose to know ourselves as primarily a rural nation, the family farm the mythic bedrock—historical, social, moral, economic—on which rested all, or nearly all, other institutions. Altogether it was a good and usable national myth, not so much fictional as allegorical, and with sufficient literal truth supporting it to keep it safely aloft.

Indeed, in 1907 President Theodore Roosevelt firmly declared: "Nothing is more important to this country than the perpetuation of our system of medium-sized farms worked by their owners. We do not want to see our farmers sink to the condition of the peasants of the old world, barely able to live on their small holdings, nor do we want to see their places taken by wealthy men owning enormous estates which they work purely by tenants and hired servants." It was a sentiment that prevailed in most regions of the country right through World War II. But in the last half of the twentieth century we came to see, reluctantly, that our favorite national family farm narrative was scarcely valid anymore. During that half century the number of American working farms decreased by two-thirds—roughly, from over six million to about two million. In the beginning we were a nation over 90 percent of whose people lived directly from the farm; today it is between 1 and 2 percent, and if that trend continues, the future of family farming does not imply a long or pleasant story. Yet the fate of family farming remains a topic so vast and significant, so intimately related to our food and health, and of such charged and hopeful interest, that one might properly hesitate to claim it as title for a book.

Many voices can be heard from the American farmland, some of them expressed in elegiac tones, and some of them employing venerable and solemn terms—"husbandry," "tillage," "yeomanry," "agrarian." We Americans may have departed the countryside in droves, we may have shut down numerous family farms, we may have watched our farmers go corporate and our farms grow huge and industrial, but we have certainly not stopped talking about them. A few years ago a National Commission on Small Farms issued an exemplary report, *A Time to Act*, with many persuasive recommendations designed to support small family farms; however, on many of these recommendations the federal government has not yet found it time to act. Meanwhile historians, sociologists, economists, journalists, and sundry others, including some commissions and politicians and, indeed, some splendidly eloquent farmers and literary people—these all have their say, one way or another, on family farming and its destiny. And although hardly any open-minded observers applaud present major trends and directions, altogether they do bring in from their many and varied fields a continuing harvest of news, occasionally some of it good news.

Here, for example, is a bit of good news: farming is still the chief family enterprise in the nation. The intimate connection that has always bound *families* and *farms* is still there, despite the bleak message in the oft told tale of the decline of the family farm. What was true two hundred years ago is true today: of all large American businesses, farming alone has the major share of its workforce made up of families; and, conversely, whenever families are in an enterprise together they are statistically more likely to be in farming than in any other single line of work. This is the literal and sustaining part of the old national myth that still holds. I call it good news, for it bespeaks a cultural bond that evidently is not easily broken or dissolved, no matter how the total numbers change or diminish. If *family farm* is a phrase no longer tautological, it is not yet an oxymoron.

So I, for one, rejoice at the clamor of all those varied voices out there, knowing that family farming is hardly the kind of topic on which some single wise person is now going to write the one definitive essay or book—though Wendell Berry came close, a quarter century ago, with *The Unsettling of America*. In general, there are too many regions and traditions for that; there are far, far too many varieties and shapes of American family farms, too many ironies and ambiguities in the story. So much the better, then, that all sorts of professionals, farmers, and writers are in on this conversation. Altogether, they have more than once surveyed and plowed up this old field; but there will always be more rocks to turn over. We need to be reminded ever and again of the vital links between farm and food. For ours is a nation where for the first time in history farmers are statistically insignificant, and usually out of sight and out of mind. Food is rarely thought of as issuing from the earth and the labors of our hands: we see it as just there, abundant, like air and water—and usually so inexpensive that it loses its symbolic value. The intimate link between the world's farms and the world's food, indeed the vital necessity of farming itself, to say nothing of its joys and hazards, escapes the focused attention of most of the people most of the time.

Therefore, I write not only for those whose personal memory or experience of a family farm is still alive, or for those who love farming or love the idea of it, or their dream of it, or who want to know where it is going and why, but also for those willing to be on more familiar terms with our long and expressive national traditions of agriculture, and with its central place in the lives of almost all our forebears. I endeavor not only to portray family farming in terms of its past and possible future but also to view farming from the inside as well as from the outside.

My own perspective is from the American Northeast. My aim is not to survey the region's farming but only to make an example of it—an example that often and in many ways extends to the nation as a whole. New England is one of our oldest farming regions, though certainly not the best; and American family farming was more or less invented on these chilly coasts and hillsides, and valued here already long before we were a nation, indeed before our founding fathers, many of whom were farmers and proud of it, laid down the premise that owner-operated agriculture, such as New England's, is the most sure foundation of a good society. Here in the Northeast former farmland is everywhere, its footprints plainly traceable in many a mossy granite wall, so farming evokes rich historical memories; and present-day farms are intermittent, invaluable, and precarious, so the state of farming is a living concern.

Throughout this book, my aim is not to forecast or prescribe but only to illuminate the fate of family farming. So this book has a bold title and a modest purpose. It engages a topic that is still morally charged in America, one that has both inspired and troubled us for a very long time, and that we may hope will be with us into the far future.

*November 2003*                                                                R.J.

# *Acknowledgments*

I am pleased to acknowledge permission from Wendell Berry and from Counterpoint, Washington, D.C., to quote from Wendell Berry's poetry in chapter 3.

My sincere thanks are due and happily paid to the farmers who welcomed me to their farmsteads and who showed and told me what they were doing and why: Bruce and Liz Bascom, Archie and Helen Coll, Erick and Susan Leadbeater, Hans and Julia Eccard, and also George and John Eccard and Margaretha Eccardt—as well as to all those who work on these farms, only some of whom I have met, but to all of whom I wish to pay my respects. I thank other friends who offered seasonal thoughts and sound advice, some of which I was wise enough to take. Ellen Wicklum at the University Press of New England was most encouraging and extremely helpful, and her sub-editor, Will Hively, was absolutely superb in saving me from slips and inconsistencies. I also wish to thank Marvin Konya. Steve Taylor, Commissioner of the New Hampshire Department of Agriculture, Markets, and Food, and Professor Otho Wells, of the University of New Hampshire, have my hearty thanks; they were especially reliable and valuable allies in this endeavor.

In many special ways members of my family were not only supportive but helped greatly by reading and offering valuable comments on the entire book: my brother Marvin Jager, who many years ago first led me into the paths of farming lore; also, my son and daughter-in-law, Colin and Wendy Jager. Most of all, with this book as with others, I owe an unrepayable debt to my wife Grace, who has read and discussed with me every version and phase of this book, and gently focused my attention on its shortcomings. Such support is beyond price but, fortunately, not beyond love.

However, if there are mistakes in this book one or several of the above should probably have caught them, so I am also willing to share the reproach with them. But most of all I am pleased to share my immense gratitude to all for their patience and help.

# Introduction: Field Survey

## *Husbandry and Farming*

The Bible is often an earthy book, much of it written by people of the land. We know that when the ancient Hebrews settled in Canaan, the Promised Land, they became farmers, and that a common ideal was that each family would cultivate its own plot and dwell in peace beneath "its own vine and fig tree." However, when you look into the King James Authorized Version of the Bible, translated into English in 1611, you cannot find a farmer in the book. But there are husbandmen all over the place. Farming is an ancient discipline, of course, but the words "farmer" and "farming" in their present meanings are not old, not nearly as old as the English language, or even the English Bible. Indeed, about the time the Europeans began shifting attention to America for their future, which happened to coincide with the publication of the Authorized Version of the Bible, the English language was undergoing a shift as well. At that time and throughout the previous century those who were stewards of the earth were known not as farmers but as husbandmen.

Why not just call it farming? Roughly speaking, in those days farming would have been leasing (farming out) something, land or whatever, but not necessarily cultivating it. To "farm" was to put out for hire the privilege or duty of getting a job done—whether it was cultivating land, collecting rent, calming the natives, defending the realm, or whatever. For example, when Shakespeare's Richard II was concerned about cash flow and said "we are inforc'd to farm our royall realm," he was not thinking about planting more corn but of collecting rent on his properties. ("Farm" is an English word, earlier often spelled "ferme," but deriving from Latin "firma," signifying that the price of the lease was fixed, or firm.)

"Husbandry" was a good English word, and it denoted an old and

honored profession, but it hadn't started out in England. The word crossed
the North Sea from Scandinavia into what was to become the English language more than a thousand years ago, and it came in two pieces: "hus"
in Old English meant "house," and "bonda" had to do with with living
within and taking care of the premises. Thus the master of a household and
its grounds, the one responsible for its upkeep, was designated a "husband," or "husbandman," and eventually "husbandry" became identified
with care of the land, and "husband" with care of the household. (Many of
these facts can be teased out of the relevant entries in the *Oxford English
Dictionary*.) English handbooks on farm life in the sixteenth and early
seventeenth centuries bore this out in their titles — *Boke of Husbandry, The
Whole Art and Trade of Husbandry, The English Husbandman, Farewell
to Husbandry, Cheape and Good Husbandry, Epitome of Husbandry*. Inasmuch as *husbandry* included the household, in effect the family and the
entire domestic economy, we see here the roots of our later concept of
*family farm*.

In America, and fairly quickly in the seventeenth century, as the immigrant people slowly and painfully learned to draw their living from the
American soil, those who were husbandmen became more and more
known as farmers. The two words — the ancient and honorable "husbandman," and the new and modern word "farmer" — diverged slightly,
not so much in meaning as in use and in overtone. The effect of this
upon our discourse is evident to this very day. A farmer labored in the soil
and did the hard and dirty work; a husbandman, especially in England,
was pursuing a profession. Moreover, tillage and land stewardship may
not have been his only profession, and many an English husbandman was
a Gentleman as well. The title "Gentleman" was often tried in America
(especially in official documents), but it did not take well here. Some
American farmers up to the time of the American Revolution titled themselves (in deeds) "Yeoman," but that did not take well either. America
soon became a land of farmers and farming, and by the time of the American Revolution, "farmer" was sometimes a proud title, even self-assertive,
a way of declaring that we are a classless society of equals. John Adams was
proud of his farmer heritage, and he often said so, and the word started
to appear in American book titles, most notably Crèvecoeur's 1782 *Letters
from an American Farmer*. But for all of that, husbandry did not just
disappear. In fact, it appeared in the title of the first American book on
agriculture, namely, Jared Eliot's *Essays upon Field Husbandry in New England* (1763).

Here lies a simple and important fact: "husbandry" and "husbandmen" were biblical terms, and they have long retained something of their elevated and biblical overtones. Professional honor and dignity, the production of life-sustaining food, a sense of history and of faithful nurture and care for a resource—these and other implications have long been attached to the idea of husbandry. God Himself engages in a kind of divine husbandry, according to Saint Paul in his first letter to the Corinthians. It may not be entirely without significance that the word "husbandry" was pushed to the background in America as restless settlers abandoned exhausted lands and moved on to new ones. To think of farming as husbandry is to think of it in exalted terms, and Thoreau remarks that "ancient poetry and mythology suggest, at least, that husbandry was once a sacred art."[1]

*Farmers*

This is a book about husbandry, which means it is about farmers and farming and families. It is also about ideas. Many farmers, many kinds of farmers, walk around in this book: some from history, some from literature, some from memory, some from books, and most important, some from today's fields, all of them living and working variations on one enduring American idea.

*Part I: Traditions* introduces farmers from history and literature who have helped to form our ideas about agriculture, about husbandry. The oldest American farms stand in a tradition of nearly four hundred years, and I assume that the condition of agriculture is not separate from its traditions. We are all heirs of the notion, confirmed by centuries of experience, that the foremost gift and promise of America was its bounteous land, a place where food and freedom would be cultivated side by side. Chapter 1, "The Idea of Family Farming," puts the spotlight on four brief and particularly revealing moments within the four-hundred-year-long saga of American farming. Chapter 2, "Farming in New Hampshire," focuses on the development of farming in New Hampshire, my own state, a place rich in natural endowments, not all of them hospitable to farming. This state's terrain was always a decisive and formidable mixture: seacoast, high mountains, fertile river valleys, rolling rocky hills, granite everywhere. (An old Granite State farmer joke has it that if this country had been settled from the West Coast, then New Hampshire, when discovered, would have been just fenced as a park and never farmed at all.) In this chapter I offer New Hampshire's farm experience as representative, not necessarily typical, of farming in the Northeast. Chapter 3, "Agrarianism," waits upon three important twentieth-century farmers who expertly cultivate literature as well as field crops, namely Louis Bromfield, Victor Davis Hanson, and Wendell Berry. These writers greatly deepen the meaning of "agrarianism" even as they sharply illuminate the contours of different agricultural ideals.

Today's farmers enter in *Part II: Four Farms*, the narrative heart of the book. These are hard-core farmers who are too busy to write about farming, though all glad to demonstrate it and talk about it. Here we can taste the maple syrup, gather eggs, milk cows, munch apples. These farms not only grow crops, but to varying degrees they are businesses as well. I have deliberately sought out farms specializing, one each, in a cross section of traditional Northeast commodities—maple syrup, milk, eggs, apples. I have visited each farm repeatedly over the course of a couple of years, to get a sense of the routines and rhythms of each place, of the nitty-gritty of its dynamics, its products and markets, and especially its farmers themselves. I sought an inside view of things.

These are the farmers: Bruce and Liz Bascom of Acworth, New Hampshire (chapter 4, "Maple"), have forty thousand maple taps on the New Hampshire hillsides. They make ten thousand gallons of syrup each year, they buy and sell more by the gallon and barrel and truckload, and they have customers all over the world. Hans and Julia Eccard of Washington, New Hampshire (chapter 5, "Got Milk?"), who farm with their two sons, George and John and their families, have two hundred Holstein cows who nearly every year produce more milk to be sold for a lower price. Archie and Helen Coll of Jaffrey, New Hampshire (chapter 6, "Cornucopia"), who farm with their son Mark and his family, have more than ten thousand big red hens who appear to think about laying eggs all day every day. Erick and Susan Leadbeater (chapter 7, "Apples") have thousands of apple trees on a Hopkinton, New Hampshire, hilltop that has been a fruit farm for nearly a hundred years. In their idealistic moments these farmers and their families and thousands like them think of themselves as stewards of the earth and as food producers, and they all get up each morning and go back to the farming chores, and often they go to bed at night exhausted and satisfied. They won't easily switch to something easier.

Perhaps in some books farms like these would be neatly sliced into statistics: bushels of apples, dozens of eggs, gallons of syrup, pounds of milk, inputs, outputs, assets, dollars, costs, ratios, profits, losses, risks, personnel, and those numbers related to further statistics, plotted on graphs, and the whole related to trends in American farming, and so on. That is good and important work, but it is not my work. My endeavor is almost the exact opposite: to slip under the radar of statistics and just look carefully at these farms as individual living objects, struggling or triumphant, and their owners as farmers and laborers. Of course, innumerable farm topics and details are omitted—things I had not time or space to pursue, that I had not skills to make interesting, that I neglected to inquire into. Although I sought to catch and convey something of the texture of these farms, I do not suppose that I have penetrated to the heart of them, or can explain what makes them work. I am fully aware that each farm that has survived in this Northeast region represents more than a dozen that were once here and are no longer. That fact has its own eloquence. However, these chapters are designed not to prove something but to illustrate much. Portraits, not evaluations.

To look at a working farm with a view to literary summary is a sobering task. A family farm still has its dual nature: way of life, way of making a living. A half century back, however, farming was not only more comprehensible but closer to the public life: then you could describe it, explain it, and expect to connect it directly with what most readers of the day might observe in the countryside. Today's farming is less visible, and today's readers are farther from the field. Therefore, immediacy with farm and farmer is one thing I seek in these chapters. Visiting these farms, I often endeavor to focus my eyes and ears on what turns up right before me, to read it as best I can. I make the assumption that four farm portraits will be more revealing, disclose a richer spectrum of accessible farm experience, and so provide a deeper insight into farm realities than a single farm portrait more rounded and complete.

The three chapters of *Part III: Prospects* are analytic and more general, and therefore comprise the most speculative portion of the book. What, I am asking, do present tendencies suggest? Chapter 8, "The Ironies of Success," is an analytic inquiry, designed to provide some conceptual handles on American farming generally and on the deep ironies that beset its various versions of success. This chapter is inescapably abstract, but in a sense it is the analytic core of the book. Chapter 9, "Biotechnology and the Future," tackles a topic so much in the news, so controversial, and so full of portents that it cannot be ignored. Mine is an observer's perspective, which strives for objectivity, in an area where many powerful interests are already deeply committed. Finally, chapter 10, "The Soul of Agriculture," is, in a sense, the political heart of the book; it attempts to survey the realm of husbandry, of farming-families-food, as an historical whole, and to suggest a certain perspective upon it.

In the background of all this is the recurring idea of how radically farming has been transformed in the last half century—since I was a boy on a small midwestern farm, expecting to become a farmer. The changes on American farms since the middle of the twentieth century, in scale and technology and diverse other ways, are surely greater than those of any other fifty years in our national history. For one thing, we've lost two-thirds of our farms in that time. My own memory and experience of that other time, of the world before agribusiness—a place of small traditional farms and close communities—was the subject of an earlier book, *Eighty Acres: Elegy for a Family Farm.* And that world will sometimes serve as a reference point for the one portrayed here.

 *Part One*

# TRADITIONS

 Chapter 1

# The Idea of Family Farming:
# Four Historical Moments

When [our ancestors] would praise a worthy man their praise took this form: "good husbandman," "good farmer"; one so praised was thought to have received the greatest commendation. . . . It is from the farming class that the bravest men and the sturdiest soldiers come, their calling is most highly respected, their livelihood is most assured and is looked on with the least hostility, and those who are engaged in that pursuit are least inclined to be disaffected. —MARCUS PORCIUS CATO OF ROME, *De Agricultura* (circa 160 B.C.)

The eastern United States has known nearly four hundred years of farming, mostly by former Europeans, a saga that goes from Indian corn to genetically modified corn, a rich and complex narrative, with many a painful early failure and many a later ambiguous success. Long before the four centuries of European occupation, there stretches back an indefinitely long period of successful farming by Native Americans, concerning which we know very little; but what we understand very clearly is that the natives' long-established knowledge of agriculture was absolutely lifesaving for many of the innocents who first came here from abroad.

The four hundred years itself encompasses a field obviously much too large to be surveyed or summarized here, so I propose to look carefully at just four isolated but especially revealing "moments," one drawn from each of those four centuries, and each of which highlights a pivotal point in the American family farm story. They are moments that enable us to see not only the realities of farming but especially the perceptions of it.

*Seventeenth Century: Beginning Failures*

From a European point of view, summers along the Hudson and the Chesapeake and the Potomac were excessively hot and muggy, and winters in

New England were bitter cold—extremes largely unknown in Europe. Moreover, almost the entire landscape of the New World was covered with huge trees, and among the trees might be hostile Indians, and, throughout most of New England, beneath the trees were rocks. None of this was good news for husbandry, or farming; and most of those who first came were not farmers and, in fact, did not even expect to become farmers. Not a good way to start a country.

What the early emigrants to Virginia and New England did expect is often not very clear. Very diverse groups of individuals, they came mainly from urban or village areas of England, often with fatally vague notions of gaining a livelihood from the land. They were religious dissenters, Separatists and Puritans, tradesmen, indentured servants, textile workers, ex-soldiers, soldiers of fortune, fur traders, lumbermen, adventurers, gold seekers, clergymen, jailbirds, fishermen, carpenters, plus, especially in the Virginia colony, a collection of riffraff from the London streets gathered up each year and forcibly sent to America to make money for the Virginia Company. Only here and there a farmer or a farmer's son among them.

Unfortunately for them, the earliest data available—to them or to us—too often presents the New World in a light extravagantly favorable to agriculture. For hundreds of years, Native Americans had farmed the eastern seaboard, and they had the good sense and the poor tools to farm only the best and most tillable areas, the fertile river flood plains and the seacoast flatlands. They were highly successful at what they did, resourceful in the use of natural fertilizing techniques—and remarkably effective in arranging for women to do most of the work. Surely they never, ever imagined that they might someday be overrun by a foreign race of "farmers" who would actually try to cultivate the rocky and forested uplands. And they had no way of knowing that their modest successes at farming probably overly impressed the earliest Europeans who first saw them, namely, the palefaced sailors who drifted along the coast and gawked and wondered if they were gazing upon the Garden of Eden. To these Native Americans belonged the first commodity farming in this region, and their chief commodity was corn—organic corn from heirloom seed, as it happens, carefully selected for more than a thousand years.

Earliest reports of European voyagers tell of huge cornfields, up to a hundred acres or more, throughout some of the seaboard regions, usually interplanted with squash and pumpkins. A century before the settlement at Plymouth, Massachusetts, Geovanni da Verrazano enthusiastically reported a countryside "adapted to cultivation . . . and of so great fertility that whatever is sown there will yield an excellent crop." Did he know what he was talking about? No one was in a position to ask. But later, Samuel de Champlain, who explored farther inland, reported "a great deal of country cleared up and planted."[2] In 1589 the Englishman Richard Hakluyt published an account of New World travelers' reports (the book's title begins, *The Principall Navigations, Voiages, Traffiques and Discoveries*, and goes on for six lines), to which he added an enthusiastic "Discourse concerning Western Planting," urging the planting of colonies in this marvelous New World. First among many reasons Hakluyt listed for colonizing New England was this: "The soyle yeldeth, and may be made to yelde, all the severall comodities of Europe, and of all kingdomes, domynions, and territories that England tradeth with."[3] New England could be the farm for the trading empire of Old England. In fact, he foresaw a new destiny for the nation: planting colonies would produce robust adventure, create new markets, provide naval stores, supply raw materials, and so on.

*The Principall Navigations* was the kind of book, and appeared at such a time (the Spanish Armada had just been defeated), as was destined to make it a best-seller; and it bent the English exploratory imagination firmly toward America. It spurred the formation of London's Virginia Company and later of the Jamestown settlement in 1607. Hakluyt's book also fired up the adventurer who became the leader of the Jamestown Colony, Captain John Smith, and *his* book, in turn, published after he left Jamestown and focused on New England, once more turned the mind of England emphatically toward America, especially New England. In *A Description of New England*, published in England in 1616, Captain John Smith lavished his heaviest praise on "the Countrie of the Massachusets, which is the Paradise of all those parts. For heere are many Iles all planted with corne; groves, mulberries, salvage gardens, and good harbours."[4] Thus was the New World—a teeming paradise where anybody could come and just harvest the garden—enthusiastically publicized in Europe. In view of the disastrous early plantation attempts, one has to suppose that far too many exaggerated reports were far too naively believed.

English settlers learned the truth the brutal way. What we know as the initial Virginia Roanoke settlement, organized by Sir Walter Raleigh, struggled, faltered, and then mysteriously and completely vanished from the earth. The next settlement, in Jamestown in 1607, was immediately another catastrophe, though it is usually called, with insufficient irony, the first "successful" colony in the New World. Beginning with 144 settlers, the group was distracted by the futile search for gold, by widespread laziness, general quarrelsomeness, and the manufacturing of pitch and tar for its London sponsors, and was reduced by desertions, by starvation, scurvy, and other disease to a mere 38 within the first year. More settlers arrived and still more sickened, starved, and died the second year, and by the third year the remnant, who had not yet learned to feed themselves, were giving up and leaving, and were stopped only by another new shipload of settlers. It was to be a pattern: new arrivals "saved" the colonists, who for a long time seemed utterly to lack the skills and ingenuity to grow and find enough food to keep themselves healthy or alive. In the first fifteen years a total of nearly 10,000 settlers came to Jamestown, many of them picked up on London streets and many of them indentured to the London Virginia Company, but by the early 1620s there were just 2,000 there. Whereupon an Indian war cost them over 300 lives in one day. An English critic was said to have remarked: "Instead of a plantacion Virginia will shortly get the name of a slaughterhouse."[5] For nearly two decades, wars, disease, famine, and returnees took a toll of hundreds every year. The stalwart few learned slowly to forget gold and grow corn, which kept them from total starvation, and to raise tobacco, which they could not eat but which pleased the London capitalists who kept sending over new innocents. Such was the "successful" Jamestown Colony.

None of this seemed to deter John Smith (who was certainly a brave and able man, and also a colorful blowhard) from his propaganda. Although the Jamestown Colony struggled to learn even basic husbandry from the Indians, New England would be much better, he prophesied in his *Description of New England* (1616). Such a message played well in both England and Holland. Those we call the Pilgrims, being mostly religious Separatists (from the established Church of England) and thus by definition a contentious and independent lot, read Smith's book, read their Bibles, said good-bye to Holland, and in late July took a leaky boat to England, where they eventually were forced to abandon it. They piled the *Mayflower* to its gunnels with over a hundred passengers and set out for the New World *in the fall* and landed in New England *in the winter!* What could they have been thinking, to go to such a world with such preparation, and in such a season?

And what did they see when they got here? John Smith, they knew, had declared this region "the Paradise of all those parts" with "Iles all planted with corne" and with "gardens, and good harbours." Perhaps they would just harvest the garden. William Bradford, in his later history of the colony, wrote of their landing: "What could they see but a hideous & desolate wildernes, full of wild beasts & wild men?" He continued: "For summer being done, all things stand upon them with a wetherbeaten face; and the whole countrie, full of woods & thickets, represented a wild & savage heiw."[6] Some paradise.

As with the Jamestown Colony there were few farmers on this boat, no farming knowledge of the New World, and little farm equipment. Presumably, no one brings a plow to Paradise. As at Jamestown many, many suffered and died that first winter, more than half of them. Perhaps all would have died if they had not been extremely fortunate to find caches of Indian corn and beans that kept them alive and supplied them with seed for the next summer. Bradford admits: "[H]ere they got seed to plant them corn the next year, or else they might have starved, for they had none, nor any likelihood to get any." In the spring the Indians offered them cleared land for use and gave them more corn for seed. And Squanto, the English-speaking Indian, taught them how to plant corn, bless or fertilize it with fish, and intersperse it with peas, squash, and pumpkins—niche farming, so to speak. Even their own seeds failed them in this paradise: "Some English seed they sew, as wheat & pease, but it came not to good, either by badnes of the seed or latenes of the season, or both, or some other defecte."[7] Without Squanto's help it would certainly have been an even worse disaster, like the first Jamestown years. Instead, we got Thanksgiving Day. But the next year was nearly as bad as the first. We celebrate the Pilgrims' tough survivalism, which is real enough, and we pity them for their suffering, which was terrible, and we politely overlook their considerable follies. But competent husbandmen they certainly were not.

Our familiar and textbook understanding of the Jamestown and Plymouth Colonies ought to include the forthright admission that they constitute thoroughly tragic and embarrassing beginnings for a nation that was eventually to pride itself on its farming traditions. The first hard and bitter lesson the Plymouth settlers had to learn was that farming in this brave new world would be absolutely essential and would not be easy at all; and in New England it would be harder, and in the winter, not possible at all. They might have figured that out before setting sail, and done more preparing, but we have no evidence that they did. Indeed, such was their wisdom about country living that it would be twelve years before they had a plow in Plymouth.

A second lesson too they had to learn at Plymouth, and this was a more subtle one, namely, that independent family farms would be more effective than the communal farming over which they struggled and quarreled for the first year. In the second and third years land was leased to individuals by lot, and on a one-year basis, but by the fourth year they had figured out that effective individual *ownership* was essential to success. Bradford tells us that individuals "made suite to the governor to have some portion of land given them for continuance, and not by yearly lotte." Under the lease and lot system "that which the more industrious had brought into good culture (by much pains) one year, came to leave it the nexte, and often another might injoye it; so as the dressing of their lands were the more slighted over, & to lese profite."[8] Thus, by an appropriate accounting—though not commonly reckoned as such in the history books—the owner-operated American farm was, in effect, invented at Plymouth in 1624, and so authorized by Governor William Bradford. Three years later, with "the division of cattle," they took the further step of creating private ownership of livestock. Later, the Plymouth Company, which had initially sponsored the venture and to which some of the colonists had been indentured, sold out to the colonists themselves, thus confirming their ownership of the farms. Meanwhile, in Jamestown, free land for tobacco growing was being offered to settlers. In short, American husbandry was being invented, step by step, from the meanest scratch imaginable.

Unfortunately, early stages of other New World settlements followed again the melancholy pattern of early Jamestown and Plymouth: terrible hardships were endemic, while the settlers struggled desperately, with multiple deaths on every side, learning how to find and raise food. A settlement in the Massachusetts Bay at present-day Weymouth failed utterly in the 1620s, "the most of them dying and languishing away," the survivors being rescued from starvation and attacking Indians by the Plymouth Colony. The Puritan Massachusetts Bay settlement of 1630 presents the same horror story for the first year: food short, sickness rampant, some fleeing to the New Hampshire Colony on the Piscataway River, many, many dying: from "April 1630 until December following there died by estimation about two hundred at the least." We learn all this from Thomas Dudley, a founder and leader and later governor of the Bay Colony (and father of the poet Anne Bradstreet), who in March 1631 wrote a long and very detailed account of that first year of the Massachusetts Bay Colony to an English friend. He reported, among other things, that "the half of our cows and almost all our mares and goats sent us out of England died at sea in their passage hither" and also that about a hundred settlers had returned to England after the first summer "partly through fear of famine (not seeing other means than by their labor to feed themselves)." Also that in the autumn, by sailing to the far side of Cape Cod, they had succeeded in buying "one hundred bushels of corn . . . which helped us somewhat."[9]

Dudley's judgment was firm and to the point: if a settler came to New England "for worldly ends that can live well at home, he commits an error of which he will soon repent him." He was writing so candidly, he said, "lest other men should fall short of their expectations when they come hither, as we to our great prejudice did, by means of letters sent us from hence into England, wherein honest men out of a desire to draw over others to them wrote somewhat hyperbolically of many things here." Nevertheless, these survivors were not utterly dismayed: "we are left a people poor and contemptible," wrote Dudley, "yet such as trust in God, and are contented with our condition, being well assured that he will not fail nor forsake us." Noble Christians, these Massachusetts Bay Puritans, but not yet America's noble yeoman farmers.

At that time the good farmers in the country were the Native Americans—or, if Europeans, they were working hard and knowledgeably on banks of the the Mauritius (later Hudson) River in New Amsterdam. Henry Hudson, discoverer of that river from the Dutch ship *Halve Maan* in 1609, was reported to have said of the surrounding areas that "this is the most beautiful land to cultivate that I ever trod upon in my life," and it probably was. In 1625 the Dutch decided to turn their trading post on the Hudson River into a permanent colony, with farmers placed at the center. They successfully shipped over several shiploads of cattle, horses, hogs, and sheep as well as farming tools and seeds, and a number of farm families specially recruited to manage them. Their ships bore the pastoral names *Paert* (horse), *Koe* (cow), and *Schaep* (sheep), which was undoubtedly a very good omen.[10]

Initially, it appears that the Dutch alone understood what needed to be done to establish a successful beachhead along the Atlantic seaboard, even a viable fur trading post, as theirs was at first. In a way it was fundamentally simple: you had to send capable and industrious farmers, equip them with seeds and tools and stock, and provide them land and incentives. The Dutch purchased the island they first named "Manhattes" from the Indians, pastured and planted portions of it, soon developed large individual farms along the riverbanks with incentives to bring more farmers over, and eventually organized a successful farming community, surrounding a trading operation. By the end of 1627 there were two hundred colonists and thirty buildings on Manhattes. Most important—and in very marked contrast to Jamestown, Plymouth, Massachusetts Bay, and other failed attempts—from New Amsterdam we read no dreary and tragic tales of deaths year after year by dozens and hundreds from sickness and malnutrition. Very soon they had European fruit trees bearing fruit, and productive farms with multiple livestock; they were growing the first successful European grains, and within two decades they were even making their own wagons and plows.

The first period of English family farming in America was mostly disastrous. It simplifies, to be sure, but not unfairly, to say that the Dutch understood immediately what the English could scarcely grasp, namely, that going or being sent in the first wave to colonize in North America was almost a death sentence unless the venture, risky at its best, were so designed as to put farmers, farming equipment, and farming know-how at the very front and center of the operation. But if the English were late to grasp this, they eventually absorbed that stern lesson extremely well, for it became the unspoken principle of almost all subsequent inland development for over two hundred years, and in terrain often far less hospitable to farming than the original flatlands of the seacoast. The remembered tradition of the New England family farm, after all, belongs primarily to generations of English immigrants and their descendants, and their farms were not made in Indian clearings, but carved from a rocky and forested wilderness.

*Eighteenth Century: Founding Farmers*

Although it was not a good agricultural beginning for New England, it was *only* a beginning. Subsequent periods of success, resiliency, and entrepreneurship on American family farms have pretty well obscured the very early disastrous memories and records, and reviews of American agriculture usually start at some point *after* these woeful beginnings. Thus Walter Ebeling writes in a well-known history of American agriculture, *The Fruited Plain*: "One remembers the English settlers of New England principally for having given Americans their initial impetus toward the free, independent, self-reliant farm family that would one day loom so large in the dreams of Thomas Jefferson for our nation. They established a unique pattern of small farms owned by the families that tilled them."[11]

Yes, indeed, "the dreams of Thomas Jefferson for our nation." We would prefer to start there, although our history did not. Despite the fact that he managed a large plantation where slaves did the hard work, Jefferson has had a great influence on American ideas about farming and the family farm. He is a principal source of the literary tradition of agrarianism in this country—a position that might more rightly have gone to John Adams for, like his father and grandfathers before him, Adams was precisely the kind of family farmer that Jefferson venerated. Adams theorized less about family farming than did Jefferson, but he, especially his family and his forebears, did rather more of it, and he always wrote with conspicuous pride of his descent from "a line of virtuous, independent New England farmers."

While it is widely agreed that as political activists and creators of government and institutions the Revolutionary generation knows no equal in American history, so too it could be said—though it seldom is—that as a generation of thoughtful and educated *farmers* they are also unmatched in our history. It happens, for example, that some leaders among the nation's founding fathers, Adams and Jefferson conspicuous among them, were trained (mostly self-trained) both in classical literature and in farming, a most rare and remarkable combination of knowledge and skills. The classical writers they preferred were those who wrote not only on government but on agriculture. Both Jefferson and Adams, for example, admired Cicero's words on farming, a topic on which he tended to rhapsodize. They would have appreciated statements such as this: "The pleasures of farming . . . come closest of all things to a life of true wisdom. The bank, you might say, in which these pleasures keep their account is the earth itself. It never fails to honor their draft. . . . Personally, I incline to the opinion that no life could be happier than the farmer's. . . . The services he performs by the cultivation of the soil are beneficial to the entire human race."[12] Washington, Adams, Jefferson, Madison didn't say it any better, but they all said it often. Adams also read the Roman agriculture writers Porcius Cato (234 to 149 B.C.) and Marcus Varro (116 to 27 B.C.), and commented on his reading in letters to Jefferson, whom he knew would be interested, and who responded in kind. Both of them would have been very familiar with the passage from the first page of Cato's book quoted at the head of this chapter. After the Romans and for fifteen hundred years we seldom encounter extended sentiments along these lines, but they became common currency again among many of America's Revolutionary leaders.

After the Revolutionary War, when Adams was minister plenipotentiary to England and Jefferson had a similar office in Paris, Jefferson visited Adams, and the two Revolutionary friends took a coach tour together of farms and gardens in England, comparing what they saw with things

American. Jefferson very often discussed farming techniques face to face with Washington, and in their letters they discuss crop rotation, moldboard plows, manure, Washington's theories about interplanting corn and potatoes, and hosts of other rural topics—much more than politics. Jefferson visited New England and promptly concluded that he had seen the moral backbone of the new nation: small owner-operated farms. Indeed, it fell to Jefferson to leave us the most memorable statements of a position that many of the founding fathers shared. In *Notes on the State of Virginia* (1785) he wrote: "Those who labor in the earth are the chosen people of God, if ever He had a chosen people, whose breasts He has made His peculiar deposit for substantial and genuine virtue. It is the focus in which He keeps alive that sacred fire, which otherwise might escape from the face of the earth. Corruption of morals in the mass of cultivators is a phenomenon of which no age nor nation has furnished an example."[13] He may well have been thinking of his friend John Adams and his fellow New Englanders as he wrote this.

Jefferson's book, incidentally, was addressed primarily to a European audience, to those used to thinking of laborers in the earth as serfs or peasants, persons without possessions and without prospects. Therefore such words might have sounded strange to their ears, and probably Jefferson knew this and intended it, thus to imply strongly that in America things are radically different. The words are strange in another way to us, for by "those who labor in the earth" Jefferson was thinking of small Pennsylvania, New York, and New England farmers, and also of his own idealized self, up to his elbows in his gardens. He was probably not thinking of the slaves in his fields as the repository of "substantial and genuine virtue."

In a letter to John Jay (1785), Jefferson later elaborated on the agrarian theme: "Cultivators of the earth are the most valuable citizens. They are the most vigorous, the most independent, the most virtuous, and they are tied to their country and wedded to its liberty and interests, by the most lasting bonds. As long, therefore, as they can find employment in this line, I would not convert them into mariners, artisans or anything else."[14] From such statements—and many of a similar kind are to be found in Jefferson's letters—derives our understanding that Jefferson really desired to see the United States remain primarily an agricultural nation. Thus we come back to one of "the dreams of Thomas Jefferson for our nation." Although it is not likely that many others fully shared this part of his vision, it was, in a curious way, the view propounded by Richard Hakluyt two hundred years earlier: let America be Europe's farm, Europe be America's factory. America would remain a virtuous nation, Jefferson tried to convince himself, so long as it remained primarily rural, community oriented, and agricultural. It seems an ideal that never had much of a chance, historically impossible for a thousand practical reasons. But will they say the same of Vermont or New Hampshire a century hence? That fate and destiny could not allow them to remain rural?

It was the decade of the 1780s when Jefferson expressed these thoughts, the decade of the momentous national Constitutional Convention, the decade, too, in which his idealized vision for rural American received impetus from the passage of the Northwest Land Ordinance (without Jefferson's personal help, as it happens, for he was in Europe). In that same decade also, an American contemporary of Adams and Jefferson, though not one of the circle of founding fathers, inaugurated the full-blown American literary tradition of agrarianism—explicitly extolling rural values and native soil in terms made familiar by the Roman classical writers. This was the work of a French immigrant, Hector St. John de Crèvecoeur, whose *Letters from an American Farmer* (1782), published first in England, gave to all Europe an eloquent and detailed portrait of life in rural America. And a most favorable portrait it is, drawn from personal travels, careful observations, and successful experience as a farmer and family man. Crèvecoeur presented American farm life in terms the European peasant could hardly imagine; and he knew whereof he spoke, for as he wrote he was practicing what Jefferson would soon be preaching. A revealing passage includes this paean to what he perceived as the very foundation of the good life in this fabulous country, namely, American farm soil:

Precious soil, I say to myself, by what singular custom of law is it that thou wast made to constitute the riches of the freeholder? What should we American farmers be without the distinct possession of that soil? It feeds, it clothes us; from it we draw even a great exuberancy, our best meat, our richest drink; the very honey of our bees. . . . It has established all our rights; on it is founded our rank, our freedom, our power as citizens. . . .[15]

The panegyric that Crèvecoeur wrote to the American soil (which goes on for several paragraphs and ends with the declaration that this is "the true and only philosophy of the American farmer") is probably unlike anything in literature at the time. You can find something similar, perhaps, in Cicero, who knew how to praise the quality of life near to elemental things; but that takes us back almost two thousand years. Yet before the decade was out similar language was to be heard independently from Thomas Jefferson and then from others. It is as if American farming and farm life—and the values they implied for freemen—reached a new and explicit level of self-consciousness at the moment of the American Revolution.

In his *Letters*, Crèvecoeur affects to be merely James, a simple Pennsylvania farmer, born on the land he farms, although he was in fact a well-educated French immigrant, and a successful farmer in New York State. Crèvecoeur's true life story, even in sketchy outline, is much more dramatic than his adopted persona: it is full of high adventure, deep tragedy, and implausible success. He had come to this country as a soldier and surveyor, fought in the French and Indian Wars, and got wounded at the decisive Battle of Quebec. Shortly thereafter he renounced his military commission and appears to have become a kind of inward Quaker, averse to war and violence. He became a British subject, traveled extensively throughout the colonies as a surveyor and salesman, then married in the late 1760s and bought a farm in upstate New York. During the 1770s, the only quiet decade of his life, his was the happy life of a family man, farming and composing his *Letters* to an English friend. (He tells of attaching a little chair to his plow handles, so his young son could sit between his arms and ride the plow in the fields.) But during the Revolutionary War he was accused of Tory sympathies and, quite independently of that, he had to get to France to arrange for his children to inherit his French property; so he fled to New York City, was jailed there, then escaped to England with his book manuscript in his backpack, sold it to a British publisher, and went on to France.

When *Letters from an American Farmer* was published in England in 1782, the author, then in France, was quickly famous, and he used that fact as leverage for an appointment as French consul to the United States. Thus he arrived again in New York as a distinguished diplomat in 1783 just as the Revolutionary War was officially ended. Crèvecoeur learned that his farm had been destroyed by Indians (he had thought they were peaceable), that his wife was dead, and his children in Boston. After some years of success as French consul, during which he was elected to distinguished societies and probably made the acquaintance of Jefferson, he returned in ill health to France, where he struggled to stay out of the way of the French Revolution and wrote, before he died in 1813, another book about the United States, this time in French. His was not exactly the quiet life of a back-country farmer . . . but there had been that wonderful decade on the New York farm in the 1770s, which had generated his famous book.

For many decades the *Letters* remained well known in both Europe and America; it was published and reprinted in many European cities, and translated into French, Dutch, and German. It faded late in the nineteenth century, but today it is in print again, as it has been continuously since the 1920s. The letters form a mixed bag: celebration of farm and family life, theory about the making of Americans, a long account of Nantucket, a spirited and impressive attack on the institution of southern slavery, charming descriptions of birds and bees and snakes and other fauna, portraits of Indians (too sentimental, as it turned out), discourses on American manners and customs, many stories of farm life, and, lastly, a melancholy chapter, "Distresses of a Frontier Man," written as the upheavals of the Revolutionary War closed in upon him and his family. Pervading the book (last chapter excepted) is Crèvecoeur's genuine enthusiasm for his adopted country, and—what is mainly in point just now—for the capacity of American freedom and opportunity to remake downtrodden Europeans into a new human beings, especially in rural environments. His famous question, "What is this American, this new man?" has become a leading theme for social historians ever since. "Here we have in some measure regained the ancient dignity of our species," he declares, "our laws are simple and just; we are a race of cultivators; our cultivation is unrestrained; and therefore everything is prosperous and flourishing."[16] There can hardly be higher praise for one's adopted country.

The second letter ends, "I bless God for all the good He has given me; I envy no man's prosperity, and wish no other portion of happiness than that I may live to teach the same philosophy to my children and give each of them a farm, show them how to cultivate it, and be like their father, good, substantial, independent American farmers—an appellation which will be the most fortunate one a man of my class can possess so long as our civil government continues to shed blessings on our husbandry."[17]

Another typical letter gives voice to prophetic sentiments that Crèvecoeur imagines as issuing from the heart of the American continent itself: "If thou wilt work, I have bread for thee; if thou wilt be honest, sober, and industrious, I have greater rewards to confer on thee—ease and independence. I will give thee fields to feed and clothe thee, a comfortable fireside to sit by and tell thy children by what means thou has prospered. . . . I shall endow thee beside with the immunities of a freeman. . . . Go thou and work and till; thou shalt prosper, provided thou be just, grateful, and industrious."[18]

For Hector St. John de Crèvecoeur, a backcountry farmer when he wrote this, later an acclaimed author and an international diplomat, the opportunities available in the vast American lands were so many and so rich, especially for farmers, when compared with anything ever available to all the ages of European peasantry, that political rebellion against England, leading to violence, was irrelevant.

It simplifies, but not unfairly, to say that the Revolutionary generation was responsible not only for the intellectual framework of our government but also for the first full intellectual expression of what they believed at the time to be the most important social institution, namely, their owner-operated system of agriculture. Both government and farm were perceived and venerated as radical alternatives to traditional European models. Farmers were not just feeding their families, as they had for generations; they were affirming a system of values, a way of life—looking to "the immunities of a freeman . . . provided thou be just, grateful, and industrious." With this Revolutionary moment American government *and* American farming became self-conscious.

## Nineteenth Century: Emerson and Thoreau

Throughout the ensuing two hundred years, and in countless times and places, writers have idealized the American yeoman farmer for his presumed virtues—thrift, self-sufficiency, authenticity, common sense, integrity, and so on, including Crèvecoeur's trinity of justice, gratitude, and industry. The farm scene itself, often an emblem of rural health and loyal family and simple virtue, has long been offered in symbolic contrast to the alleged decadence of urban existence—an easy and cliché-ridden contrast that goes back to the Roman writers on agriculture and was enthusiastically amplified by Jefferson. Indeed, from its native materials rural America has been manufacturing virtue in Currier & Ives settings for a very long time. In the middle of the nineteenth century few were better at manipulating such symbols and giving them voice on a grand scale than Daniel Webster—now posing as a humble landed aristocrat, now Massachusetts yeoman, now farmer entrepreneur, now simple farm boy from the New Hampshire hills. In an 1840 Boston speech Webster said typically: "We live in a country of small farms . . . a country in which men cultivate with their own hands, their own fee simple acres; drawing not only their subsistence but also their spirit of independence and manly freedom from the ground they plow. They are at once its owners, its cultivators, and its defenders."[19]

Historical vision, plain history, romance, idealism, and cheerful hum-
bug—by the middle of the century, they all mingled and merged in the
many-sided pastoral symbolism of the American family farm.

Two famous mid-nineteenth-century neighbors and friends who voiced
sharply contrasting views on these images, as well as on the realities behind
them, are, rather surprisingly, Henry David Thoreau and Ralph Waldo
Emerson. Neither is typically placed among the nation's agrarian spokesmen. Indeed, neither was really a farmer, although Emerson was a serious
gardener and Thoreau did some cultivating and pruning on Emerson's ten
acres of orchards and gardens, where hired farmers did more of the work.
And of course Thoreau famously farmed beans one summer on Emerson's
land at Walden Pond. Both frequently mingled with Concord farmers—
Emerson because he lived among them and hired them, and Thoreau
because he watched them daily on his rambles through the countryside and
worked with them as a surveyor. We may be confident that both knew
much more about both the practice and the state of farming than someone
in their position would have a century and half later. They were responding within a culture, unlike our own, where everyone understood that local
family farming was the essential and ever present support of life and of the
economy, and that a majority of the citizens were involved in it.

But Emerson and Thoreau were not, like Jefferson and Crèvecoeur, pro-
jecting a broad and rural vision for a restless and expanding nation; theirs
are spectators' impressions, but perhaps the more useful for just that reason. And they are innocent of vested interest. Thoreau and Emerson reflect
to us different slants on an American agrarian project already well articulated and, indeed, fully implemented; and their views enlighten us not only
because of who they are but because, while contemplating the same realities, their perspectives contrast so sharply with each other. Emerson, it
turns out, is entirely on the side of the agrarian idealists, fully in the tradition of Jefferson and Crèvecoeur. Thoreau will not indulge such romance
and, except in rare moments, he adopts, or at least affects, a negative and
occasionally hostile view of farming as he observed it.

When Thoreau speaks of farming there is often a severe irony in his
tone, and we cannot always be certain how to interpret this. Here is a typically jaunty *Walden* passage: "I see young men, my townsmen, whose mis-
fortune it is to have inherited farms, houses, barns, cattle, and farming
tools; for these are more easily acquired than got rid of. Better if they had
been born in the open pasture and suckled by a wolf, that they might have
seen with clearer eyes what field they were called to labor in. Who made

them serfs of the soil?"[20] The images here are certainly striking. Of those in my ken who were suckled by a wolf, one came to a bad end and the other founded Rome—and that's as remote in time and circumstance from inheriting a Concord farm as I can imagine. Which is probably the point. The farm is an unworthy career: those so destined are "serfs of the soil." A stern reading of American history, this. Thoreau is importing the harshest European imagery and planting it brutally in the American landscape. Had not Crèvecoeur, but seventy years earlier, laid down a warm and affectionate panegyric to that same American soil? Thoreau may not have heard of Crèvecoeur, whose *Letters* were no longer in print.

We surmise that Thoreau understood that he might conceivably have married and become a family farmer himself but, realizing that he had eluded both, he may have felt a need from some obscure source to ruthlessly distance himself from that hypothetical career. His official supposition, as we discern it between the lines, is that his escape gave him "clearer eyes" to see his neighbors. In any case *Walden* offers no respite from such judgments. The beanfield chapter contains a diatribe against the farmers' misuse of the land and landscape, and of nature generally. "By avarice and selfishness, and a groveling habit, from which none of us is free, of regarding the soil as property, or the means of acquiring property chiefly, the landscape is deformed, husbandry is degraded with us, and the farmer leads the meanest of lives. He knows Nature but as a robber."[21] Between serfs of the soil and robbers of Nature, there is not much to choose. A plague on both your farms, thinks Thoreau. He could probably have named names and pointed to specific farms, for undoubtedly much husbandry of the time was degraded. A man of Thoreau's sensitivities would have been cut to the quick by the exploitive misuse of farmland.

Yet it is not clear that he was willing to applaud what was ostensibly the proper use of farmland either. Somewhere, surely, Thoreau would recognize a husbandry not degraded, somewhere, perhaps, a genuinely model farm with modern improvements? He observed such farms on his way back from the Maine woods: "The journalists think that they cannot say too much in favor of such 'improvements' in husbandry; it is a safe theme, like piety; but as for the beauty of one of these 'model farms,' I would as lief see a patent churn and a man turning it. They are, commonly, places merely where somebody is making money, it may be counterfeiting."[22] Nothing farmer-friendly there, certainly; but that, of course, is the public and published Thoreau, and there may still be some posturing in it, some assumed crankiness, enabling him to keep the whole complex subject at a safe distance.

One might suppose that Thoreau's voluminous journals would include perspectives with broader sympathies for farming as vocation and way of life, and for the traditions and rural economies that sustained his own community. He was, after all, willing to eat bread from meal that farmers had grown and ground. But while his journals record a great deal of observed farming detail—cutting hay, cradling rye, spreading manure, digging potatoes—his is almost invariably the stance of spectator and critic. In February of 1851, while *Walden* was in preparation, his journal recorded: "Consider the farmer, who is commonly regarded as the healthiest man. He may be the toughest, but he is not the healthiest. He has lost his elasticity; he can neither run nor jump. Health is the free use and command of all our faculties, and equal development. His is the health of the ox, an overworked buffalo. His joints are stiff. . . . It would do him good to be thoroughly shampooed to make him supple." That's the vaguely sarcastic Thoreau again, slightly off stride when talking about farmers. A few years later, in December of 1853, Thoreau stares coldly at an aspect of farm life that is seldom reported upon, except in novels. He has been working at surveying for three days, and writes: "All I find is old boundmarks, and the slowness and dullness of farmers reconfirmed. They even complain that I walk too fast for them. . . . It is remarkable how unprofitable it is for the most part to talk with farmers. They commonly stand on their good behavior and attempt to moralize or philosophize in a serious conversation. Sportsmen and loafers are better company."[23]

Thoreau is often a lively bundle of contradictory opinions and, from somewhere in his massive writings, he can often be quoted on both sides of an issue. Thus, in a very few isolated moments, he too was capable of imagining agriculture in loftier terms. The spring of 1852 was such a rare moment. Thoreau had just read a "report on Farms by a committee of Middlesex husbandmen." It told of acres cleared, swamps drained and turned to farmland, of stone walls built; and on March 1 he wrote: "I have faith that the man who redeemed some acres of land the past summer redeemed also some parts of his character. I shall not expect to find him ever in the almshouse or the prison. He is, in fact, so far on his way to heaven."[24] Generous sentiment, for Thoreau, and the next day, March 2, he ventured a step further: "I think that the history (or poetry) of one farm from the state of nature to the highest state of cultivation comes nearer to being the true subject of a modern epic than the siege of Jerusalem. . . ." The previous summer (August 1851) he had already compared soldiering very unfavorably to farming: "Mexico was won with less exertion and less true valor than are required to do one season's haying in New England." Pregnant thoughts, indeed, but forever undeveloped by him, belonging to Thoreau's literary imagination and to husbandry in the abstract, but not to his enduring feelings about farmers themselves.

In 1857, Thoreau composed a longish journal passage about "cracking the nut of happiness," which includes these sentences: "Farming and building and manufacturing and sailing are the greatest and wholesomest amusements that were ever invented (for God invented them), and I suppose that farmers and mechanics know it, only I think they indulge to excess generally, and so what was meant for a joy becomes the sweat of the brow. . . . No amusement has worn better than farming. It tempts men just as strongly today as in the day of Cincinnatus." Such thoughts might have been nurtured until they developed into something, and one wishes Thoreau had done it, but in the very next sentence he briskly nips them in the bud, and firmly declines to take a grave view of farming: "Healthily and properly pursued it is not a whit more grave than huckleberrying, and if it takes any airs on itself as superior there's something wrong about it."[25] With that, he dismisses about a century's worth of national image making. Farming is not a whit more grave than huckleberrying.

It seems more than likely to me that Henry David Thoreau's friend and neighbor Ralph Waldo Emerson was very much aware of these sentiments about farming, and thought them quite misguided. Was there ever an extended dialogue between them on farming and farmers? If so, I can find no record of it. We have to peer between the lines of what we have. Shortly after Thoreau jotted the above passage in his journal, Emerson accepted an invitation to present his thoughts on farming at the September 1858 Middlesex Cattleshow, a gathering of Boston-area farmers. His speech was called "The Man with the Hoe." It seems entirely possible to me that Emerson's speech was directly prompted by his reaction to Thoreau's views.

When Emerson arrived at the cattleshow—it would be called a county fair today—he certainly came to talk about something he regarded as much more grave than huckleberrying. At the very outset he promptly and firmly installed the American farmer on a pedestal. "The glory of the farmer is that, in the division of labors, it is his part to create. . . . He stands close to Nature; he obtains from the earth the bread and the meat." Moreover, "every man has an exceptional respect for tillage," he declared, "and a feeling that this is the original calling of the race, that he himself is only excused from it by some circumstance which made him delegate it for a time to other hands."[26] On such a view, farming is not serfdom to the soil, but the classical and the noble profession.

Emerson's portrait of the American farmer could draw upon a long tradition. What most of the founding fathers believed had been often reaffirmed in different words as the spiritual promise of America before it got to Emerson, who affirmed it again: "The first farmer was the first man, and all historic nobility rests upon the use and possession of land"; moreover, the farming profession has "in all eyes its ancient charm, as standing next to God, the first cause." John Adams and George Washington would have approved. Thoreau might have winced.

We have no direct report on what the farmers gathered at the cattleshow thought. But we can imagine silent bystanders edging into the jostling crowd, perhaps nudging an already bemused listener to ask what's up, and getting a whispered response: *That's Mr. Emerson talking. He's not really a farmer. Ten acres is what he's got. Fruit's what he raises mostly; won a prize here last year. Can't really imagine him digging potatoes or milking cows, though. He's a philosopher, actually; gives lectures all over the country, England too. Listen.*

In the great household of Nature, the farmer stands at the door of the breadroom, and weighs to each his loaf.

Then the beauty of Nature, the tranquillity and innocence of the countryman, his independence and his pleasing arts—the care of bees, . . . of hay, of fruits, of orchards and forests, and the reaction of these on the workman, in giving him a strength and plain dignity like the face and manners of Nature—all men acknowledge.

The farmer is a hoarded capital of health, as the farm is the capital of wealth; and it is from him that the health and power, moral and intellectual, of the cities come.

Now the listeners are shifting their feet and exchanging approving glances: a speech worth turning aside for, on a profession they take as far more grave than huckleberrying. What cheerful yeoman would not leave off digging spuds to come and hear the philosopher talk about him like this? Every cider-from-the-jug farmer is at attention as the speaker warms to his subject. The city is always recruited from the country, he says, and those who drive the wheels of trade, practice statecraft, preserve the arts— they and the "women of beauty and genius are the children and grandchildren of farmers, and are spending the energies which their fathers' hardy, silent life accumulated. . . ."

By now the speaker has to warn us, as well he might, that the "farmer's office is precise and important, but you must not try to paint him in rose-color." Nevertheless, we learn some rosy things: that farmers learn patience from the daily encounter with Nature, gain health from the country, strength from the land. And they do the world's indispensable and hard work, work not done by "scheming speculators, nor by soldiers, nor professors, nor readers of Tennyson; but by men of endurance—deep-chested, long-winded, tough, slow and sure, and timely."

It develops that the principal term of value in Emerson's image of husbandry is Nature. He was heir to generations of thought, reaching back through the founding fathers to the European Enlightenment and back even to classical Rome, Cicero and Virgil especially, wherein Nature was comfortably allied with virtue, or at least innocence. This Eden-like linkage of ideas easily suggested another, namely the association of the city with degeneracy, or at least artificiality, a squandering of moral capital. Himself a refugee from Boston, Emerson said it at the cattleshow directly: "Cities force growth and make men talkative and entertaining, but they make them artificial." Meanwhile, the potency of Nature is linked in Emerson's mind with its moral force: "Nature never hurries: atom by atom, little by little, she achieves her work." The farmer times himself to Nature, and "acquires that lifelong patience which belongs to her. Slow, narrow man, his rule is that earth shall feed and clothe him." Yet, though he would not shine in palaces, the farmer "stands well on the world." Nature speaks to what is best in a man, to his resilience, his inner strength, his natural endowment, not to an acquired sheen. There is "no arrogance in his bearing," and the drawing-room heroes put down beside him "would shrivel in his presence; he solid and unexpressive, they expressed to goldleaf." Emerson is telling these rapt farmers: Nature and farm labor mold the stolid solid citizen yeoman while the city makes the dandy.

There are long and philosophical passages on Nature and on what we today would call ecology—most of them perhaps more than a little baffling for this audience. Baffling but uplifting. Here the humdrum shape of their daily concerns assumes a loftiness of purpose and meaning just barely recognizable—as if farming, for one hour at least, has more to do with lofty vision than with bushels per acre. They hear again, or perhaps for the first time, that America's enormous moral capital, even its daring notion of human equality, is somehow linked with the promise and fertility of its land, thence with its agrarian economy and its rural society, hence with its farmers as stewards of the land, keepers of the nation's promise. This vague ideal, somewhat elevated and loose-jointed, was, Emerson knew, supported by a powerful blend of moral fact and moral fable. Major premises of his scheme of these things were a spiritualized image of Nature and the raw abundance of the American continent. The farmers didn't catch all these big ideas, surely, but they would not have failed to feel the proud association of their strenuous and humble labors with things large, historic, and noble—which is surely what Emerson intended. More grave than huckleberrying, certainly.

As for the social and moral standing of farmers and farming, perhaps we may say that Emerson developed his ideas from the top down, and Thoreau from the ground up. Thoreau *looked at farmers* around him, and so drew his conclusions, largely negative, about farming; Emerson *thought about farming* and so drew his conclusions, largely positive, about farmers. Opposite perspectives on the same facts. In the cattleshow speech Emerson proceeds from first principles: Nature and life in its presence, Nature as lawgiver and teacher, sustainer of life, whose face and manners the farmer comes to know: the rest is working out the details. Thoreau is focused on details, on fields and farmyards, on narrowed lives and exhausted soil, of which there was a depressing abundance—how else to draw conclusions about American farming?

One is reluctant to say it, but surely there are important truths in both perspectives. When Emerson says of the farmer (he would prefer to call him Farmer) that he obtains from the earth the bread and the meat, he means to direct us to very fundamental moral and economic facts. Thoreau shrugs, and points to the eroded hillside and the impoverished serf. They are disagreeing not about the facts, but about the relative value to be assigned to the facts. The difference is not likely to be resolved by more facts, or even by discussion—though it would be exciting to know if they had that discussion and what they said. But already then the contest was old; and it is as new as today's newspaper. How do we value and evaluate the farmer's life and labors?

The upshot is that in this mid-nineteenth-century moment it is Emerson and Thoreau together—but only together, and in opposition to each other—who offer a useful snapshot of American husbandry.

*Mid-Twentieth Century: Husbandry and Harmony*

As Emerson spoke at the cattleshow that day hundreds of Irish immigrant famine-fleers were struggling for livelihood in nearby Concord, Massachusetts, and they were to be followed in the next half century by millions more European immigrants, mostly impoverished peasants, many to take up family farming. We may be confident that most of them had never entertained such lofty sentiments as those expressed by Emerson, or by the immigrant Crèvecoeur before him. The nobility of farming was not part of the peasant outlook they brought here, and they did not intend to add weight and color to America's secular religion of the family farm. But eventually they did that too, for they learned soon enough about the Homestead Act, signed by President Lincoln in 1862, offering free land to citizens. When they came, the immigrants knew only that they were poor, that there was land in America, and that there they might succeed. And by succeeding, they fell in step with "the dreams of Thomas Jefferson for our nation." In their own way they actually heeded the land's silent proclamation as imagined and voiced by Crèvecoeur a hundred years before: "I have bread for thee . . . fields to feed and clothe thee . . . independence . . . if thou be honest, sober and industrious."

It was a Dutch second-generation immigrant community in which I happened to spend the first two decades of my own life; I lived there, in Michigan, from the mid-1930s to early 1950s. It was a period that coincided with massive shifts in the American economy, including the rural economy, shifts that hearsay and memory collect around certain vivid poles—the Great Depression, Second World War, postwar recovery. As I and my siblings and contemporaries arrived at young adulthood in the 1950s, all the rural world we knew seemed poised at a new and optimistic threshold. True, we were young and the future was wide open, and this colored our vision, but we were conscious that the very recent post–World War II years were good years on the farm, especially when measured against our own dim memories of earliest childhood. We could see that the whole countryside itself had recovered from the tedious shortages of the recent war years, could see that the strains of the Depression, which had demoralized rural communities like ours, were now but a bad and distant memory. When we arrived at midcentury it seemed—especially to those of family and community with long immigrant traditions and memories—as if the promise of America was to be fulfilled again, and with interest. It was tempting to think that family farms and farm life had now resumed their historic rhythms and would prosper along familiar lines. We did not then know that this was to be a brief and somewhat unusual moment in American agriculture.

For myself, I had assumed without qualm or question that I too would be a farmer—like my father and his immigrant father and *his* serf father, and like twelve of my thirteen uncles and their fathers. At that time one could remain, as we did, largely unaware that, as Emerson emphasized, it is a fact of our history that the city recruits from the country, and that it might eventually recruit us. Although all my ancestors, both sides, so far as records and memories report, had been people of the land even before they arrived in this country around the turn of the twentieth century, my siblings and I all went off, one by one, to other professional careers. None of us farmed for a living, as had our ancestors; we just talked warmly about farming, as we still do, and some of us have long been avid readers of farm lore and farm history. Eventually, I would begin to write about it. I write now from a perspective of the fifty years since I worked seriously at farming, then as a boy. During that time I have observed, with sidelong glances, a very different farm world emerge from the one familiar at midcentury. Most of that old world has been swallowed up, but it can still be summoned as a measure of what has changed and what has remained the same.

Our farm was then typical of thousands and thousands of traditional American farms, and one brief way to depict that mode of agriculture is to think of it as highly *diversified*, and highly *integrated*. In our region of the Midwest, even in the middle of the twentieth century, mixed farming was still firmly believed to be the better part of wisdom, especially by those who had begun farming in the era of the Great Depression. In *Eighty Acres: Elegy for a Family Farm* (1990), a memoir focused on this midcentury moment in American agriculture, I wrote:

Crop diversification, based on the farm's needs and the market's demand, put everything into a modest scale: ten acres of any one row crop was a lot. Moreover, the soil itself, not especially fertile, required crop rotation, and that imposed variety in field crops. The soil also required manure, so the farm required livestock. Diversification was also a financial necessity, a hedge against failures: the potatoes might be blighted one year, but the bean crop could be depended upon; milk prices might drop, but egg prices would hold; if not, we could sell some chickens, feed the grain to the cows, and sell cream. Thus all the major demands of the system—cash flow, feeding the family, insurance against hard times, predictability, and the need for the farm to pay for itself steadily over the course of three decades or less—were exactly geared to the rhythms and the variables of small-time mixed farming.[27]

This is a version of traditional American farming—hundreds of years old, diversified, horse powered and hand powered, extremely labor-intensive, not notably efficient but quite self-sufficient—that was still thriving at the midcentury, unaware that in the next half century it might evaporate like the morning dew. It was a place of many and varied enterprises, of many small hedges against total failure, and internally bound with a certain tight logic. Beans, corn, potatoes, hay, wheat, oats, sugar beets, string beans, cows, pigs, horses, chickens, dogs, cats, woodlot, swamp, pastures, pond—all of that and more packed into eighty acres. For most farmers at that time and place it would have seemed chancy to break out of that diversified and modest scale.

In retrospect one concludes, and the record confirms, that throughout the country this idea and ideal of farming was then very much keyed, as well it might be, to the mentality of the Great Depression, a bleak era of the clearly remembered past. Although it was indeed past, older adults felt no assurance whatever that a Depression would not reappear after the first flush of postwar boom, just as it had after the economic boom following the First World War. Farmers of that day still looked to the remembered past for guidance and wisdom, and they could scarcely have imagined that this mental habit would become almost obsolete in a few generations. Theirs was a farming style designed as much to avert or face disaster as to achieve some abstract notion of success.

Self-sufficiency on these farms was not so much an idea or byword as a habit; and the farm woodlot, a vast warehouse of raw materials, was a visible token of this fact. I wrote in *Eighty Acres* that whenever possible my father did not buy his supplies but grew them, and not just fuel and lumber, which were of indispensable importance, but many other things, tangible and intangible, such as "sleigh runners, wagon tongues, rafters, tool handles, hen roosts, ladders, fence posts, and a dozen other things, not to mention maple syrup and spring flowers or brush piles for rabbits or browse for deer or shade for cattle or a playground for kids or a quiet destination for a Sunday afternoon walk."[28] For a relatively small and highly diversified farm the woods was often an essential part of its integrated economy.

Traditional farmers found their farm's diversity, and the variety of challenges it imposed, valuable in themselves, and many regarded farm specialization as a step away from history and self-sufficiency and toward business. I think that traditional farming did not appear outdated to most of those of my own community, for they saw it as visibly successful. And they were not psychologically ready to put all their eggs into just a few baskets, let alone one. I wrote of that era that most farms shaped up in remarkably similar ways: "a half dozen standard field crops, some wasteland in pasture, at least two cash crops, six to ten cows, a team of horses, a hundred chickens, some pigs, an orchard, a garden, a woodlot. On every farm every one of those elements was intimately tied to each of the others. . . . We hauled the hay that fed the cows that fertilized the fields that grew the grain that thickened the milk that fattened the pigs that supplied the bacon that fed the family that hauled the hay."[29]

There are limits, of course, to how far this portrait of mixed farming can be generalized across the country or across time. But in most respects it is an image that would be recognized, at least, by John Adams and Crèvecoeur in the eighteenth century, as well as by Thoreau and Emerson in the middle of the next century, and by unnumbered American farmers in the first half of the twentieth century. Such diversified farming could, of course, be well or badly executed, and nothing assured that it would be well or wisely done. In earlier centuries when it was well done it was called husbandry.

The heart of the matter, I believe, is that on such farms, commitments and even objects themselves, flocks and fields and tools, had a scale that was comprehensible, humanly manageable, for they presented themselves as already integrated, organically related to each other and, when properly husbanded, mutually supportive. Every farmer knew his own land intimately, knew its quirks, its strengths and weak spots; and to a very large extent it was the produce of that land that was brought to his own table. And he knew his neighbors, and worked with them, and in harvesttime exchanged work with them, each lending a hand to the other. Community, farm, ecosystem, crops, woodlot, animals, family, gardens, work, neighbors, worship, leisure—together they promised and, when effective, shaped a coherent system, a total community of life. Consequently, farm families would find therein a kind of intangible *harmony* of many and diverse elements, such as is hard to find or create within a one-dimensional twenty-first-century commodity farm.

For some observers, that traditional idea, through its many variations in diverse sectors of the country, seems as close as Americans have come to a finished system of agriculture and of rural life—a view of things helped along by the relative prosperity and security of those midcentury years. Though very imperfect, and seldom an epitome, each family's farm did offer the prospect, within its own limits, of a satisfying order and completeness. To most of those who participated in that lifestyle at that time, the devouring forces of industrial agriculture, its specializations, complex technologies, its scale, vertical integrations, corporate consolidations, and so on, were only vague threats still hidden just over the horizon. To some, the resilience and apparent success of that postwar moment made it appear to be something toward which history had long been pointed.

It is undoubtedly true that this sense of things might have the effect, easily unnoticed, of fostering a too selective reading of farm history, of encouraging the mistaken idea that there is indeed one timelessly superior mode of agriculture and that it is rather like this one—the diversified and integrated mode that flourished for a brief moment just before the full onset of specialized agribusiness. So it is to be remembered that the same moment in time meant very different things in different regions of the country. And, moreover, that system was utterly vulnerable in ways it did not know; it could not endure, and it did not. Although the great rural depression so widely feared to follow the post-war boom never materialized, on most midcentury farms the modest scale and age-old harmonies of traditional husbandry did dissolve and recede. But it is to be remembered, finally, that much successful Amish farming, even of the present day, a full half century later, remains very firmly rooted, historically and economically and psychologically, in precisely that same style of diversified and integrated hands-on farming.

From fifty years' distance one can see that the rural certitudes of midcentury were not all historically or economically well grounded, and that so singular a moment could not have endured while all the surrounding world changed course. But it did contain and express certain complex truths about rural America and its family farms. Therefore, reflection on this particular moment will return in the next chapters, through different eyes.

This chapter has put just four dots on a very wide agrarian canvas. Four stops on a four-hundred-year journey, mere snapshots of fleeting moments within teeming centuries. It takes books and more books to connect the dots properly. Not everyone's snapshots would be the same, either, and mine are taken as much with an eye to what Americans were thinking about farming as to what they were doing on the farm. Partly for that reason these particular moments figure only obliquely in most of the farming accounts I know—testimony, undoubtedly, to the immense richness and variety within the traditions of American agriculture.

# Chapter 2

# Farming in New Hampshire

Agriculture in New Hampshire is often perceived as "dying out" when, in truth, it is relatively stable in terms of numbers of farm units—and is actually growing moderately in economic value. —STEPHEN H. TAYLOR, Commissioner, New Hampshire Department of Agriculture, Markets, and Food, 2001

New Hampshire is tucked into New England atop Massachusetts and wedged between Maine and Vermont. Most of our New England winters are cold, most of our summers are short, most of our autumns spectacular. Our favorite is spring, with its beloved sequence of frost heaves, mud season, blackflies. It is all ideal for living, but only selected portions of New England and the larger Northeast are ideal for farming: Maine is hard to beat for potatoes, New York has great vineyards, New Hampshire and Massachusetts take pride in apples, and Vermont in its dairies; maple syrup is a proud and favorite product of every state in this broader region. No state in the Northeast is quite like any other, yet in agriculture we all followed somewhat similar paths to the present—with hundreds of individual variations. If you were to choose one state in the Northeast to look at closely to capture the gist of the development of the region's farming, you could pick the wedge of New Hampshire as well as any. Most of what can be said of farming in New Hampshire has its analogues in the other northeastern states.

## Corn and Potatoes

An early summary of New Hampshire farm products, taken at Piscataway (now Portsmouth) in 1635, shows that "Indian corn" was far and away the largest commodity crop of these new American farmers. The settlers had been in New Hampshire just over a decade, but they had assimilated the message being picked up simultaneously in Massachusetts and elsewhere, namely, that Native Americans had much to teach innocent Europeans about growing food. The heart of the lesson was simple and direct: grow corn.

The words "corn," "wheat," and "grain" were used in special ways in the seventeenth century and, moreover, they got stirred into European politics. In England "corn" was a general term for cereals, so "Indian corn" had the right specificity for what we now call simply corn. On the other hand, "grain" was the term not for cereals generally but for the kernel itself, as for a grain of salt, sugar, sand. Thus what we now would call a kernel of wheat or rye was then called simply a grain of corn. Europe had not known (American) corn until Columbus brought it back from the Americas, and during the following century, for complicated political reasons, it came to be widely called "Turky wheat." In some countries it was called "maize" (a Spanish adaptation of an Indian word Columbus had also brought back), a word disliked by the English, who were usually at war with Spain. Furthermore, Indian corn, alias Turky wheat, née maize, was often arrogantly disparaged as food in sixteenth-century Europe: Gerarde's *Herball* of 1597 said of Turky wheat: the "barbarous Indians which know no better . . . think it good food; whereas . . . it nourisheth but little, is of hard and euill digestion, a more conuenient foode for swine than for man."[30] Consequently, many of the colonists came to America firmly prejudiced against Indian corn. It proved to be merely a life saver.

Although the English New Hampshire farmers had brought their traditional cereals with them from Europe—rye, wheat, barley, oats—it was decades before growing any of them was regularly successful here. Indian corn farming, however, following Indian teaching, was an immediate success. The ripened crop could even wait in the field a month or more until harvested and still be undamaged. Despite the New Hampshire settlers' early prejudice, Indian corn soon became their chief field crop, their commodity of exchange, their main product for export (to Virginia and even to England), feed for their livestock, and the leading ingredient in dozens of domestic food recipes, many of which were also learned from Native Americans. It was their miracle crop and for the next century their principal crop.

From the beginning the settlers had supplemented their corn farms with squash, pumpkins, Jerusalem artichokes, and beans, which they also got from the Indians, as well as the wild rice and wild onions the Indians led them to. The colonists could often add six or ten kinds of native wild berries and fruits, several kinds of nuts and, again following the Indians' lead, maple sugar. From Europe they had brought cabbage, turnips, carrots, parsnips, cucumbers, and, of course, their own domestic animals, so they added beef, mutton, and pork, as well as milk, cheese, and butter to the fish and game they often found in abundance. Thus early New Hampshire farming, and hence New Hampshire diets, could soon be quite diversified (at least seasonally), even as corn still predominated.

The staple item missing in this early picture is the lowly potato (*Solanum tuberosum*). It is astonishing to realize that the first hundred years of American colonizing got along without potatoes; almost as astonishing to realize that the potato is native to the Americas, where it had been known and eaten by Native Americans for millennia, but had to be taken to Europe first, then domesticated, transported to England by Walter Raleigh, then to Ireland, and had to become a dietary mainstay there, before being returned to these shores and—so the record suggests—first seriously planted as a colonial food crop in New Hampshire.

Five shiploads of Scotch-Irish immigrants arrived in Boston in 1718, and eventually many of them settled in Nutfield (now Derry and Londonderry), New Hampshire, where they were soon joined by others. The English-American farmers looked askance at them: these newcomers talked a funny English, they farmed without pigs (for nearly a hundred years pigs had been the easiest and most successful of New World livestock), didn't even care for pork, they were devoted to raising flax, they had strange spinning wheels in their homes, and they dug their main food out of the ground. Near the end of the eighteenth century, New Hampshire historian Jeremy Belknap reported that the Scotch-Irish immigrants had brought to this country spinning wheels, "turned by the foot," for the manufacture of linen, and that they had also "introduced the culture of potatoes" to New England. By Belknap's day, the grubby tubers dug out of the ground and the numerous weird ways of processing and eating them (boiled, fried, mashed, roasted, baked, buttered, flavored with other vegetables and herbs, in soups and stews) had been enthusiastically passed around from the immigrant Irish settlements to most of the larger communities of English farmers. Thus the Irish and their linseed oil, their fine and famous linen, and their versatile potato entered American history. So, for that matter, did another short-lived Irish favorite, namely, potato whiskey, though eventually it could not hold its own against imported rum and local hard cider. But that is another story.

*Settling the Land*

Most of New Hampshire's terrain is not readily hospitable to farming. The question arises, therefore, how it developed that within less than two hundred years (early seventeenth to early nineteenth centuries) this once "howling wilderness" was reduced (except for the White Mountains) to over two hundred highly organized towns, each with an average of a hundred or more individual family farms, with agriculture accounting for the overwhelming share of the state's organization and economy. How did this happen?

The answer is not unique to New Hampshire but has firm analogies across New England, with the experience of Massachusetts the central piece of the story. In fact, most of what became New England farmland, divided as it was into rather neat family farms with more or less precise, often stone-walled boundaries, was originally settled through a surprisingly orderly process. Surprising, because the rules for land division had to be improvised from scratch under pressure both from a restless and growing population and from sometimes hostile Native Americans. From 1630 onward literally thousands of immigrant Europeans came ashore every year. New England's population was thirty-three thousand by 1660 and it doubled every thirty years until the Revolutionary War, when it was over half a million. These newcomers landed on the edge of a raw and apparently unending wilderness, a formidable world of trees and rocks and mountains, lined with a few seductive and grassy valleys. ("It is fortunate that there is one thing that even God cannot do," Ethan Allen is said to have said: "He cannot make two mountain ranges without a valley between them.") How on earth would they divide and settle and gain a peaceable living from this landscape?

There were two principal early models for turning New England wilderness into ordered townscapes of farms. The first model, prominent in seventeenth-century Massachusetts and Connecticut, started with a defensive nuclear village, as erected initially at Plymouth, with outlying individual farms. By the eighteenth century, especially in New Hampshire and Maine and in the unsettled parts of Connecticut and Massachusetts, this model gave way to a different style whereby a new town, from the very outset, was composed of individual and widely scattered farms, each family living upon its own land. In such a town, villages of clustered houses were not planned but grew up naturally and haphazardly, a convenient grouping of private homes and community entities, often centered about a tavern and meetinghouse.

By the last half of the eighteenth century a new town (often called a *township* before it was incorporated) typically consisted of an integrated community of pioneer farms and mills, and had been created from wilderness by a very stereotyped process. It started when a group of prominent men, perhaps living in the vicinity of Portsmouth or Boston, would petition for a particular grant of land. In New Hampshire the petition went to the royal governor, or to the Masonian Proprietors (a group of large New Hampshire landholders), or, after the Revolution, to the General Court (legislature). At issue was invariably a slab of raw wilderness, marked out on a crude map, usually about six miles square; but its terrain and its potential for farming were often largely unknown. The petitioners were really land-and-development speculators. Having secured the grant of land (the government had vested interests in settling the land and making the grants, including competition between Massachusets and New Hampshire over lands along disputed boundaries), the new owners then sent a delegation to survey it and lay it out in lots of several hundred acres each. Invariably, the surveyors came back with a very rational-looking map, with hundreds of lots parceled off in straight lines. The actual terrain might be something else. The lots were then distributed randomly among the new owners (usually called proprietors), who also taxed themselves to pay for the survey and the construction of the first roads to and through the grant. Benning Wentworth, the royal governor of New Hampshire for a quarter century (1741–1766), made dozens of township grants and always reserved several hundred acres of each one for himself, thus consolidating his personal and financial empire.

Significantly, the charter of the land grant came to the proprietors with strings attached, and failure to adhere to them could forfeit the grant. A few dozen townships were forfeited in New Hampshire and later regranted, but five or six per year succeeded in the decades before the Revolutionary War, and they continued (but at a slower pace) right through the war and after. Strings: the new township had to have a specified number of settled families with permanent homes built within a certain number of years (five or sometimes ten), each with a specified minimum number of cleared acres; minimal roads had to be laid out, a sawmill erected, acreage set aside for the minister, for the school, and so on, and usually within ten years a meetinghouse had to be built. Another common early string, absurdly attached even to grants many miles from a navigable river, decreed that all pine trees "twenty four inches in diameter or more and fit for masting his Majesty's Royal Navy be reserved for his Majesty and Successors forever" (this from the 1768 grant of what is now Washington, New Hampshire, whose mast trees could never have been reasonably shipped out). This string was ignored in dozens of places, and its lack of enforcement set the pattern for slack on other strings as well, such as the time limits. But, in general, this process of land development was both remarkably methodical and effective, and the particular strings attached to ensure orderly settlement of the granted lands constituted a distinguishing New England mark.

To achieve their goals the proprietors had to make the future town look attractive, make the farming prospects sound good, make the land accessible, inexpensive, and so on. They needed settlers swiftly. Often they sold portions of their lots, typically a hundred acres, or granted them freely to committed settlers, sometimes sight unseen—easy to do, perhaps, when consulting a shiny new map in Portsmouth, but afterward the prospective pioneer farmer might find it hard even to locate the lot among the rocks and trees in the remote wilderness, let alone farm it. In any case it was understood that the proprietors would reserve most of the best lots for later and much higher sale, after the town had developed—their only chance of profit. Thus, when the Scotch-Irish and their potatoes came to Nutfield in 1719 they entered a partially settled community, but one with much land still available for easy purchase. Often, whole groups of friends and neighbors moved into a new township; and sometimes some of the proprietors themselves came and took up farming on their land.

If things went smoothly, and the land was quickly settled, the proprietors stood to make a profit eventually, though in many cases the land under the forest was quite unsuitable for farming. The original grantees of what became the town of Bradford, New Hampshire, for example, looked their gift horse in the mouth in 1738, said no thanks, and wrote to the General Court, "showing that ye lands in said township are so rocky and mountainous on a View thereof that renders ye settlement impracticable; praying they may be allowed to take up a Tract of land in lieu of ye aforesaid Township, lying West. . . ." Well, westward the land was just as rocky and mountainous and the grass was no greener, but nevertheless Bradford was eventually settled and, like its neighbors, became a successful farming community.

*Towns of Self-sufficient Farms*

When a new group of farmers and millers and their families had settled into a firm community they could apply to the state or province's legislative assembly for incorporation as a town. This would give them a representative in that assembly, certain judicial privileges, the ability to levy taxes for roads, meetinghouse, school, for paying a minister, and also the right to hold town meetings and elect town officers. In just this way town government and the town meeting, still today deeply cherished in New England, sprouted and grew in each locale anew, directly from the process of land development. The settlers of New England's backcountry almost inadvertently invented the rudiments of an entire culture: not only their politics but also the fabled Yankee qualities of independence, localism, thrift, tenacity, and so on were the accompaniments of the way the land was assimilated into their lives. This was agrarianism before that word was even firmly installed within the American vocabulary.

Although it included plenty of friction along the way, and was early disturbed but not stopped by the French and Indian Wars, this overall scheme for reducing the northern wilderness to farmland and incorporating independent settlements into a civil society was a remarkably rational and coherent process. Other regions of the country (occasionally the Northeast too) had innumerable problems deriving not only from conflict with Native Americans but also from the competing interests of squatters on the public lands and the speculators who came to be owners, and so required more complex processes of land settlement. New England had developed, almost inadvertently, a generally successful working model, even though it proved hard to follow elsewhere. Of land settlement in America, it was once said, "the farther it got away from Boston the messier it got," and there is some truth in that. Moreover, when Congress created the Northwest Land Ordinance of 1785 it had its eye firmly on the New England precedent, and thus provided for a survey of all public lands that would endeavor to mark them into blocks six miles on a side, like New England towns.

While the settlement process itself in New England, and New Hampshire in particular, was comparatively simple, executing it involved labors of epic proportions by the settlers themselves. Here was a people that shaped the land, and here too was a land that shaped a people. The granite hardihood of these pioneer New England farmers and families is almost beyond praise. However, unlike their pioneering predecessors of a hundred years earlier, namely, the first colonists who came to the New World as naked innocents, these inland farmers knew exactly what they were in for, and those unequal to the challenge usually did not attempt it. Most were second- or third-generation immigrants who went inland from coastal towns to create a new life for themselves on the frontier. Some were restless types, pioneering for the second time: they might clear new land, build, settle, then sell out and move farther west once more.

Those who settled the bulk of inland New Hampshire—which took place essentially during the eighteenth century—faced a raw wilderness, and by the time they had hacked down or girdled enough trees to let the sunlight in they had exposed a lot of rough terrain that could never accommodate a plow, and sometimes hardly a hoe. They built post-and-beam homes (the story-and-a-half Cape Cod was a standard farmer's style), and for several generations they continued to roll the movable rocks into durable stone walls. In 1872 the U.S. Department of Agriculture reported that a recent study had indicated that there were approximately 240,000 miles of stone walls in New England and New York. Half of these are now estimated to be gone. One of the few towns that has completely inventoried its stone walls is Petersham, Massachusetts, near the New Hampshire border. This typical town, six miles square, has 280 miles of stone walls. All across the rough inland portions of the Northeast, except for the genuine mountain ranges, an extremely rugged and resistant terrain was systematically measured and recast into a mosaic of working farms and rural towns. For a time, most of them prospered. And it happened remarkably quickly—the biggest settlement was the work of but a few generations. In New Hampshire a hundred new towns were chartered in the decades preceding the Revolutionary War, and in the next forty years the population of the state doubled.

The farm life in upstate New York that Hector St. John de Crèvecoeur had described and endorsed in high spirits (chapter 1) in the years just before the Revolutionary War seemed still possible throughout the Northeast for the next fifty years. Farm prices were good; the population was expanding; demand for farm surpluses was high in the growing cities and towns. New England farming appeared to be successful, though not everyone agreed that it was good agriculture. Shortly after 1800 Timothy Dwight of Yale traveled through New England and published an extensive report, including comments on the farms: "The husbandry of New England is far inferior to that of Great Britain," he said, and blamed the lack of labor, poor manuring practices, and "the want of a good rotation of crops." New England farming was often wasteful and careless, but the bill for that did not come in for a couple of generations. Meanwhile, most farmers prospered. In 1821 one wrote to a London paper from Merrimack, New Hampshire: "We have now a comfortable dwelling and 2 acres of ground plowed with potatoes, Indian corn, melons, etc. I have 2 hogs one ewe and a lamb. . . . Half my land which was wood I have cleared this spring. . . . I can assure you I have made every possible enquiry and can safely invite you to this happy country. Bring all the furniture you can. . . ."[31]

In 1839 the governor of New Hampshire reported that he thought farmers were better off than any other class of men: this was at the height of the successful sheep-raising era. Another writer observed in the widely circulated *Farmer's Monthly Visitor* that the "almost universal condition of the inhabitants of Lyme [New Hampshire] is the possession of abundance of the good things of life."[32] There was talk of railroads. By 1840 many New England hill towns had reached a peak both of population and of rural prosperity, even though they did not then know that it was the peak. For the most part, these farmers thought of the wilderness as tamed, and they and their fathers had done it. New Hampshire could think of itself as living out the Jeffersonian agrarian ideal. It was summertime in New England, and the sheep were in the meadow.

However, the next two generations were not destined to see their rural lives as such an unqualified success story.

The term most commonly associated with this era and style of New England farming is "self-sufficient," meaning that most of life's necessities and the farm's needs were supplied by the farm: grown or made there, or at the mill down the road, or acquired by barter or work exchange with the neighbors. Accurate enough—but it is evident too, as recent social historians have made clear, that pioneer farm life involved a good deal of interdependence among farmers as well, just as we know that despite the many accounts of rural prosperity, there were also many who struggled with mortgages on impossibly difficult farmland. But in the days of self-sufficient farming, cash was far less a measure of success or failure than was the quality of rural life, and quality of life was often defined in terms of improvements over the struggles of the immediately preceding decades of pioneering.

## More Sheep Than People

The sheep saga represents Northeast agriculture as well as anything, partly because it once seemed a galloping success story, perhaps in the long run a way to sustain the vigor of the region's farms. But there are few long runs in this region. It was ever true that Northeast hill country is hard to plow, but it appeared that it should be relatively easy to pasture, and that it might more readily produce meat and wool than wheat and corn. Accordingly, Vermont farmers led the way into serious sheep farming as early as 1810 with the importation of merino sheep from Spain, a fancy breed with exotic and heavy, oily wool. All across the Northeast farmers began to look at sheep raising and the sale of wool as a potential cash crop. Something to put beside maple sugar.

Initially, in the early days of homespun and self-sufficiency, nearly every home had a spinning wheel and a loom, and many farms had a flock of sheep to serve the family's immediate needs. But the demand in the city for manufactured woolen products was increasing rapidly, as was the New England population. Eventually, new woolen mills with power looms made the products cheaper, thereby increasing demand still more. Lamb and mutton were plentiful and inexpensive, thereby increasing demand again. The era of serious sheep farming came to the Northeast and peaked and faded during the fifty-year period from about 1820 to 1870, and for those early decades high tariffs kept foreign competition comfortably at bay. During the 1830s and early 1840s wool sold for 40, 50, and up to 60 cents per pound (equivalent to several days' wages), while careful breeding, especially of the prized merinos, brought wool production up from two to four and five pounds per sheep, and eventually even higher. So farmers bought more sheep. Vermont always led the way, but New Hampshire and Maine were not far behind. By the 1840s the Upper Connecticut Valley seemed one vast sheep run, and the New Hampshire river towns Walpole, Lebanon, and Hanover had 12,000 sheep apiece. In the 1840 census there were over 617,000 sheep in New Hampshire, more than twice the number of people. Vermont, with no large cities, had more than a million and a half sheep, five for every person.

The bubble could not grow forever—even with a growing population demanding ever more manufactured cloth goods. Cotton started to pour into northern mills from the South, and tariff laws changed in the 1840s, eventually letting in Australian and New Zealand wool. Then tons of wool began streaming east through the Erie Canal from the Midwest, where, it turned out—surprise!—you can raise large numbers of sheep more cheaply than in New England hill country. In the 1850s the price of raw wool fell to half of what it had been. Fickle fashion turned away from merino wool. From the Northeast farmers' point of view the Civil War held off the collapse of sheep farming for nearly a decade, through its heavy demand for woolens and the sudden loss of southern cotton imports. But by 1870, with sheep numbers less than a third of what they had been and declining, it was clear that sheep farming was no longer a sustaining but rather a dying industry in New Hampshire and in the entire Northeast. A few voices remarked that the decades of intense sheep grazing may not have been good for what there was of the New Hampshire soil.

*Trouble on the Farm*

A writer noted in 1853 that times were changing: now a New Hampshire farmer needed a hundred dollars in cash a year to meet his basic expenses. Soon larger changes were afoot, and within the next decades their combined effects would be utterly transforming. From this convenient distance we can summarize them in a sentence: an Industrial Revolution in the cities that would drain local manufacturing from the New England countryside, a harrowing Civil War that deeply wounded nearly every community, market upheavals created by the railroads and the Erie Canal, the flight of youth to the manufacturing cities, the opening and the promise of the West—all of it leaving in its backwash a more commercial, more complicated, and ultimately less successful agriculture for the Northeast and for New Hampshire. Suddenly it was possible to raise corn in Illinois and ship it by canal or rail to Boston, where it would undersell the corn slowly wagoned in from the hills and valleys of New England—stunning, to be sure, and, as it turned out, but a token of a hundred such economic dislocations for the northeastern farm.

In the heroic days of self-sufficiency, farm life had been much less dependent on cash crops and a major market. Modest amounts of surplus maple sugar, cheese, butter, potatoes could almost always be traded or sold in this town or the next. This was still true two decades after the Civil War, but no longer sufficient for cash needs. Many farms were heavily mortgaged, requiring cash for solvency. Rural household industries, from spinning and weaving to coopering and smithing and a dozen others, were moving wholesale to factories downriver. By midcentury and beyond, agriculture was shifting slowly but inexorably from self-sufficient to more commercial farming (and, indeed, sheep farming had already encouraged this trend), but the conditions for a successful transition in the Northeast were not good.

Within the climate of industrial and transportation and social change always loomed the formidable New England terrain. For a hundred years these tough and stubborn Yankee farmers had demonstrated that the forbidding land which their fathers had subdued would never defeat them. And as long as they were a world unto themselves—their own farms, their own communities, their own region, their own markets in their own cities—it did not. But in the generation following the Civil War, Northeast farms inevitably became American farms, and their destiny became bound up, through tenuous ties at first, with all the farms of the growing Midwest and the South. The news was brutally simple: what happened elsewhere mattered here. As wool from Australia and New Zealand and Ohio arrived in Boston and began to sweep thousands and thousands of sheep from the rocky New England hillsides, it began to look like defeat.

If not sheep, then what? Cows? In fact, as sheep decreased, cows did increase. Farmers began to appreciate that the market for milk, cheese, and butter was actually more certain and stable than for raw wool. So, for that matter, some of them noticed, was the market for fruit, especially apples; and as New England cities grew, the local urban market seemed more secure. But although the rural readjustments in the decades following the Civil War seemed to be just that, in fact farming in New Hampshire never fully readjusted, because its challenges were ever multiplying and its real problems were so much larger than could at the time be easily imagined. In hindsight we can more easily appreciate the combined and crushing effects of vast intangible forces sweeping over the entire American landscape, far outside any one community's, any one state's, tinkering or control. They are chilling even to enumerate: industrialism, Midwest imports, volatile markets and tariffs, rural isolation, the pull of cities, the call of the West; the list goes on—ending, always and forever, with that tough and stubborn granite landscape.

Several major initiatives at this time had a long-term beneficial effect upon New Hampshire agriculture—but chiefly slowing the decline, not arresting it. The first was the Morrill Act, signed by President Lincoln in 1862, which created the national system of land grant agriculture and mechanical arts colleges, and put the national government squarely on the side of agriculture. Another, quite independent, initiative was the Grange movement, officially the Patrons of Husbandry, begun in New Hampshire in 1873. The numerous granges—local associations of, by, and for farmers and their wives—created a sense of solidarity among farmers and assisted them in forming co-ops for purchasing, processing (local co-op creameries made butter and cheese), and marketing, and also in establishing fire insurance companies.

A third initiative in New Hampshire was the 1870 legislative creation of the state Board of Agriculture, which labored mightily to assist local farmers in many practical ways, holding regular "Farmers' Institutes" in all parts of the state, disseminating information, demonstrating new farm technology, reporting and encouraging research; and they also regularly published a huge annual report, loaded with data and statistics. In 1880 members of the New Hampshire board held a total of four hundred local meetings and sponsored over a thousand lectures—a virtual traveling university, and a prodigious amount of work for an unpaid board. Some of the printed speeches presented were of the cheerleading sort: a very successful farmer, J. B. Walker, wrote in the 1871 annual report: "Our agriculture is just now in a transition state, from a lower to a higher plane." Indeed! The good old days had been days of an expanding rural population; now the reverse was true. New Hampshire's rural and agricultural problems were deep, systemic, historical, and ultimately beyond any available therapy. It seems almost inevitable now, but it seemed merely depressing then: by the 1880s rural New England had plunged into the winter of its discontent.

The migration of people out of rural New England during the last half of the century was one of the largest internal movements of people in the nation's history. New Hampshire's total population was relatively stable from 1860 to 1890 (the rest of the country was growing), but the truth was that New Hampshire cities were growing and rural towns were shrinking. Farm production statistics highlight the facts as well, and wheat is a dramatic example. In 1860 New Hampshire produced over 200,000 bushels of wheat, but by 1900 the production dropped to a mere 4,000 bushels. Similar but less drastic numbers hold for the state's production of corn, oats, rye, and barley—everywhere, a one-way trend. Significantly, this was precisely the era of new farm equipment, such as mowers, binders, and threshing machines—equipment that slowed but did not stop the decline in farm production. Thousands of farms that had been so laboriously and methodically shaped upon the rocky hillsides in the last half of the eighteenth century were being literally abandoned to the forest and the elements a century later. Many had been heavily mortgaged when acquired, payments could not be met, and the family just pulled up roots and left for the city or for Illinois or Michigan to start over. Almost every rural town counted dozens of such gaping, empty homes and falling barns.

Undoubtedly, not all the causes of decline were external and entirely beyond the farmers' control. One thoughtful spokesman put his finger on a problem in the 1870s:

Had a judicious course of cultivation been pursued on a larger portion of the now abandoned farms, they would have been today paying investment. The selling of hay and grain from the farms, close feeding of the mowing fields every autumn [he is thinking of sheep grazing], and reckless waste of the manurial resources of the farm, together with the natural restlessness and love of change that seems to belong especially to Americans, are, I believe, the principal causes of this decrease of the rural population in so many of the farming districts of New England.[33]

Still, there was the cold fact that much of this land was unsuited to cash crop agriculture. New Hampshire had had such a remarkably successful wilderness-conquering past that it was almost impossible for some people of the last quarter of the nineteenth century (grandchildren and great-grandchildren of the pioneers) to believe it could not continue or be re-created. Surely, it was a matter of finding the right formula, or the right sort of people, the right cash crop, or the right tools. Or for the Board of Agriculture to do the right thing. New England's plight was a theme of the press of the time, and the article titles alone suggest the tone: "The Decline of Rural New England" (1889), "A Good Farm for Nothing" (1889), "The Decadence of New England" (1890), and dozens like them. The Board of Agriculture tried to do the right thing: they began advertising, throughout this country and through northern Europe, that cheap and settled farms were available here, and they produced a booklet, *Price List of Abandoned Farms in New Hampshire*. Good idea, bad title. The board reported the next year that three hundred empty farms had been reoccupied, some by Scandinavians, whose descendants are still here. The next booklet in 1891 bore a better title, *Secure a Home in New Hampshire—Where Comfort, Health and Prosperity Abound*. But prosperity is a relative thing, and did not always abound. A New Hampshire woman, Kate Sanborn, wrote a smart how-to book, *Adopting an Abandoned Farm* (1891). Soon thereafter she wrote another, wiser book, *Abandoning an Adopted Farm* (1894). In the latter she notes the joys of farming in New Hampshire:

Haying is a terrible ordeal. There's real poetry about emerald-tinted dewy grass, and the waves of growing grain, and the tall and blithely nodding oats, and the stalwart bronzed haymakers, and the merry sun-kissed maidens in broad brimmed hats. But the real man in actual prosaic haying is like a woman on washing day—so outrageously and unreasonably cross and irascible that the very dogs dart outdoors with tails between their legs.[34]

*The Twentieth Century*

New England hill towns—which in New Hampshire means more than half of them—were in trouble, but many valley towns continued to have good and prosperous farms on into the twentieth century, as did valley towns in neighboring states. Indeed, New Hampshire agriculture looked better in the first half of the twentieth century than it did in the last decades of the nineteenth century. Two of the strong players during most of this era were dairy and poultry. The Granite State Dairymen's Association had been formed as early as 1884, and at the same time the extension of railroads (twelve hundred miles in New Hampshire by 1884) to ever more remote regions of the countryside meant that milk and other perishable farm crops—butter, cheese, fruit, vegetables—could be rapidly transferred to the cities. Dozens of New Hampshire hill towns were added to what was known as the "Boston milk shed." In 1910, over half the people in New Hampshire still derived their living from farms, and that year the census listed 27,000 farms in New Hampshire and over 100,000 dairy cattle. Sheep, having once numbered well over half a million, were down to less than 50,000.

Numerically, New Hampshire farms diminished steadily, but even as they became fewer and fewer a variety of important initiatives assisted those remaining. The Farm Bureau was founded in 1911, and eventually rivaled and then superseded the Grange as a farmers' organization; the New Hampshire legislature created a Department of Agriculture in 1913, with a full-time commissioner, and the work that the board had done was greatly expanded; a Co-operation Extension Program began in 1914 under federal legislation, included a system of county agricultural agents; New Hampshire's land grant institution, which had begun life successfully as an adjunct to Dartmouth College in Hanover, namely, the New Hampshire College of Agriculture and Mechanic Arts (now the University of New Hampshire), had been moved to Durham, New Hampshire, and assumed a significant role as locus of training and research for farmers and future farmers.

In 1930 the census showed that only 11.3 percent of New Hampshire residents derived their living from farms. By 1950 there were only half as many farms (13,000) in New Hampshire as in 1910, and by far the largest source of farm receipts now came from poultry and eggs—which were worth $35 million annually. Four years later, 1954, just a half century ago, the number of farms was down to about 10,000. These declining numbers no longer had the shock value of similar numbers in the last half of the nineteenth century, and undoubtedly the reason was that the self-image of the people of the state had altered. New Hampshire now was heavily industrialized, as it had not been in the 1880s, and was no longer primarily an agricultural state. The farm was still extremely important—as tradition, as food source, as heritage, as experience, as ideal, as way of life, even as scenic amenity—but it was already being driven to the economic margins in New Hampshire. The Jeffersonian ideal of the family farm, while still a daily enactment, was also on its way to becoming an historical icon.

### A Personal Window

Sometimes—especially if you are very fortunate—you may find that one complicated artifact incorporates within itself a long stretch of historical experience. In the late 1960s when my wife and I bought a derelict New Hampshire farmstead, hoping to create of it a home, it had long been neglected and finally deserted. The barns were gone. Although it had been a family farm since 1780, it had not been farmed and only occasionally pastured since the 1940s, and in recent years it had been intermittently occupied by renters, by transients, by nobody, and finally by raccoons. The house was small, post and beam, Cape Cod style, center chimney, and built to last—which it had. And has.

The virgin forest here was opened and the house built about 1781 by Ebenezer Wood, a former Massachusetts minuteman and volunteer in the Revolutionary War, then with a wife and three young children. The land on which it stood, "a hundred acres more or less," and marked out in straight lines with absolutely no reference to the character of the terrain, he had purchased for almost nothing from the speculator who had acquired it from the original proprietors of the township. It was standard stuff: the town had needed settlers. So the farmstead entered into and eventually passed through two hundred years of very typical New Hampshire rural evolution. As we recovered it, we found that the outline of its particular history recapitulates the larger rhythms of much of New Hampshire agriculture. The labors of Ebenezer Wood and his family and of the successor family turned out to be but a personal and concrete version of what happened nearly everywhere in the hill towns of New England to untold numbers of families.

Ebenezer Wood was a farmer, like all his neighbors, and he did coopering and carpentry on the side for barter and for the small amount of cash he needed. He would immediately have cleared the forest from a few acres where he could raise wheat, which he would have had ground two miles down the road at the mill where the boards for his house were also sawed out. To this day, throughout the woods I can spot several dozen large rocks with heaps of smaller stones on top of them—there they were out of the way of Wood's scythe and hoe, and there they have remained for more than two centuries now. (This is one of the signs I look to when wondering whether a given forested area was once a field.) After constructing a typical farmer's story-and-a-half Cape Cod post-and-beam house, Wood had to raise food for his growing family, and he built stone walls to keep his animals at home: a deed of 1790 refers to one boundary wall, so I know he went to wall building near the beginning of his time here, and he probably continued it all his life long. And on the evidence, so did all his neighbors. The Wood family grew to eleven children, twice the average size of the time and surely a challenge for self-sufficient farming. Tax records show that there were oxen and a few cows, and not much acreage cleared for crops. For the first forty years, the Wood farm chiefly fed the large family, never had a mortgage, and slowly drove the forest back.

In 1825 the youngest son, Timothy Wood, took over the family homestead, and the senior Woods moved to a small house across the two-track public cart road. Self-sufficient farming was now thriving all across the settled parts of New Hampshire, in the valleys certainly but in a hundred hill towns as well, and as was to be expected, sheep appeared on this town's tax roles. So did more people: the town was growing rapidly, heading toward a peak of over eleven hundred in 1830. According to the town tax records, in 1832 Timothy Wood had three oxen, seven cows, and twenty-five sheep. Undoubtedly, that is the time when he built more stone walls, with oxen and tripod, to enclose the growing livestock. There are today three or four miles of walls on and enclosing the original hundred acres, and there are blank spaces too, where the job was never finished. Piled brush would probably have filled the gaps. Timothy experimented with horses too, as many New Hampshire farmers were doing: in 1833 he had three, but the next year he was back to three oxen. And more land was readied for crops, especially hay and pasture for the livestock, which could be accomplished on pretty rough terrain. For several years "orcharding" was listed as among his taxable assets. The Woods were living out the Jeffersonian ideal of family farming.

Altogether, the evidence of what was accomplished on this place, in clearing and building, by the two generations of Woods is staggering to contemplate. While the senior Woods, the pioneers and builders, lived into the 1840s, son Timothy Wood, second-generation farmer, turned this into a successful farm, always with more than twenty sheep and sometimes ten cows. And, significantly, always without a mortgage. Around him the town population expanded, as did that of all neighboring towns. Tax records suggest that the farm prospered, just as the town and the state did, through the era of self-sufficiency and homespun and sheep and into the brink of a new era. The Wood farmhouse and its hand-hewn beams, the hand-planed boards of its walls, the carefully chiseled fireplace hearthstones, the small stone piles on large rocks, and the miles of surrounding and crisscrossing stone walls, all reflect the history of successful New Hampshire farming of that time and place.

The next stewards of the homestead were also father and son, and altogether Anson and Auren Powers labored here for nearly ninety years—from before the Civil War to the end of World War II. But this was a different farming era. Unlike the Woods, the Powerses, father and son, were usually heavily mortgaged, so they always needed cash. Anson Powers was a young man when he took up farming here in the 1850s; he had grown up in the region, so he may not have had many illusions about it. But he could hardly have known when he set out that New Hampshire farming was headed into a bleak period. The population of the town had peaked and already begun to decline when Anson began, and this trend would continue unsparingly for the entire forty-five years of his tenure.

In 1850 the Washington town population was over a thousand, and when Anson Powers died at century's end, it was less than five hundred: that loss of over five hundred people was primarily a loss of *farmers*. The town history, written in 1886, makes clear that many of Anson Powers's very near neighbors had abandoned their farms, which had fallen into ruin. Farmers who survived and stayed in one place for that entire period were uncommon, and Anson Powers was undoubtedly good at just hanging on. Tax records suggest he tried to meet his cash needs somewhat as Timothy Wood had done decades earlier—wool and butter, sheep and cows. But we can be certain his twenty sheep in 1881 didn't bring him nearly the income that Wood's twenty-four did in 1840. And we can only speculate what fifty or sixty years of continuous sheep grazing had done to deplete the soil of the meadows—was this generation paying for the exploitations of the previous generations? At any rate, some of the pastures eventually grew back to forest during Anson Powers's tenure, and the next generation harvested timber from land that the Woods had fenced and grazed.

When Anson's son Auren took over just at the beginning of the twentieth century, it would have been hard to have high expectations. Maybe he did initially, for when his barns burned in 1905 he promptly built a large new one. Auren Powers lived in a New Hampshire hill town, and for those regions his experience was to be fairly typical, but not wholly typically for New Hampshire farming as a whole. Good dairy and fruit and poultry farms continued, and many thrived in more favored regions of the state, as they long had, while he merely hung on.

In 1900, tax records show that Auren Powers had two cows, two oxen, and two horses; but for many like him a reliable and significant cash crop was hard to come by. Potatoes thrived in this soil and climate, and in some parts of the state farmers did very well by them, but only small patches of his ground were free enough of rocks for row crops. Maple sugar and syrup were important cash crops, and in 1909 he sold some timber and also built a big sugarhouse. The population of the town declined relentlessly every year during his entire tenure, just as it had during his father's time. The deed shows that Auren took out a mortgage in 1915 that was not fully paid off until 1940; and in 1927 he took another one. For decades, and in a pattern not unusual in regions like this one, Auren Powers pieced together a living from odds and ends. At a minimum he had to have cash to pay the taxes, pay the mortgage, buy some groceries. Always he had a few cows, so he sold milk, sold butter; intermittently he put up ice to sell to summer cottagers; he worked for the town, boarded the schoolteacher, made maple sugar, maybe raised potatoes, put up hay, and in the 1930s disposed of his oxen (but not his horses) and got seriously into hens and eggs for a few years. Thus he finally paid off his mortgage, but by that time he was sixty-eight years old. Meanwhile, the remaining neighboring farms were going out of business, one by one.

Somewhere, to be sure, thousands of New Hampshire farms were surviving, and some were thriving, but many were dying like this one. From 1939 to 1944 the tax valuation on Auren Powers's farm went steadily downward when, because of wartime inflation, it should have gone upward. Indeed, New Hampshire's total farm income actually doubled during those years. Not his: the farmer was getting old; the place was on the skids; the house developed a deep sag on the far side. In the forty years from 1910 to 1950, 14,000 New Hampshire farms went out of business, and his was just one of these. When Auren Powers died without descendants late in 1944 in the old house where he had been born, it was in the last occupied farm-house in a district that had been reported in the Woods' days as one of the most "thickly settled" farm regions of the town.

When my wife Grace and I arrived in the mid-1960s, old farm equipment still lay collapsed and scattered about the yard and nearby woods, the larger pieces being horse-drawn or oxen-drawn implements, mostly iron or steel, and still sufficiently intact to be identifiable. Here a mower, there by the stone wall a collapsed dump rake and a harrow, and yonder a cultivator and the broken frame of a buggy; in a distant pile near the woods was a sled or parts of a sleigh, and over there the remains of a plow. I recognized them from my days as a youth on a farm, and here in display they offered a weird sense of homecoming, making even the very neglected farmhouse some-how less unattractive. To be sure, such had been the fate of thousands of New Hampshire farms, only this one was not a statistic but a palpable fact before our eyes. The basic story could be read from the surface by a careful observer: sometime in the 1940s this old farm had died in its tracks, and now it just lay there, its bones sticking out.

And such bones as these secrete volumes of rural history. Sometimes you can find and read part of the mixed narrative of New England agriculture right where it lies in the countryside, in the residues of overgrown farm-steads, in gaping cellar holes, in broken farm implements. Eventually, the implements we had inadvertently acquired with our old farmhouse gave up a few hints about their last days. The cultivator testified that there had been some row crops, possibly potatoes, or perhaps corn for the chickens; the mower and dump rake said that haying had once been too serious for a mere scythe; the buggy suggested that the horse had had its uses getting to town and back and delivering ice in summer; the plow and harrow that the land had been, at least for a time, tilled and planted; the absence of a potato digger suggested that Auren Powers had never been too serious about that crop.

Altogether, they clearly said something else, namely, that this farm went out of business in the twentieth century before the tractor came in. Not one of these scattered implements was equipped to be drawn by a tractor. In many American farming communities, and not only in New England, it happened that the tractors on some farms sent the horses and oxen—even on other farms—out to pasture. And this eventually brought it about that these same pastures grew up to brush, and then to forest, as many now stand. It was horsepower (oxen, mule) and its limitations as much as anything that long restricted the size of many farms, and as a consequence it was tractor power that often created the real watershed among smaller American family farms. The tractor transgressed the limits of size and farming style that the horse or the ox had rigidly imposed; and on the broader and more open regions of the country especially, this opened the way wide to new levels of scale and efficiency and technology.

Looking at those old relics reminded me again that an essential fact about horse-drawn (mule, ox) farm equipment is that its technology is wonderfully uncomplicated, and it was all largely in hand by the beginning of the twentieth century. Horse-drawn equipment, which has no mysteries and no black boxes, can be repaired by the farmer or his blacksmith. Unsurprisingly, most of the tools used on the farm up to World War II were replicas of the ones in use in 1900 and before. Often, they were the very same tools: harrows, mowers, wagons, plows, rakes, potato diggers, cultivators—which were mostly steel that rusted but did not rot. Those old tools lying in my newly acquired farmyard could date from any time between 1875 and 1940—almost as ageless and undated as a pitchfork. One wants to ask, How many farm tools from 1950 are in use today? That change, too, can be largely related to tractors. Once the farmer bought a tractor and replaced his horses with the equivalent investment of, say, three or four cows, he had taken a long step on the road to agribusiness, though most would not have thought of it in this way in the 1940s. The limitations of horsepower include the crucial fact that most farm implements adapted to horses are not directly usable by tractors without radical alteration, without so-called "new attachments." That too shows how the horse put a check on the scale of agriculture, as the Amish understand very well.

Tractors have been around in some form since the beginning of the twentieth century, but they were revolutionary only after World War II: historians point out that the number of tractors on American farms leaped from 1.8 million in 1945 to 4.7 million in 1960. And new implements themselves followed tractors as a matter of course. And since the power was there, or could be put there in next year's design, the new implements were that much bigger. Soon enough, so were the fields. So then was the tractor itself. The tractor was transforming for agriculture, as the automobile was for transportation. But tractors and their elaborate equipment are not well suited to much of the New Hampshire terrain, indeed, to most of the acreage that was once farmed in this state. Most of this hilly and rocky land is reasonably comfortable to oxen, some of it to horses, but only a small proportion of it to large machinery. What is farmed in New Hampshire today does not include most of the land once farmed with oxen or horses. So, I was forced to reflect, Auren Powers could never be a tractor farmer on this farm. Which meant that he would not have a successor.

Having admired and studied the old farm machinery, and having read as much as could be found legible in it, we reluctantly called for help and had two large dump truck loads of it picked up and hauled away for recycling. Farewell, old New Hampshire farm.

*New Century Landscapes*

To form a clearer perspective on Northeast farming at the beginning of the twenty-first century, I stopped in to talk with Stephen H. Taylor, commissioner of the New Hampshire Department of Agriculture, Markets, and Food; and I also attended the annual midwinter New Hampshire Farm and Forest Exposition in Manchester, New Hampshire.

Commissioner Taylor is a quick study, and he rapidly sketched for me one way to view present-day Granite State agriculture. Look at it in terms of two streams, he said: on the one hand there are, as there have been for a couple of hundred years, still a fair number of "commodity farms," whose produce is largely wholesaled; and these are often single-commodity farms (though many vegetable, fruit, and greenhouse farms are diversified), often driven by the need for efficiency. Many commodity farms are owned by older farmers, he observed, and some often carry considerable debt simply as a way of doing business. Such are New England's remaining dairy farms, chicken farms, apple, berry, Christmas tree, hay, vegetable, and greenhouse farms, and also some few of its maple syrup farms; they rely precariously upon a commodity that has a more or less certain market, but not necessarily a price-favorable one. On the other hand, said Commissioner Taylor, obviously warming to his subject, there are hundreds of "niche farms": individual, entrepreneurial, sometimes part-time operations that have found and carefully targeted a special market niche for what is often a specialty product—fish, honey, lambs, goats, cheese, strawberries, alpacas, roses, mushrooms, wool, or, again, maple syrup. Taylor said that this is often the direction in which younger farmers are pointed.

These two types of farms—commodity and niche—overlap, of course, but in a rough and ready way anyone can see the difference between these kinds of farming. It is notable that both contrast sharply with the older and traditional several-crop or mixed livestock farm of New England history and idealized memory. Steve Taylor would certainly not have summarized New Hampshire farming in this bifurcated way even fifty years ago. The niche farm is occasionally an elaborate hobby that is also sometimes fortunate enough to turn a profit. The commodity farm, on the other hand, had better be profitable, or perhaps a whole family, maybe of several generations, is in trouble. New Hampshire dairy farms—of which there were precisely 156 on January 1, 2003, down from 167 the year before—have an average herd size of about a hundred cows, and produce more milk than we can consume in this state. Also, commodity apple farmers yearly pick over a million bushels of apples in New Hampshire, nearly a bushel apiece for every citizen of the state. We could handle that amount nicely, but in fact we ship them the world over, just as we eat apples from a dozen countries. Maple syrup is another major commodity, and seventy-five to a hundred thousand gallons of it come each year from New Hampshire, and more and more of that is going to foreign countries. Poultry and eggs today make up a much smaller part of the commodity market, and indeed most of the eggs produced in the state come from just a few farms.

Now in the new century, Steve Taylor tells me, there are about 3,000 farms in New Hampshire, and their numbers are *increasing*. He means that to surprise me, and it clearly pleases him. Of these New Hampshire farms fewer than 400 could be classed as commodity farms, a large proportion of them dairy farms, but they also include some serious vegetable farms, many with an important retail component. He remarked that New Hampshire farmers were once famous for their potato crops, grown in our naturally cool and acid soils. (Checking on this, I learned that in 1925 potatoes were New Hampshire's leading cash crop, and that today no New Hampshire potatoes are raised for the major commodity markets.) But if some commodity farming, such as dairying, is still declining in New Hampshire, niche and retail and other diversified farming is definitely on the rise, with a growing variety of activities and exotic products—goat cheese, sheep cheese, buffalo steaks, alpaca lambs, angora wool, emu eggs, and the like. Meanwhile, farmers' markets and organic farms are increasing in number every year, as they are throughout the entire country. Taylor admits to having been skeptical for a long time of the prospects for alternative-animal agriculture, but he finds it growing a little every year and now says: "I'm convinced it's here to stay. Across New Hampshire we've got elk, deer, bison, llama, alpaca, emu, and ostrich farms and plenty of enthusiastic owners."

Still, the modern economy does not deal more kindly with farming in many areas of the American Northeast than do climate and terrain. Cross-country transportation on public highways powered by cheap oil, Midwestern productivity, Californian agribusiness, and the global market bear down heavily upon New England family farms. All kinds of anomalies appear in the wake of the drive to streamline, make efficient, and rationalize the food industry. During our own apple-picking time, apples from New Zealand, South Africa, and Washington State, usually indistinguishable from local fruit (except that they are not so fresh), are all over New Hampshire stores. Much of New England's commodity farming—dairy, apples, maple syrup, eggs, beef—moves now among remote economic and food industry institutions and pressures that appear to originate as far away and remain as unappeasable as the stars themselves.

Nevertheless, festivals that celebrate farm and country life in the Northeast are thriving. The summer is hardly long enough to contain all the agriculture fairs, for in the Northeast several states mount one in midwinter. In fact, if you (along with ten thousand others) were to attend the New Hampshire Farm and Forest Exposition when it is held each February in Manchester, New Hampshire, you might form the impression that New Hampshire farming, despite its long and rocky road from colonial days to the present, is not only still alive and well but even exuberant.

Perhaps this winter exposition is just an elaborate excuse to have an off-season country fair, an effort to drive out the northern doldrums and liven up the dead of winter. But it puts an inviting face on twenty-first-century New Hampshire farming. Walk through the door of this place, hear the bleat of sheep and buzz of honeybees, catch the aroma and good cheer, linger a few hours among the tools and workshops and displays, and you may find yourself thinking that this is the year to become a serious niche farmer. The two-day event is many things: trade show for equipment dealers, a heavy schedule of solid workshops on everything from food labeling to invasive species to equine management; also an animal minishow, awards festival for exemplary farmers, an opportunity for several dozen New Hampshire farm-based organizations to tell their story and distribute their literature. It's a general get-together for the landed folk. And if you are of a certain type you will also find yourself picking up reams of available literature.

The first brochure in my hand tells me that agriculture contributes annually nearly $700 million to New Hampshire's economy, that it directly engages well over five thousand people and thousands more indirectly. One reflects: if such an enterprise were entirely concentrated in one place it would be a large and impressive business; but it is in fact a business scattered over nearly five hundred thousand acres where, as a social by-product, it is largely responsible for maintaining the visual architecture, as it were, of the state's beloved landscapes. No other business in the state does anything nearly so benign. If today New Hampshire has 3,000 farms, you can count that as a major drop from the 13,000 of 1950 when the Wood-Powers farm sank from sight; but you can also reflect that the current numbers appear to have bottomed out and are slowly rising.

Stop at the booth of the New England Agriculture Statistics Service and you can come away with piles of data.[35] Here you learn that a farm is still defined, as for decades past, as any place that raises for market a thousand dollars' worth of produce. As this bureau measures things, the principal growing edge of New Hampshire agriculture today is not dairy, apples, or syrup, but something called environmental horticulture. "The fastest growing and largest segment of our agriculture" says the official pamphlet, "includes greenhouse and nursery production, flowers, turf, landscape materials, etc." I continue to collect pamphlets, brochures, and handouts on subjects that interest me, and soon I have acquired a deep stack of local farm lore, a week's worth of worthy bedtime reading. I have a young library of information from all sorts of New Hampshire farm organizations, and a dozen market directories and information bulletins. I learn where to get barn plans, where to find a lambing clinic, where to get my soil tested, how to fatten and process pigs, and I now know how to get in touch with everybody from the New Hampshire Compost Association to the New Hampshire Maple Producers Association. Were I to become a farmer this year I could draw upon far more than just my own wits. What might traditional farmers, like the Wood and Powers families, have done with all these workshops, with all this learning and lore, with all this assistance? My local farm library grows rapidly. It now occupies a fat niche on my bookshelves, running from angora goats to zinnias.

At the exposition I met Otho Wells, of the University of New Hampshire, a horticulture specialist. He has a remarkably favorable view of Northeast agriculture, a subject he has researched and taught for thirty-five years. Indeed, by some direct measures of agricultural "productivity," he suggests, New England is a national leader. This region, he notes, has the heaviest concentration in the country of retail farming operations; moreover, at least 75 percent of the population is within ten miles of a retail outlet selling fresh produce on a seasonal basis. Looking at New England fruit and vegetable production, for example, he relates yield per acre, or income from farm retail sales, to the average number of frost-free growing days per year. Growing days are few in our case, as compared with double and triple the number in more southern regions. "Productivity" in these terms, says Wells, puts this region's retail farming in the forefront. Moreover, because the New England landscape is "a hodgepodge of small communities interspersed among pockets of tillable and fertile soil, diversified crop production and marketing are very closely and intricately intertwined," he says. And that is one of the reasons Wells finds that New England has "the most exciting agriculture of anyplace in the United States."

My gleanings from various authorities yield a partial perspective, to be sure, but on the basis of this showing at least, the end of Granite State farming, pending for a hundred years, is certainly not yet. New Hampshire farming as a whole is undoubtedly more diversified than it ever was, its productivity is remarkably high, and its numbers more or less stabilized. Moreover, such evident signs and symbols of vital farm life are not unique to New Hampshire. Similar grass roots are native to many regions, and they continue to sprout and spread throughout the country.

# Chapter 3

# Agrarianism: Three Defining Voices

Certainly one of the happiest of men is the good farmer who lives close to the storm and the forest, the drought and the hail, . . . whose sense of beauty and poetry is born of the earth, whose satisfactions, whether in love or the production of a broad rich field, are direct and fundamental. . . .　　　　　　　—LOUIS BROMFIELD, *From My Experience* (1955)

By any yardstick one uses, we are now in the penultimate stage of the death of agrarianism, the idea that farmland of roughly like size and nature should be worked by individual families.　　　　　　　—VICTOR DAVIS HANSON, *Field without Dreams* (1996)

But the care of this earth is our most ancient and most worthy and, after all, our most pleasing responsibility.　　　　　　　—WENDELL BERRY, *The Unsettling of America* (1977)

Husbandry breeds literature. Forceful spokesmen on behalf of family farming are part of the American literary tradition, and in this chapter I feature three of them. These are voices of twentieth-century farmers, none of them connected directly with the American Northeast, as it happens. But prophetic writers they certainly are, each bearing singular and eloquent witness, each very much alive to the historical moment and context for which he speaks. These voices arise from the American heartland and from the Far West, and all three are *agrarian* voices—a term to be explored in this chapter.

### Three Agrarians

For the true agrarian, the land is everything. This may be an oversimplification, but the land is where the agrarian scale of values is grounded. The term itself—which comes from the Latin *agrarius,* pertaining to land— has long been on the margins of our public discourse, never central but always relevant to a nation whose land and farms have been so vital to its identity. Figures as far apart, and as similar, as Cicero and Jefferson might not have called themselves agrarians—but we do. Until the twentieth century the word was rarely used with its current rich connotations—which now imply a philosophical outlook and a scale of values related to the land and to people, and to the care and husbandry of soil and the earth. Still, the term is a bit precious for daily use, and sometimes more evocative than precise.

By "land" agrarians mean not just soil but also air and water, landscapes and farmscapes, place and home, habitat, entire ecological communities— in any case, not just real estate. Agrarianism's central idea that land is the principal locus of value is often associated with the more developed and polemical idea that a truly humane life is fostered not by cities and industry, which tend toward acquisitiveness, but by the nurturing disciplines of nature and husbandry and by local economies and landed communities. To the historically minded the term is widely suggestive of the special dignity accorded to agricultural pursuits and values, a theme always present but often recessive throughout our entire Western culture. Our three authors are recent American agrarians, but each in his own way.

The first of the three—Louis Bromfield of Ohio—speaks for agriculture at the middle of the twentieth century, for family farming recovering from Dust Bowl, Depression, and war. The second—Victor Davis Hanson of California—writes of family farming at the end of the twentieth century, especially as it cringes before the onslaught of the metropolis and corporate agriculture. The third—Wendell Berry of Kentucky—is today widely known and admired as poet, novelist, farmer, essayist, who marches to a different and traditional drummer. Together, they frame and directly illuminate the recent half century during which family farming has been radically transformed and the meaning of agrarianism has assumed sharper and more vivid contours.

As the quotations at the head of this chapter suggest, each of these writers approaches agriculture with an attitude: Bromfield is exuberant, Hanson combative, Berry pensive. This may suggest that these agrarians do not have a lot in common, and in a way they don't—except that they all write a lot, and much of it is about agriculture, and all of it bespeaks a powerful empathy with American landed traditions. Each provides a highly individual and forceful literary variation on the struggle that is family farming, even as they imply rather different ideals of character to be forged in that crucible. None of these writer-farmers is in the least bit typical, either of writers or farmers, or anything else; and they might find it strange to see themselves linked in this chapter. But they are all agrarians.

Louis Bromfield has been dead and gone almost fifty years, and his Ohio farm is now preserved as a state park. Victor Davis Hanson is still very much around to stimulate and engage us today, farming in the San Joaquin Valley, writing a new book almost every year; he probably expects his California farm to be buried under a shopping mall. Wendell Berry, explicitly calling himself an agrarian, has been exploring that commitment in poetry and prose for over thirty years, and he doubtless hopes his Kentucky farm will be farmed by his descendants.

## Louis Bromfield: Quest for the Good Farmer

Louis Bromfield (1896–1956) of Ohio was probably the most interesting and informed spokesman among American farmers around the middle of the twentieth century. He was a novelist, farmer, and self-appointed agriculture prophet and visionary, whose unusual life and work provide a clear window on American farming in the middle of the century. To his farming enterprises he brought not only his own personal wealth but the even greater wealth of his enormous idealism and ambition, to say nothing of his natural capacity for being provocative. Bromfield actually sought to change the course of American agriculture, and he aimed to do it, not by preaching from a university chair, but by example, by the hard-won wisdom of practical and personal experience on his own farm, and by publicizing the results in books and lectures and conversations. Doing so, he made himself into probably the most visible farmer in America at the time.

Born a country boy in Ohio, and reared on a succession of unsuccessful farms at the beginning of the twentieth century, young Bromfield was prompted by his mother, who hated the dismal life of the rural poor, to escape the bleak countryside for the city and a career in journalism. He did this successfully in New York but soon left that for the greater adventure of ambulance driving in France during World War I. He participated in battles, was awarded the Croix de Guerre, returned to journalism, then switched to novel writing. He was a quick study and a swift success. From the first, and for more than two decades thereafter, all his many novels were moneymakers and best-sellers, and many were critically acclaimed. With his second book (*Early Autumn*) he won the Pulitzer Prize for 1926, then secured Hollywood contracts and friends and started to make piles of money. Eventually a dozen of his novels and short stories became films. He traveled widely, secured a venerable home with large gardens outside Paris, acquired a wife, beautiful daughters, and also money, celebrity friends, and international fame.

In 1933 Bromfield published his seventh novel—mainly autobiographical it turned out—with the uninspiring name *The Farm*, about a young man who had achieved success in the city but whose heart was lodged in the ancestral soil of his native place, to which he returned years later to find the family farm a melancholy and neglected ruin. At the time, America was in a deep economic depression and nearly every working farm was on the skids, but still Bromfield's *The Farm* sold well. More of his stories became movies, and he eventually wrote screen scripts for Hollywood friends, such as Samuel Goldwyn, and for money. More, perhaps, than any of his Parisian American-expatriate literary friends, Bromfield was the man who had everything, and in 1935 he wrote a successful novel titled *The Man Who Had Everything*.

If this yarn sounds like a strange way to begin breeding a farmer, that's because it is. Exiled, as he felt he was, to the sophistication and decadence of old Europe, a culture he saw drifting out of depressions into wars, increasingly doubtful of the value of fame and fortune, Louis Bromfield admitted to himself that the one thing he didn't have was the one thing he really wanted. He wanted to own and live on and work a farm in Ohio, to take a typically run-down piece of American land and make it into a good and productive farm, and there put down family roots. He wanted to come home to his native land. It may be that some agrarians are born and not made.

Later, he wrote of his European experience. "It occurred to me that the honors I valued most out of all those I had received was the diploma given me by the Workingmen-Gardeners' Association of France for my skill as a gardener and the medal given me by the Ministry of Agriculture for introducing American vegetables into popular cultivation in the market garden area surrounding the city of Paris." He thought he knew why he valued those honors in particular: it was because they spoke of "a permanence, a continuity which one seldom found in America. When I returned home, I knew that permanence, continuity, alone was what I wanted, not the glittering life of New York and Washington, not the intellectual life of universities. What I wanted was a piece of land which I could love passionately, which I could spend the rest of my life in cultivating, cherishing and improving, which I might leave together, perhaps, with my own feeling for it, to my children who might in time leave it to their children, a piece of land upon which I might leave the mark of my character, my ingenuity, my intelligence, my sense of beauty."

Louis Bromfield loved being a man of the world, but his preferred and chosen self-image was to be that of a farmer. In 1938 he and his family left Europe—then rapidly disintegrating—and bought a farm in Ohio, bought three of them, in fact, then a fourth, and soon leased a fifth. He settled down to work out his dream and, not incidentally, to have an impact by precept and example on American agriculture, which he correctly believed to be in a sorry condition. He called his enterprise Malabar Farm, using a name he had picked up in his travels in India, where several of his novels were based. Succeed or fail, it would be a life more significant to him than making pots of money writing novels. For a time he could afford to be indifferent to fortune and to fame, though, given his character, it was unlikely that Louis Bromfield would be out of the limelight for long.

When he began farming in Ohio in the late 1930s the reputation of American agriculture was perhaps at the lowest ebb in its history: what hung in the public mind was a gallery of bleak images of the Great Depression, forlorn scenes of rural poverty, woebegone farm foreclosures, and the once fertile western prairies degraded to the infamous Dust Bowl. In less than ten years that rural picture changed considerably, stimulated in part by the demands of a nation at war, by government prodding and assistance, by the new markets everywhere, and by the spectacular profit and productivity of wartime—stimulated also, undoubtedly, by the conspicuous propaganda of rural visionaries like Bromfield.

Bromfield's first report on his farming experience, *Pleasant Valley* (1945), tells the story of his return to Ohio, his rather grandiose plans for his farms, and his ambitions for a revitalized American agriculture—which he then imagined would be along very traditional lines, widely diversified and largely self-sustaining. The "good farmer" is now the Bromfield hero: "A good farmer in our times has to know more about more things than a man in any other profession. He has to be a biologist, a veterinary, a mechanic, a botanist, a horticulturist, and many other things, and he has to have an open mind, eager and ready to absorb new knowledge and new ideas and new ideals. . . . We have been inclined in our wild industrial development, to forget that agriculture is the base of our whole economy . . . the cornerstone. It has always been so throughout history and it will continue to be so until there are no more men on this earth. We are apt to forget that the man who owns land and cherishes it and works it well is the source of our stability as a nation. . . ."[36] *Pleasant Valley*, which was an immediate publishing success, called widespread attention to Bromfield's farming experiments with soil conservation, crop rotation, contour farming, the use of brown and green manure; so too did his frequent lecturing, his newspaper articles, his NBC radio programs, and his engaging welcome of the growing crowds of curious visitors to his farm. By now he was a famous novelist of fading reputation and a famous farmer of growing reputation. His next book gave an account of what he had attempted and learned and accomplished as an exemplary farmer, and an equally candid account of his failures.

*Malabar Farm* was published in late 1947, and it immediately became a kind of oddball agricultural classic. It is still, or again, in print today. E. B. White wrote a charming and favorable review of it for the *New Yorker*. Almost everybody praised it; some probably even read it, maybe all five hundred pages of it. As a book it has no particular order; it is verbose and opinionated and frequently entertaining—in part a farm journal, a tract for the times, a scientific treatise, a diary of daily events on the farm, an eloquent plea for land stewardship—altogether a long-winded lecture that not every farmer or agriculture professor wanted to sit still and listen to. It contains engaging vignettes of animal life: a sentimental farewell to a favorite dog, the story of a ram named Haile Selassie who developed a fierce addiction to tobacco, an account of a cow who chewed her cud in rhythm to whatever musical tune was playing on the milking parlor radio (surely the most accomplished cow since Mother Goose's moon jumper), and the like. It is a thoughtful book too: full of ideas and idealism, a fine historical sense, chockablock with soil science and with passionate love and respect for the land and advice to landowners. And the book is prickly with stinging passages about "a whorish, greedy, ignorant agriculture which fastened the label 'hick' to the farmer of the last two generations." It is clear that this farmer-author-critic actually likes farmers, as individuals and as a class. He especially likes the "good farmer," but in this book he just can't see many of them. He focuses a strong dislike on something slightly more abstract, namely, American agriculture.

*Malabar Farm* does not linger over rhapsodies to the family farm and its widely alleged place in the history of American virtue—the author takes that all for granted—nor does it often sing the song of the noble American yeoman farmer of yore. Bromfield does not quote Emerson or Jefferson or Crèvecoeur. More often he looks at one-crop farming and soil erosion and decries a heritage squandered. He might have cited Thoreau, with whom he has a temperamental affinity, though he is really far more interested in his own opinions. Everywhere he assumes or asserts that the farmer's life, at its best and when properly lived, is the model of the good life, by far the most significant, worthwhile, and challenging life. After all—though he never says this—he himself with the world at his feet has simply chosen to be an American farmer. But his real interest is, How good a farmer is the American? Typically, not good enough, in his blunt opinion. Too often the farmer wastes his soil, exploits his land as if farming were mining, and shows little respect for what Bromfield calls "the eternal natural laws" of fertility, management, and stewardship. "There is as much original sin in poor agriculture as there is in prostitution," he says, "and a good deal of the agriculture practiced in this country is itself no more than prostitution. The speculating wheat farmer, the farmer who 'wore out three farms and was still young enough to wear out a fourth,' the miserable one crop cotton farmer. . . . All three represent a whorish agriculture. . . ." Bad farming is a blatant sin against any worthy religion, thinks Bromfield. "I am aware," he admits "that many factors have contributed to the waste and dissipation of our abundance—the absentee landlord, tenant sharecropper systems in which the evils of a parasitic agriculture are doubled, subsidies by government which tend only to preserve and maintain such systems . . . exploitation of the farmer by fertilizer and feed merchants. . . ."[37] Bromfield is even more exasperated with bad farmers than is Thoreau.

Bromfield's hurried glance at poor fields and negligent farmers is withering and, at times, without much sympathy for those who struggled through the Depression just trying to avoid foreclosure. When he returned to Ohio he had some definite—sometimes dogmatic, sometimes tentative and experimental—ideas as to the kind of improvements necessary; so he set out to try them himself and to publicize the results. He was, of course, a well-to-do farmer, and he could afford to think long-term and do what he thought best, and buy the machines and seed and livestock he needed. He asserted, however, that it was a rule at Malabar not to practice or recommend strategies that the typical farmer could not afford, or that were not designed to be eventually self-supporting. By now he had become an effective and much respected missionary for the cause of soil conservation, especially erosion prevention, and restoring fertility through the incorporation of vast amounts of organic materials. He often preached agrarianism but seldom called it by that name: a nation's security and prosperity, he declared forthrightly, are "dependent upon the fertility . . . of the farmer's soil and the efficiency with which he cherishes and manages it."[38]

Bromfield had genuine successes reclaiming his worn-out Ohio farms and making them experimental and productive showpieces, which he did with heavy use of organic materials, and only moderate and always decreasing use of chemical fertilizers. His last and perhaps his best farm book, *From My Experience* (1955), gives a fifteen-year retrospective on his efforts, and his new concern at this time about the use of chemicals in farming is especially impressive. Although he was never doctrinaire about pure organic methods, he did early and often voice emphatic and remarkably prescient warnings about the multiple dangers of chemically intensive farming. He was concerned that "even a mild insecticide such as rotenone could also have a serious toxic effect upon certain living soil bacteria and even upon earthworms and other beneficial living organisms which are essentially a part of any truly healthy, living and productive soils." He expressed early and very deep suspicions of arsenic, DDT, and other pesticides. "Nor do we have any desire," he said, "to act as laboratory specimens for the testing of viciously poisonous inorganic chemical by-products dumped on the market without proper tests or research into their lethal qualities"; and he worried that we simply do not know whether many of these pesticides might "do real harm and serve in a general way to impair the health of the whole nation and to create an increase in degenerative diseases. . . ."[39] Remarkable insights for the 1950s; clearly, Bromfield was on the frontier.

Throughout the summers of the 1940s, hundreds of people would show up at Malabar Farm on a Sunday afternoon, when the farm was open to visitors. For many, it was a kind of farmers' pilgrimage to learn firsthand what this new and noisy book writer was up to with his thousand-acre farm. Initially, he had been devoted to the idea of a farm as a widely diversified and largely self-sufficient entity (a rather old-fashioned concept for someone deeply committed to modern methods), which included the ideal that almost everything consumed at Malabar—by his own extended family, the four or five families who worked for him, other hired help, and his numerous guests—was to be raised there. After a decade he acknowledged that this made more sense during wartime scarcities than in the late 1940s and, moreover, that in the final analysis it just was not an efficient way to conceive of modern farming. His own successes with soil preservation, crop rotation, incorporating organic material, land use, tool purchase and use, animal care, in harvesting and marketing, and so on, brought the question of efficiency sharply to the fore. Some crops and some operations made money; others did not.

At the same time, efficient farming began to matter more for him as the income stream from his novels and Hollywood contracts (now fewer and less lucrative) began to run thin and threatened to run dry. He also had to support his experiments, his workers and their families, his own family, and innumerable friends and visitors; so while the farms and gardens were in many ways successful showpieces, undoubtedly good farms with high yields per acre, and certainly an educational and inspirational focus for the many thousands who came from far to pay attention, it was never exactly clear that they were always financially successful. There were always new investments needed. Moreover, Bromfield was able to develop special markets, such as for registered dairy cattle to be shipped to Pennsylvania and New York dairy farms, that his neighbors could not expect to match.

By the late 1940s Bromfield was urging—for himself first and also for others—that farmers consider relinquishing the type of mixed farming that he himself had advocated ten years before, "a little of this and a little of that." Farmers, he learned, could do a better job by focusing on doing fewer things well. Step by step he abandoned his own heavy investment in poultry, then in his apple orchards, then in raising potatoes, finally in corn: raising chicken feed also did not pay, he found, row crops were hard on the soil, and the equipment rather expensive to buy and maintain. Although he continued his heavy investment in a diversified vegetable retail business, he turned more and more to grass and clover and cattle as the commodities that his Ohio farms, his particular soil and climate, and his markets were best suited to. Bromfield's experience and his own farming practice turned out to be a most explicit metaphor for this stage of American farming generally. In the 1950s he began looking steadily toward a more specialized agriculture, and away from the mixed farming he had idealized and stumped for in the early 1940s. Bromfield's experience dramatically demonstrated, if demonstration was needed (but it seemed to surprise him) that there is not one right way to farm, independent of surrounding economic and cultural conditions. Skill at adaptation became for him another hallmark of the good farmer.

The result of all this—though not of this alone and not fully foreseen by Bromfield or anybody else—was that as American farming became more specialized and more efficient, food prices at the grocery dropped. Efficient farming matured to create, not necessarily higher profits at farm, but almost inevitably cheaper food at the grocery. A glance at the statistical tables of the U.S. Agriculture Census shows that the historical moment in the twentieth century when Americans, as a whole, spent the highest percentage of their disposable income on food was 1947 (the year *Malabar Farm* was published); since which time this percentage has steadily dropped right to the end of the century, when it was the lowest. This is pretty exactly correlated with the growth of efficiencies in farming and food processing—and this is the issue taken up later in this book, in chapter 8. Bromfield had begun, about 1940, to be properly concerned about the high price of food for consumers and about the misuse and depletion of soil, and then he became concerned about the need for farming efficiency and the lack of specialization. If we put aside for a moment the important concept of who owns the farm and think only of the farming method, then we see that what Bromfield eventually came to practice and advocate was, in many respects, a *forecast* of what developed in America during the next fifty years. Today, unlike the 1940s, retail food is both abundant and cheap, farmers are specialized as never before, and they are also heavily mechanized, often deeply indebted, not diversified, and prodigiously efficient. But this still does not mean that all is well on the farm.

It is to be expected that the author of *Malabar Farm* did not foresee the degree to which the efficiencies and specializations its author came to recommend, and the scientific tinkering they encouraged, would eventually overwhelm and transform agriculture. Today, there are very few of the kind of poor run-down farms that Bromfield so deplored in the late 1930s, farms that offered a poor livelihood then and would now offer none at all. Of the poor farms he criticized, and took to be typical of the majority of American farms at that time, those that have not been converted to something like his way of thinking have been brusquely pushed to the margins or absorbed by better farms or driven out of business, simply because they could not today sustain a family.

He did not then fully imagine that "the good farmer" whom he idealized might somehow, in some places, give way to a large corporate agency wherein something properly called a "farmer" can hardly be picked out and identified within a cadre of machine operators and computer-wielding technicians. To those who wrote about farming in those days, Bromfield among them, it may have seemed that it would always be the case that a substantial percentage of the American populace would be farmers. Maybe it didn't seriously occur to Bromfield and others that if farms and farming improved, if farms became more productive and efficient, and if other continents and nations (China, India, Africa) became food self-sufficient, then the American farm population and farm communities would *necessarily* decline in numbers and therefore in social importance. Hardly anyone foresaw that they would shrink in half a century to include only a tiny percentage of the population.

As much as anything Louis Bromfield yearned to see the profession of farming itself, which he passionately loved and idealized, restored to what he took to be its proper place: socially honored and solvent, professional, devoted above all to land and animal stewardship, healthy and health giving, backbone of community, and pride of the nation. When this agrarian novelist-turned-prophet was not spinning out a new farm idea every day, he was stirring up controversy by handing out praise and blame to American farmers. "Never forget," he wrote with emphasis in the introduction to *Malabar Farm*, "that agriculture is the oldest of the honorable professions and that always the good farmer is the *fundamental* citizen of any community, state, or nation."

### *Victor Davis Hanson: Embattled Family Farmer*

It is sometimes suggested that California is a decade or so in advance of the rest of the nation. It is also sometimes responded that this is quite true, and that it represents a decade's advance toward disaster. If the original maxim holds for family farming, it may be worth glancing across the continent to see what the weather has in store for the rest of us. We can hear some of the news from an articulate farmer right there on the front lines. Victor Hanson is a classics professor, author of a stack of books on modern agriculture and on ancient Greek rural history and warfare, and in addition he is a fourth-generation California fruit farmer. He works and writes under both hats, always interestingly, usually irreverently, and sometimes with a sizable chip on his shoulder.

Some decades ago, after completing his doctorate, Hanson left the university to help manage his family's fruit farm, where Thompson raisin grapes have been one of his family's chief crops for generations. After about a decade on the farm ("the disastrous 80s," he calls it) he came to regard small farming as pretty much a failure, as did thousands of other American farmers at the time. Many of them concluded that family farms like theirs were doomed by agribusiness and its attendants. So Hanson returned to teaching and to academic scholarship, but he didn't leave the farm or farming. California State University at Fresno was down the freeway, and there he helped to start a classics department. For more than a decade now he has divided his time between teaching, academic research, family fruit farming, being very irritated, and doing a prodigious amount of writing. As befits a man who earned his academic spurs studying the sciences and arts of warfare, almost all his writing, ancient or modern, has a polemical edge. Indeed, farming is warfare by other means, and potential enemies are all about: fungi, bankers, insects, developers, bacteria, food processors, weeds, university people. Despite his embattled stance, Hanson's is one of the most interesting and arresting voices writing today on family farming. He speaks directly as a farmer and on behalf of the farmer, although not all farmers would approve of what he says, and probably not many farmers will read what he writes. He draws his agrarian inspiration from wide-ranging sources, principally from Crèvecoeur and the ancient Greeks and his own ancestors. Not all of what he has to say is edifying, but most of it is arresting and important.

In *Field without Dreams* (1996), Hanson concentrates on California fruit farming. He does not linger over the ways in which that compares to, say, farming hogs in Iowa or corn in Ohio or poultry in New York; but in fact nothing on the American horizon suggests to him hopeful prospects for small family farms. So he generalizes boldly from his own experience, much of it unsatisfactory. A recurrent theme is that the combined effects of corporatization, vertical integration, economies of scale, global markets, subsidized transportation, and even university research and government loan and support policies have now thoroughly conditioned American consumers: we expect large quantities of very cheap, good-looking, and fresh food, regardless of season and largely regardless of taste. And this is exactly what American agribusiness supplies by the truckloads. There are, he knows, various niches in this formidable structure of food supply, but not many, not large, and not for long—once the preying corporations spot another candidate for buyout. Thus the vivid imagery of predator and prey permeates his farm books: as he sees it, the American family farm and farmer are usually prey. In short, he is writing biting elegies for what he regards as a vanishing species, even as he is extravagantly celebrating the strenuous and heroic life of the farm. So these, which he is celebrating, are fields without dreams. "Any book about farming must now not be romantic nor naive, but brutally honest: The American yeoman is doomed; his end is part of an evolution of long duration."[40]

So what is it of value that America is losing? Hanson has a well-delineated conception of the American farmer as naturally blunt, brutal at times, taciturn, and in various ways unattractive; and then, as if to illustrate the point, he sometimes comes across that way himself. Perhaps he would like us to think of him, too, as tough and nasty if he needs to be. Thus his dislike for field men, company reps, salesmen, brokers, agribusiness agents, bankers, and all their kith and kind is palpable on many a page. But even as he sounds hard or sarcastic, sometimes angry, he is often eloquent and insightful; and now and again he turns the other cheek and waxes positively poetic about some remote aspect of farming. In one book, for example, he lays down warm paragraphs about the marvelous Thompson grape and intersperses them with glowing descriptions of the rather different marvels of his beloved vineyard tractors. All in all, his is a point of view that mixes appreciation, passion, and even wonder with large doses of cantankerousness, and he portrays and illustrates the American farmer in his natural state as defiant, no-nonsense, and contrary. He is preparing us for the argument, later in the books, that a democratic society absolutely requires such farmers, not despite such qualities but precisely because they are so different, so rough hewn, so stubbornly independent.

In *Field without Dreams* Hanson declares that there really can be no serious controversy over the status of agriculture in America. "By any yardstick one uses, we are now in the penultimate stage of the death of agrarianism, the idea that farmland of roughly like size and nature should be worked by individual families." All studies, he says, by both conservatives and liberals alike "point the same way and can be reinforced by personal anecdote and direct observation." He reels off statistics: 1 percent of farmers now account for more than half of all farm income; nearly 90 percent of all farmers earn less then $20,000; two thousand family farms a week vanished in the decade of the 1980s; and so on. Hanson tries to give his due to those who say these trends are inevitable. But what exactly *do* they say? This is his summary of their view: "Based on proven economies of scale, they say farm corporatization is as American as the rise of the industrial state in the nineteenth century. As small car companies gave way in the early twentieth century to Ford, GM and Chrysler, as oddball tinkerers and nuts like Studebaker and Tucker were absorbed by their more extensive brethren so that we in America might enjoy at last air bags, antilock brakes, and power windows, so too agriculture will be and must be transformed."[41] This is the view that agriculture has no special status that might exempt it from the unyielding "canons of capital, finance, and production." That's what they say, says Hanson.

In the face of that, family farmers and those who would save them might suppose that Hanson would be forthright in joining their side. But he is no ordinary liberal, and no ordinary farmer: "We few left in farming mostly despise those who are dedicated to saving us," he says. Such a sentence gives reflective pause to anyone writing a book on the fate of family farming. How are those sympathetic with family farming being perceived? "Some are the radical environmentalists and utopians at the fringes of every reform school . . . the majority . . . are an idealistic but often rather protected species of conservationist and renegade university professor."[42] Having put the do-gooders aside, Professor Hanson puts on his contrary farmer's cap and reminds us that the dilemmas of American farming are also loaded with bitter ironies; and he lays them out without mercy for fellow farmers especially to contemplate:

Farmers, baffled at foe and ally alike, stand in the vortex, dumbfounded that conservatives like themselves now advocate radical farm policies that destroyed their land and families; they are even more surprised to hear distasteful liberals champion their notion of conservation and protection from continuous government onslaught and corporate subsidy. Democrats have outlawed farmers' beloved chemicals that have poisoned their well water and made them sick and sterile; Republicans have protected the hated laissez-faire world of the broker that has robbed them. Democrats demand fair and managed trade overseas that enriches domestic farm export. Republicans champion absolutely free international commerce that has dumped subsidized foreign products on the market and helped to ruin the American farmer.[43]

We come shortly to what may be the harshest irony of all. We Americans generally, he says, would declare that we love and respect and treasure the family farm, but in reality we don't, as witness our collective actions and our permissive inactions. In myriad ways we abandon and flee the farm. Says Hanson: the verdict on the American family farm does not lie with either the farmer or with those who would devise policies to save him, "the verdict lies rather with the American people, and they have now passed judgment." The hard fact, he says, is that, on the whole, Americans no longer care much where or how they get their food; "as long as it is firm, fresh and cheap," they have little interest in preventing the urbanization of their farmland "as long as parks, Little League fields, and an occasional bike lane are left amid the concrete, stucco and asphalt." They feel no need for knowing the farmer, "someone who they are not," and especially they do not wish to be confronted by someone "who reminds them of their past and not their future." Indeed, he declares that all of us have been running from "the isolation, uncertainty, boredom, toil, and drudgery of the farm" for a century now, and today we have largely escaped it entirely. No longer need we "worry about rains and hail that wipe out years of labor and capital . . . or brokers who devour our young." What Americans really desire is "the security of the corporation and bureaucracy even as we hate what we become." We run from the farm "only to dream that it might save us all yet."[44]

Is this only Californian hyperbole speaking? A decade or two in advance of the rest of us?

Hanson writes out of both sides of his career: the nuanced and deferential academic, the blunt and angry farmer. Eloquent chapters detail his battles as a farmer: with weather and weeds and plant diseases, with equipment and neighbors and developers and vandals, and with the unsettling metropolis, creeping implacably over the hills and devouring his neighborhood. In our times, serious farming ultimately instills a tragic view of life; he is sure of that, but sure at the same time that it may occasionally be a great, even a splendid and heroic life. Bad things happen, and are to be expected: crops freeze, disease spreads, debts multiply, the rains fail, the land is divided. Strength of character derives from how one responds to the stern hand of fate.

In *The Land Was Everything* Hanson explores these darker themes. "Farmers see things as others do not," the book begins. "Their age-old knowledge is more than the practical experience that comes from the art of growing food or from the independence of rural living. It involves a radically different—often tragic—view of human nature itself that slowly grows through the difficult struggle to work and survive from the land."[45] The frustrations of farming bend the farmer out of shape, when he wants desperately to concentrate only on his land and his work. For a multitude of reasons, many having to do with the daily battles with weather and markets and crop losses in a society of ease and abundance, "the last generation of American farmers have become foreign to their countrymen, who were once as they." Farmers, he believes, are now almost alone in understanding their tragic fate, and accepting it, "this doom of the universe that has no solution on this earth, this law that freedom, drive, ambition, and self-interest alone create all of what we have, and yet make us become what we do not like."[46]

And Hanson is frequently not satisfied even with his own dark view: "Sometimes I think the agrarian comes even to not like himself for what this insight from agriculture, this daily testimony to plant and animal ruthlessness has done to him, this unhappy insight that character more often comes from tragedy, virtue rarely from success."[47] But this too helps to explain the farmer's nature and character: "Sometimes I see why at sixty he is gnarled, and tough-tongued, and apart from this world." But more than tough stoicism is involved here. Throughout these books Hanson's argument is rooted in the question of the relation between a healthy agriculture and a healthy society, between making a living from the land and making a nation of citizens. What ultimately is required to sustain a good society and democratic institutions? For one thing, Hanson reasons, we need at a minimum (just as the Greek *polis* and Roman *civitas* needed, just as the Revolutionary founders of America needed and had) a reservoir of "tough, unpleasant, skeptical and independent" people—individuals, families, communities who daily battle nature and the elements with their muscles and their wits, who force food from the soil, who tame the wild, and who, stoically or joyously, take the rough encounter of the countryside, not the blandness of city and society, as their everlasting challenge and their measure. They are those who cultivate and symbolize for the rest of us the ancient virtues of liberty and frugality and industry: and to the degree that they can remain independent of some larger economic system, to that degree they are free to contribute to the public good. This is Jeffersonianism with an attitude: the attitude is that the Hansonian yeoman on whom the democratic order depends may be a fellow we don't much like.

Hanson believes that our liberalism and our cultured leisure, our capacity for social nuance and evasion and irony and knowingness—these need to be forever confronted, somehow, somewhere by the Other, and by citizens who forcefully embody that force and presence. "Democracy and capitalism . . . will ultimately bury us all beneath a sea of affluence and liberality if there is not a body of independent thought and action outside our reach. And that counterpoint and corrective to the evolution of American culture . . . is not to be found in the corporation, the government, or the university."[48] To be sure, this is also a plea for a culture less decadent—one not wholly dominated by the weakling who "depends on someone else for everything from his food to his safety." But (to repeat): as a "counterpoint and corrective to the evolution of American culture," we need persons of "independent thought and action outside our reach." This is vague and heavy stuff, to be sure, but that is what is needed to sustain a democratic society, we are being told. And precisely that, according to farmer-professor Hanson, is the historic calling of an American yeomanry, and is ultimately why he and we should care about the fate of family farming.

Hanson doesn't just make this stuff up out of whole cloth: he extracts it from his reading of history, especially Greek history, which he knows as intimately as his back forty. "I have argued at length elsewhere [he means

*The Other Greeks: The Family Farm and the Agrarian Roots of Western Civilization*] that the entire history of Greece, the origins of Western civilization itself, lies in the countryside."[49] All the ideas we now associate with the Greek *polis* "followed from, did not precede, a vibrant agrarianism." Athenian democracy, Hanson says, was not a radical departure for the Greeks but rather a "further and logical refinement of a prior two centuries of agrarian egalitarianism."

If indeed—omitting niceties—we can say that in significant ways Greek civilization followed from the way the Greeks had organized and related to the economy of their countryside, then we touch upon a profoundly important parallel with American history. Both point emphatically to the historical and cultural significance of a vigorous and more or less stable agricultural class, providing, as it were, a leaven for the entire national ethos. Of course, one of the founding ideas of America itself involved an ideal of self-reliant, self-employed rural individuals: Jefferson's "independent yeomen farmers," or Hanson's "eccentric, independent citizens vital to consensual government." But if the family farmer is forever beleaguered, and his mundane prospects anything but bright, Hanson still has a Jeffersonian confidence in the fundamental moral importance for society of the agricultural life. Ultimately, it is farmers and laborers, the independent and resilient ones, people who work with their hands and wits and hearts, families dedicated to the land through the generations, who embody the virtues that make nations strong and who give to democracy its initial impetus. The Greeks knew this, he constantly reminds us: they too believed in equality, in private property, in political dissent, in political rights and independent responsibility; and it was the life of the countryside that nourished these things. Agriculture, he says, will "always be a war. At the conflict's most dramatic, during an unseasonable storm or foreclosure warning, the agrarian fight becomes real bloodletting, a brutal, horrific, yet sometimes heroic experience." In this battle, individuals are ultimately temporary, even dispensable, but the land with its legends and its possibility and its meaning is permanent, the locus of value.

*The Land Was Everything*—so Hanson titled his book, and so it was for his great-grandfather, and grandfather, and for his parents, who had once farmed his fruit lands. So too was this entire limitless American landscape to the French immigrant farmer Hector St. John de Crèvecoeur, whose *Letters from an American Farmer* serve Hanson as foil and inspiration. Like any good farmer Hanson is eager, even desperate, to keep faith with his forebears on his ancestral land—which once was everything. That land was limitless possibility, the place to employ one's labor and invest one's hope, and it nourished freedom itself; it was livelihood and security and the promise of the future; in hard times it meant food and survival, it represented community and heritage, it was the great equalizer, and it would endure, with careful stewardship, though crops and families failed, and would bind together and outlast individuals and generations. American land gave birth to American character. It was the great and good gift outright of which the poets sang. The land was everything.

And what is it now? Hanson's conclusion comes on the book's last page. "That the land is now nothing is the real diagnosis of modern man's mysterious spiritual illness."

The farmers Louis Bromfield in 1950 and Victor Davis Hanson in 2000 contemplate very different realities: different times, places, crops, different economies, and utterly different challenges. Both write out of their own, often wrenching, sometimes exhilarating, and utterly different experience, but also out of long and personal family traditions of farming. They are spirited spokesmen for the issues, cultural and agricultural, of their own day, for the history they live and lived through, for the promise and plight of family farming. And both are disposed to see these trials and triumphs in epic terms.

It remains remarkable that in the middle of the twentieth century the American countryside could raise up freewheeling adventurers, could still give birth and shape to the buoyant and sometimes cranky idealism of a fearless farmer like Louis Bromfield, and could give to that singular outlook and career a voice that resonated clear across all the farming valleys of the Midwest. But at the end of the century such a rallying call for realistic or daring farming entrepreneurship is hardly to be imagined. More to be expected perhaps is the melancholy voice of one, such as Hanson, experienced at casting a long and backward glance with furrowed brow over troubled history, as if to take the full measure of a venerable tradition that, he deeply regrets to say, may have run its course. The heroic days are in the past. Whereas Bromfield sought to reinvigorate the charter of American agrarianism, Hanson offers to write its elegy.

But the time for elegies is not yet, and maybe not ever: such is the word from somewhere deep in the American heartland. Today the voice that succeeds Bromfield's of a half century ago has a more philosophical and reflective tone, and it belongs to an essayist and poet. The message does not tell us how to plow and plant and harvest, but it reminds us yet again why it all matters and why we should care. If Victor Hanson belongs temperamentally to Thoreau's party, Wendell Berry belongs to Emerson's party.

*Wendell Berry: Agrarian Traditionalist*

Wendell Berry of Kentucky, writer, poet-farmer, seer, foe of agribusiness, has in common with Bromfield and Hanson an unwavering commitment to agrarian ways of thinking and feeling, and a good part of his life's work has been to express and defend that outlook through poems and fiction, through essays, books, and lectures.

Like that of Hanson, Berry's life journey has involved a shuttle between the land and the university. He was born and reared in the Kentucky farm region where he now lives and works, and although he taught and wrote for a time in New York and elsewhere, by the early 1960s he sensed that his ancestral land, in all its history and drama, its people and tragedy and poetry—six generations of Berrys in the same region of Kentucky—was inescapably his life's theme. He bade farewell to New York City and returned to rural Kentucky, a move that may recall Louis Bromfield's leaving Paris for his Ohio homeland, or Hanson's quitting the university for the family farm. Returning to the land—this is, of course, a powerful and evocative theme in both history and literature and, indeed, in every personal life in which it is seriously enacted, and it may sometimes become one of the spiritual taproots of agrarianism itself.

For nearly forty years now Berry has poured out a stream of stories, poems, novels, essays that speak to an ever widening circle of readers. Sometimes complete strangers develop an instant rapport with each other when they mutually discover that they are Wendell Berry readers. It is not usually his plots or arguments or fictional characters that they are responding to but rather an entire perspective on life, a system of values, which includes a deep spiritual kinship with the earth and its human and ecological communities, indeed, a quietly subversive perspective on modern life, together with a remarkably rich and wide-ranging literary and poetic expressiveness. Many, even urbanized individuals, sense the deep appeal of his sensitive agrarian outlook, though they may not be able to say just why. Altogether, Berry's writing constitutes one of the most impressive, certainly one of the broadest and most effective, single-authored bodies of agrarian literature we have. Moreover, much of his work, with its resolutely rural orientation, glides well beneath the verbal radar of the urbanized literary establishment. I do not know that most of his books are especially widely reviewed or extensively discussed in the urban press, but I keep finding that they are very widely read and admired.

Berry returned to Kentucky in the mid-1960s and in 1977 published his fifth volume of poetry, called simply *Clearing*—a slim volume whose chain of poems, borne on a light prose cadence, are remarkably accessible and forthright. The poems yield a candid portrait of a farmer-poet in a beloved but beleaguered landscape, and they display his passionate involvement, sensually and morally, in his own newly acquired old farmstead. This is the place where "The woods drew in the rim / of the pasture like an eyelid / closing." It is a figure that will register instantly with anyone who has been privileged to live in the countryside. "The house weathered / on its perch of stones."

The poet seems to inwardly adopt as his ancestors all the generations of farmers—good and bad, but mostly bad—who for two hundred years have farmed and misfarmed this region along the Kentucky River. By conscious decision, all "those who sleep / in graves no one remembers" are part of his moral community. His eye is merciless and gazes upon a landscape of misused farmland, a legacy of eroded hillsides, gullied fields, farms neglected and grown up to brush. It is a burden he takes upon himself:

> All the lives this place
> has had, I have. I eat
> my history day by day.[50]

The poet is now steward of a little piece of this land, and what he owns bears all its troubled history in its bosom:

> By this earth's life, I have
> its greed and innocence,
> its violence, its peace.

How to make amends for the old generation's mistakes? How restore these newly purchased fields, reclaim the worn-out pastures, reseed the eroded slopes?

> Through my history's despite
> and ruin, I have come
> to its remainder, and here
> have made the beginning
> of a farm intended to become
> my art of being here.

The art of being here—that is a central Berry theme, whether in poetry or prose: to live responsibly on the land and with it, within the community and for it, to find delight in useful labor and turn it into praise. The art of being here. The farm is the means and metaphor for the life. A later book of essays is foreworded with this statement: "My work has been motivated by a desire to make myself responsibly at home both in this world and in my native and chosen place. As I have slowly come to understand it, this is a long term desire, proposing the work not of a lifetime but of generations." Being grounded for generations—such is Berry's agrarianism.

In "Work Song" the poet is momentarily energized by the vision of a far future—an agrarian future, to be sure, when the art of being here is fulfilled, when "The river will run / clear, as we will never know it, / and over it, birdsong like a canopy." This is to envision a moment when "The veins of forgotten springs will have opened. / Families will be singing in the fields." In such a time

> Memory,
> native to this valley, will spread over it
> like a grove, and memory will grow
> into legend, legend into song, song
> into sacrament. The abundance of this place,
> the songs of its people and its birds,
> will be health and wisdom and indwelling
> light. This is no paradisal dream.
> Its hardship is its possibility.

Bearing a legacy as well as a vision, the poet turns to his hard physical labor. In these poems strenuous labor is usually figured not as punishment but as delight: "But work clarifies / the vision of rest. In rest / the vision of rest is lost." Work is a gift, but it is also banally connected with all the traditional arduousness of the farm, such as clearing the fields of brush.

> The sorrel mare eager
> to the burden, you are dragging
> cut brush to the pile,
> moving in ancestral motions
> of axe-stroke, bending
> to log chain and trace, speaking
> immemorial bidding and praise
> to the mare's fine ears.

The poet's farm, its history of abuse and his present labor and care for it, restoring it — these things and more find their place within a vast economy, a brotherhood of all creation, such as is never far from Berry's writing, whether poetry or prose. One of the *Clearing* poems speaks directly:

> Little farm, motherland,
> made, like an abused wife,
> by what has nearly been your ruin,
> when I speak to you, I speak
> to myself, for we are one
> body.

Elsewhere the poet had written: "My fields and walls are aching / in my shoulders." Here too the mutuality is complete. Still addressing the farm:

> When I speak to you,
> I speak to wife, daughter, son,
> whom you have fleshed in your flesh.
> And speaking to you, I speak
> to all that brotherhood that rises
> daily in your substance
> and walks, burrows, flies, stands:
> plants and beasts whose lives
> loop like dolphins through your sod.

This last striking figure epitomizes eloquently the sense of delight and song and community that permeates all these *Clearing* poems. In the book's last specimen, "Reverdure," the poet rescues an old word to name precisely his new work: "The slope whose scars I mended / turns green now."

> Though I came here
> by history's ruin, reverdure
> is my calling:
> to make these scars grow grass.

Spiritual themes, mostly Christian, and a spiritualized view of the natural world run throughout Berry's writing, everywhere inform his sensibility, and are implicit in his judgments. His work breathes a sacramental consciousness. Perhaps the entire sequence of *Clearing* poems can be read as parable, though perhaps not explicitly intended as such. The poet takes on the ancestral burden of an agriculture that has wronged the land; innocence assumes the guilt that cannot be borne by the perpetrators, and bears it away with love and labor — that is the art of being here. Only thus, perhaps, could it come about that meaning and legend will grow "into song, song into sacrament." Surely, its hardship is its possibility.

What may be Berry's best known book is less a work of literature than of polemics. *The Unsettling of America: Culture and Agriculture*, published in 1977, calls to mind Rachel Carson's *Silent Spring* of the preceding decade: each gave eloquent and precise expression to a hitherto vague apprehension and at the same time alerted hosts of others to issues they hadn't considered. Berry's book is a spirited and many-sided critique of industrial farming and agribusiness, of its origins, theory and practice, and consequences; and in particular the book includes a withering report on its enablers and apologists in government and in land grant universities. Altogether, he sees these forces as systematically spelling doom for small farms and small farm communities. When this book came out, many who had admired Berry's writings suddenly realized that there was more to be reckoned with here: the poetry and fiction and essays that expressed an oppositional way of life were now flanked and undergirded by diligent research and uncompromising argument. Berry argues that present trends in agriculture are not necessary, not inevitable, and certainly not good; his charge is that agribusiness is an explicit version of a thoroughly skewed, indeed, a rapacious and destructive system of values. The book marks a watershed in the rhetoric of agribusiness.

Hitherto, the most noticeable voices in the farm conversation—the USDA and the American Farm Bureau, for example—were those that applauded the new agricultural efficiency, its scale, consolidation, productivity, voices that usually ignored the human and social and ecological costs and side effects. And these were the sore points where Berry put his probing finger. Much of the book is trained not just on what is happening in agribusiness but on its defenders, witting and unwitting. Berry includes long quotations from USDA officials and agriculture professors; he lines them up and mows them down. In one passage, much like a dozen others given the same treatment, he quotes an Iowa professor of agricultural economics who began an essay in *Scientific American* thus: "Over the past 200 years the U.S. has had the best, the most logical and the most successful program of agricultural development anywhere in the world." Best? Logical? Successful? This, as an unargued *premise*? By the time Berry gets through with this author the reader has developed sympathy for the mangled underdog. A striking thing about this polemical book is that it came from the hand of a gentle and sensitive writer who carefully cultivated a small piece of Kentucky farmland. This from a poet?

This deliberately unsettling book is subtitled *Culture and Agriculture*, and reading it straight through is a bracing experience, like an icy shower on a sweltering day. You will be invited into a different world of associations and values and ideas, and much of the time Berry is talking not just about agriculture but about culture, about history and morality and politics. You glimpse a positive vision centered on ideas of respect and restraint, of humility and limits, whether in nature or mankind, also on the nuanced values of family and work, of place and community—in short, all the value-laden assumptions of America's rural traditions that are threatened by corporate invasion.

In contrast, as Berry sees it, modern agribusiness is essentially a contemporary variation on age-old rapacities. Therefore he often reaches far back, beyond farming to culture, beyond culture to history and to parable. There is even a splendid section on Homer and the idea and meaning of home and fidelity in the *Odyssey*, and in another typical passage he harks back to the Spaniards who first came to American shores. "And so at the same time that they 'discovered' America, these men invented the modern condition of being away from home. On the new shores the old orders of domesticity, respect, deference, humility fell away from them: they arrived contemptuous of whatever existed before their own coming, disdainful beyond contempt of native creatures or values or orders, ravenous for their own success. They began the era of absolute human sovereignty—which is to say the era of absolute human presumption. . . . An infinitely greedy sovereign is afoot in the universe, staking his claims."[51]

In such lights Berry sees modern agribusiness: Columbus estimating the prospects of the slave trade as soon as he arrives in the West Indies, the strip-mining for coal that has made a desert of much of eastern Kentucky, the bottom-line agribusiness whose economic leverage and efficient machinery has caused a rural community to wither—they are of a single piece. Accordingly, Berry sometimes speaks of the specialist or expert (whether in mining or in modern agriculture) as one without fundamental historical and moral bearings, one who has "no very clear sense of where he is," one who arrogantly assumes "there is nothing he *can* do that he should *not* do, nothing that he *can* use that he should *not* use." Such a one is not at home in the world—the ultimate indictment—he does not respect and he does not know a genuinely nurturing habitat. In this book Berry aspires to clarify what we lose in America to the degree that we relinquish our ·

commitment to the value of living well on the land and to being at home in the world.

Many sentences in Berry's prose have an oracular quality—and this may be connected with the allusiveness of his poetry. It is, at any rate, the same voice. Here are sentences from a prose paragraph like hundreds of others. "A healthy culture . . . reveals the human necessities and the human limits. It clarifies our inescapable bonds to the earth and to each other. It assures that the necessary restraints are observed, that the necessary work is done, and that it is done well." You could carve that in granite, and it wouldn't look bad. Here an entire universe of values is alluded to (and "alluded" is the right word); you find yourself nodding in assent: yes, this is what we want to affirm. Inwardly we urge him to go on, not to explain but just go on, and he does: "A healthy *farm* culture can be based only on familiarity and can grow only among a people soundly established upon the land; it nourishes and safeguards a human intelligence of the earth that no amount of technology can satisfactorily replace."[52] A lot of large and important ideas and allusions are packed in there, named and drawn upon, certainly more than a just a sentence's worth. Berry has agribusiness in the back of his mind—that's why he commends "familiarity," disparages "technology," and contrasts it with "intelligence of the earth," which we are invited to prefer. And undoubtedly we do prefer it, unsure, perhaps, just why. It sounds reliable, solid—well, down-to-earth. But exactly what is it to be "soundly established upon the land?" Even if we are not certain, we are quite certain we agree, for who would favor being *un*soundly established? We are encouraged to think, Maybe we can't define it but we would know it when we see it, and that's good enough. Berry's prose, his very idiom, his whole scheme of implied and stated values, is thus utterly seductive. If you are not in sympathy, you will forage elsewhere; but if your antecedent sympathies fall along his lines, you readily get in step with him and are carried forward. Almost effortlessly he delivers the insights you may have dimly sensed but did not fully grasp until he pointed.

Fast-forward now a quarter century. It is the spring of 2002, at a Kentucky conference on the future of agrarianism timed to celebrate the twenty-fifth anniversary of the publication of *The Unsettling of America.* When Wendell Berry speaks he begins with a rather bleak review of the quarter century since the book's appearance:

The conditions it describes and opposes, the abuse of farmland and farming people, have persisted and become worse over the last twenty-five years. In 2002 we have less than half the number of farms in the United States that we had in 1977.

Our farm communities are far worse off now than they were then. Our soil erosion rates continue to be unsustainably high. We continue to pollute our soils and streams with agricultural poisons. We continue to lose farmland to urban development of the most wasteful sort. The large agribusiness corporations that were mainly national in 1977 are now global, and are replacing the world's agricultural diversity, which was useful primarily to farmers and local consumers, with bio-engineered and patented monocultures that are merely profitable to corporations.

There would be much more to his reflections, of course, most of it less melancholy. Statistically, these opening remarks are undoubtedly true and must be acknowledged. It is also true — though perhaps more appropriate for us than for him to say — that twenty-five years ago there was no thought of a congress of miscellaneous agrarians gathered to explore agrarianism and to commemorate a book of this kind! That itself signifies a huge change in climate, possibly a change in public consciousness, and it may portend more for the future — a theme that recurs in the last chapter of this book. Berry's writings, which have continued uninterruptedly throughout this quarter century, have done as much as anything else to bring this about.

His effectiveness and appeal may be linked to the fact that there are many themes in his agrarianism not in the work of others. Berry has notably expanded the agrarian discourse, and despite the polemical stance, this remains an agrarianism without aggressiveness. His language is his own, usually pacific, and terms such as "wholeness," "domesticity," "gratitude," "household," "community," "economy," "fidelity," "song," "limits" are common in his writings, poetry and prose, and usually given an uncommon richness and depth. This is not Victor Hanson's idiom. A recurring theme is that of being at home in the world, which Berry skillfully wraps in layers of moral meaning, including our own well-being, and especially he explores the innumerable ways in which our well-being is inextricably tied to the well-being of the earth. There is a serenity in his tone that comes fully to the fore in his "Sabbath Poems," published in *A Timbered Choir*. These poems reiterate the idea that well-being on earth, though requiring labor, is not a battle but is fundamentally a gift wrapped in mysteries, whereat the appropriate human posture is gratitude and humility. Often, this outlook is distilled into exquisite lyricism:

> The mind that comes to rest is tended
> In ways that it cannot intend:
> Is borne, preserved, and comprehended
> By what it cannot comprehend.

Your Sabbath, Lord, thus keeps us by
Your will, not ours. And it is fit
Our only choice should be to die
Into that rest, or out of it.[53]


## The Making of Agrarians

"Agrarianism" and "agrarian" (noun and adjective) are terms of ever evolving meanings. Certainly, the core idea behind them is that expressed, with permissible hyperbole, in the title of Victor Hanson's book—the land was everything. And this is not a metaphysical proposition but a value judgment, opening up into a family of ideals, pointing to certain loyalties and hopes, recommending particular habits of feeling and practice. Inescapably, these will focus upon the care and culture of individual and specific lands, upon agri-culture.

But ours is now an industrial culture in an urbanized environment, wherein the majority of people no longer have any daily interactions with agriculture, or even a meaningful encounter with the earth, and certainly do not regularly experience the grand economies of nature as source and sustainer of life. In this context, "agrarian" is sometimes taken to characterize anything that would genuinely tend to reestablish—spiritually, physically, morally, economically—those vital and severed ancient bonds of humankind and the land. It is undoubtedly with this understanding that the editor of a fine recent book, titled *The New Agrarianism*, wrote:

With no fanfare, and indeed with hardly much public notice, agrarianism is again on the rise. In small corners and pockets, in ways for the most part unobtrusive, people are reinvigorating their ties to the land. . . . Agrarianism, broadly conceived, reaches beyond food production and rural living to include a wide constellation of ideas, loyalties, sentiments, and hopes. It is a temperament and a moral orientation as well as a suite of economic practices, all arising out of the insistent truth that people everywhere are part of the land community, just as dependent as other life on the land's fertility and just as shaped by its mysteries and possibilities. . . . It is the land—as place, home, and living community—that anchors the agrarian scale of values.[54]

There is a natural inclination—too tempting, perhaps—to expand such a land-and-community ethic into a more comprehensive system of evaluation and diagnosis, to put the emphasis not upon agrarian attitudes and loyalties but upon an abstract doctrine of *agrarianism*. This makes it into a philosophical platform for a sweeping point of view, such as for a negative critique of industrialism. Wendell Berry does this in several places, but it probably does not serve him well, since agrarianism is not a sharp enough instrument for social diagnosis. Perhaps Berry is agreeing with this by saying in another place: "Agrarianism is primarily a practice, a set of attitudes, a loyalty, and a passion; it is an idea only secondarily and at a remove."

"Agrarian" and its cognates are terms that have been bent in several directions. Since Americans generally no longer live in an agrarian culture as they once did, many of the associations of the term "agrarian" have veered more toward the *literature* of land and agriculture than toward direct encounter with them. The term is sometimes now applied wherever there is some intimate interplay, not between people and the land, but between *writing* and the land, or writing and agriculture. I think we can discern a specific explanation for this conceptual shift toward what may be called "literary agrarianism."

Seventy years ago, "agrarian" was applied to the work and ideas of a particular group of conspicuous men working not in agriculture but in literature. The Southern Agrarians, as they were called, were professors, writers, poets, essayists, many of them associated, in one way or another, with Vanderbilt University in Nashville, Tennessee. They were spokesmen for that part of the southern tradition, its society and culture and landed traditions, which they saw as threatened, in the 1920s, by industrialism and urbanism; indeed, they were still responding to the Industrial Revolution. Their 1930 book *I'll Take my Stand* was a kind of manifesto in defense of a particular system of values, which they associated historically with (certain select strands of) southern culture, thought of as essentially agrarian in character. The real axis of their outlook was not so much rural versus urban as man versus machine, the ideals of a humane society as against those of an industrial society. Their lingering influence is indicated by the fact that their book has been reprinted several times and is in print today, more than seventy years later.

Although this particular form of southern agrarianism is often passed by in silence today by agrarian writers (Wendell Berry, who belongs to a nearby region, mentions it only in passing), the link, as illustrated by the long succession of writers such as Emerson and Crèvecoeur, between American agrarianism and literary culture is there to stay. The three writers featured in this chapter confirm that. Indeed, in a nation where agrarian values have long been esteemed, there is almost bound to be a tradition of literary agrarianism. Inescapably, most agrarians that come to our attention, or remain there, are in some sense literary people. Thomas Jefferson is usually named the founder of the agrarian tradition in America, not because of what he *did* along these lines, but because of what he thought, speculated about, and wrote. In terms of *doing* agrarian work, of living and savoring and exhibiting the whole of a fully integrated agrarian life, John Adams in Massachusetts far surpassed Jefferson; but he did not commend it to us in such engaging and persuasive terms. It was the agrarianism that Adams and his neighbors practiced that Jefferson preached. And history has remembered the preacher.

This intimate interplay between two lines of work, writing and farming, between literature and the life of the land, is in the final analysis what I have been exploring here. For agrarians traffic not only in values apprehended but also in values expressed. And for some, the natural mode of expression is through a harvest of ordered words, whereby poems and paragraphs are cultivated fields in slightly different forms. For all agrarians, farming is *the* foundational and inspirational discipline, *the* sustaining activity for life and for democratic society. For the three agrarians considered here, this fundamental commitment is expressed in their writings and in their lives in different ways—as a great and good adventure, as an heroic epic struggle, as a dedicated pastoral mission.

Louis Bromfield was a facile and successful wordsmith, and when he committed himself to an agricultural life, it was not to stop writing but to forge a different literature out of earthier themes: down-in-the-dirt farming and all its rough and delicate details warmed his prose for nearly two decades. Indeed, he exhaustively ran his farm and wrote it up as a great adventure until his health failed and his finances collapsed. (Jefferson also ran out of money and ran into debt; Adams, ever the thrifty New England agrarian, was careful not to.) One gathers that Victor Davis Hanson's farm is also regularly beset. Often, it seems, his fruit farming does not repay his efforts in strictly economic terms, and he sees only a dim future for it. For him writing is a perfectly natural, perhaps inevitable, way to continue by related means the epic struggle that is farming itself; and evidently each skirmish sustains and energizes his writing in many a mysterious way. When his farm does not supply him with raw capital, it supplies him abundantly with raw experience and evidence. If he were not still a family farmer, whether solvent or not, whether satisfied or not, he would not be equipped to write, nor we to admire, his passionate elegies for family farming.

And why did Wendell Berry, urban writer and professor, take up farming when he returned to Kentucky? Why buy a team of horses and tools, as he did, and clear the pasture and reseed the eroded slopes? Why bother "to make these scars grow grass"? Surely not for the basic reason his ancestors did, not to make a living, nor to help feed the world. Not even for the reason Bromfield gave himself for going back to the land—to see if he could succeed where others had failed. Evidently, for Berry it was a task that insistently asked to be done, as a poem or an essay may ask to be written, for his gullies were a landscape in visible pain: he was the land's steward and custodian of its spotted history, so he obeyed the summons. One senses within Berry's writings what the writings need not say, namely, that ultimately he began to farm in order to cultivate in all its manifold forms the poetry of farming—surely one of the deepest agrarian impulses there could be. Now that his hillsides are green again, and a good harvest secured, it seems fair to say that he made the right choice for the right reason.

 *Part Two*

# FOUR FARMS

# Chapter 4

# Maple: The Sweet Good-bye of Winter at Bascom's

In times past, a new crop of maple came at the end of the dreariest part of the year for country families. . . . The fresh taste of new maple syrup must have been an even more wonderful sensation than it is today. —LAWRENCE AND MARTIN, *Sweet Maple*, p. 106

Maple Weekend is this Saturday: Tour Sugar Houses and Maple Orchards, help gather sap on horse drawn sleds, enjoy collections of maple memorabilia, musical entertainment and horse drawn rides. Treat your taste buds to samples of Maple Products, including "sugar on snow," homemade donuts, sap coffee, and pancake breakfasts!!
—ADVERTISEMENT in *Concord Monitor*, March 2001

## The Sugar Season

Early springtime in New England, season of hope and much backsliding. The countryside is drab at this time of year, and the roadways with their slush and dirty snow plead for some dressing up. One is happy, then, to spot here and yonder a dignified row of ancient knotty maples decorated with old galvanized buckets, or with plastic pails and recycled milk jugs or even juice jugs—a springtime flowering of sorts, scenic and colorful in its own hopeful way, and probably the work of a true backyard amateur sugar maker. "Maple syrup" is a loaded term in our regional culture, and the annual sight of tapped maple trees releases a cascade of favored and familiar images, most of them long ago mellowed to comfortable clichés. Milk and eggs and apples may come from anywhere and everywhere in the nation, but maple syrup and all its clinging clanging clichés belongs to the Northeast.

There is the rustic sugarhouse, with steam oozing or billowing from its roof, also the snowy hillside sugarbush and the everlasting sap buckets (pictured, they are often still wooden buckets) clinging to unimaginably ancient maple trees, and perhaps (when very lucky) we may spot the real thing—a yoke of patient oxen drawing an enormous barrel mounted on a sled. Here is the sentimental and sugary rural icon of New England; and here and there, maybe on a tourist-inspired "Maple Weekend," it still all comes to life. Remembered, imagined, or actually glimpsed in the round, it remains a regional favorite, quaint certainly, sweet with the aroma of nostalgia, but still warming the heart of knowing Yankee and visiting flat-lander alike.

The moment actually arrives, of course, within a larger season of test-ing for rural spirits: to the dour and the melancholy New Englander this is a bleak period of rotting snow and frost heaves and mud season. But to the gentle of temper and the pure of heart it is the thrilling season of maple syrup, the sweet good-bye of winter. To be sure, the oxen are going or gone, fading away for a century now; even horses are very rare, and the sap buckets, which long ago turned from wood to metal, are swiftly yield-ing to plastic tubing, and inside the sugarhouse there is almost certainly some clever new gimmick to simplify the labor-intensive operation. And, indeed, to visit the Bascom Sugarhouse in Acworth, New Hampshire, for example, is to experience the full force of how the quaint and beloved maple ways of old have been conquered by the cheerful onslaught of modern technology.

For ready comparison and perspective, I try to keep this in mind: the last time I myself made maple syrup in my own little evaporator (although I didn't work at it very hard) I thought it was a good day if I made a couple of gallons of syrup. A few good days like that and we were set for the year. A few more good days and we had a year's supply of sweet gifts for friends and relatives. When I last visited the Bascoms it was a very good day and they were cranking out syrup at the rate of a gallon a minute—sixty gal-lons an hour. I was doing it for fun, of course. At Bascom's they do maple for a living.

That word *maple*, in its migration from adjective to noun to verb and back again, sometimes works as an all-purpose word covering the entire subject, or any aspect of it—trees, tapping, gathering, syrup, production, marketing, and so on. ("He talked maple for an hour." "Dairy farm, berry farm, maple farm.") In my own state, the local trade organization is known as the New Hampshire Maple Producers' Association. Milk producers pro-duce milk, so maple producers produce maple? Short for maple products, perhaps. But *maple* in this usage will not easily dislodge the word *sugaring,* the verb that has ruled this realm for hundreds of years. Old-timers talked *sugarin'* in their youth because in their father's day more sugar than syrup was made from maple, sugar being much easier to handle and store than syrup. That is why they now gather sap in a *sugarbush* and make syrup in a *sugarhouse.* If *sugarmaking* and its cognates are now verbal anachronisms, that doesn't mean they will soon go away. It's likely that there will always be, as there has been since 1894, a Vermont Maple Sugar Makers' Association, and its publication will probably forever be called *Sugaring.* Anyway, we do our sugaring during the maple season, by making syrup. Please bear with us: that's just how we talk here.

And the whole enterprise is still and always a mixture of primitivism, romance, and arbitrariness. And it lives by absolutes. It depends absolutely upon the climate and the weather, and it absolutely cannot be coerced. You cannot do it in Florida, or on the Fourth of July or Christmas or on a cold day at the height of the season in New England. Why not? There is a legend that for every question, maple people will supply two or more plausible but contradictory answers. The authors of a recent and superb book on the maple business (*Sweet Maple,* James Lawrence and Rex Martin) remark that they found the making of maple syrup to be "an astonishing labyrinth of folk art and modern science, primitive craft and high technology."[55] They were probably right about that, although I suspect there may be another opinion down the road.

It is harder to find a second opinion on the delights of eating maple syrup, though there are many favorite ways. Poured over pancakes, buttered toast, or vanilla ice cream are some traditional ways of consuming it, and making it into maple candy is another favorite. My own preferred candy recipe fearlessly bypasses the industry standard ("pure maple syrup" as *sole* ingredient) as yielding a product too sweet; I cut it by putting in as much butter and nuts as it will hold. Granulated maple sugar, which was routine for centuries but almost disappeared in the twentieth century, now has a growing market—often used on toast and on ice cream, and increasingly now as an alternative to brown sugar in recipes. To eat maple syrup by the spoonful from a bowl is an addiction easy to acquire, especially by those who are laboring in the sugarhouse. Maple syrup is also an ingredient in many kinds of foods, most notably baked beans (also in some smoking and chewing tobacco, incidentally). Commercial firms frequently add maple syrup to hams, salad dressings, barbecue sauces, and to corn syrups that want a maple flavoring. Merely tasting maple syrup has also been implicated in destroying many people's taste for corn syrup.

Maple producers often start with a very small operation, not intending to be very professional: they just adopt a springtime hobby, not to be taken too seriously. But there is an occupational hazard for the backyard sugar maker, namely, the temptation to expand. The marketing end of the enterprise then takes on more significance, more complexity, and its challenges come in stages. First, it was just a matter of making enough syrup for home use and for gifts; then you make a little more and sell some at the dooryard; then you get a good evaporator and start consignments to the local grocery; after that, you grow a bit larger and find a regular market retailing by mail. It turns out to be fun and not unprofitable to send a gallon by UPS each March to those folks from Arizona who stopped by a few years ago. By now you have trapped yourself into marketing more than syrup, for you are actually selling many other commodities: you are dealing in *nostalgia*, and *New England*, and *homemade*, and *cottage industry*, and *family business*, and *country* and *romance*, and various other sweet intangibles, all very marketable and all neatly wrapped into the maple syrup package. You expand a bit more and then you may start wholesaling to people like the Bascoms. Pretty soon, and especially if you are suggestible, you are in the maple business, and you are both incredibly busy for at least two months each year and also unreasonably good-humored about it.

The Bascoms are serious maple farmers, and their operations have progressed light-years beyond these early stages. Maple is their thing. (Not their only thing, to be sure, for there is also a two-hundred-cow dairy farm on the side.) Serious maple farmers like the Bascoms are forever exploring new frontiers of technology, production, and marketing, and forever hosting surprises from the weather. They do a lot of all that at this place. It is worth focusing on the Bascoms precisely because they are not typical of maple people: they not only make syrup in record amounts, but they buy, process, and sell syrup in record amounts as well.

*Bascom Maple Farms, Inc.*

It is early April in southern New Hampshire and the snow is almost gone and there are tinges of green on some southern slopes. I am sitting with Ken Bascom in his kitchen and we are discussing the joys and trials of a lifetime of farming and the maple syrup business. Ken Bascom has a mountain of experience in these things and he also has a head full of stories that his father and grandfather have told him about farming on these unforgiving New Hampshire hills. The maple season has just concluded and yesterday was the last boiling day. Ken Bascom has lived here and made maple syrup from these trees—many of the same trees—every spring, one war year excepted, for more than sixty years. Most years the operation—first his father's, then his, now his son Bruce's—has expanded a bit each spring. Ken well remembers the year when he was a very young man and his father and his family had finally moved to the farm that they had owned for a decade. It was 1939.

More than six decades ago—a vanished world. "That first year we hung six hundred buckets." Ken grins and shakes his head. In the ensuing years and especially after he took over the farm about 1950, Ken tried his hand at poultry farming, at potato farming, and dairy farming, and maple farming, and at all four, all with hard work and moderate success, but nothing spectacular. The natural conditions here, the hills, the rocks, the climate, are too austere for any great farming successes. Sometime in the early 1960s he decided to sell his dairy cows, sell his summer's hay instead of turning it into milk, then expand his sugarbush and try to make a living on maple alone. It was an unusual and a brave decision for one man and one family: only someone who loved sugarmaking would do a thing like that.

The keeper and chronicler of the Bascom legends is Ken's brother Eric Jr., whose memoir (*Up Where the House Burned Down*, 1996) reports that there have been Bascoms in these hills since long before the Civil War. Many of them, he wrote, had "something like granite in their bones and maple sap in their veins." The Bascom sugarhouse is today on the farm that Ken's father Eric Bascom Sr. bought in 1929—bought the farm as a hedge against the Great Depression, for he was a clergyman serving a poor church in Canterbury, New Hampshire, and he hoped the farm would help pay the bills and help feed the family. Ken's father served his parish and also farmed eighty miles away in Acworth, arranging his vacations to coincide with sugaring in the spring and digging potatoes in the fall. He took a break from parish work to peddle his syrup door-to-door in Concord, New Hampshire. Ken knew pretty early that he wanted to be a farmer, though both his parents were ordained to the clergy and soon his brother Eric Jr. was too. Not theology but maple sap was in Ken's veins, and he is glad to have eventually done a bit of pioneering in the maple business.

"We were innovators in some respects," he says cautiously. "We introduced plastic tubing pretty early, and we probably led the way with reverse osmosis around here." This is not a man who could ever afford to put much stock in the storied ox sled and the wooden bucket. But time was, during

Ken's prime, when the Bascoms did a lot of catering to the tourist trade. "Oh yeah, the whole bit," says Ken. "Sugar on snow, pancakes, maple candy, donuts, busloads of tourists used to drive up, the place was full of cars, and we'd entertain them all." (This reminds Ken of an old joke told to tourists, told in opposite ways in Vermont and New Hampshire. The New Hampshire version, he says, is this: Occasionally the syrup maker may unfortunately find a drowned squirrel in one of his sap buckets. In New Hampshire the practice is to discard that bucket of sap; but in Vermont they just wring out the squirrel, discard it, and save the sap.)

Here at Bascom's the real tourist era is decades in the past now, and the place where the tables stood for guests is now warehouse space, and those days seem to be gone without much regret. I imagine that the Bascoms are glad that many other sugarhouses, such as the Clark's just down the road, do a fine job of welcoming the public, with far more typical and traditional facilities than Bascom's. The traditional working sugarhouse is still virtually an open invitation for passersby to stop in and observe the process. People don't usually stop by just to watch you hoe the garden or prune the apple trees or feed the chickens, but syrup making is different. If they see the steam rolling from the roof they assume they are welcome to knock on the door and sniff the aroma. It's a kind of understood New England hospitality. If it is your neighbor's sugarhouse and you don't stop in sometime during the season, you may be reproached for standoffishness.

But the Bascom sugarhouse no longer fits any such stereotyped traditional image. When you arrive on a paved driveway here, you are confronted with a blank wall and small door marked *Office*, with hours posted. Inside is a corridor and row of offices, and beyond is a cavernous warehouse and work space where there are syrup bottling machines, filtering machines, several reverse osmosis machines, stacks and stacks of boxes, barrels of maple syrup, and other equipment and merchandise. There is an evaporator off to the side, small, very effective and efficient, but entirely unromantic, and there is no wood and no fire, for it runs with steam heat. In fact, nothing here looks like the sugarhouse of lore and yore. It is the farm sugarhouse of the twenty-first century, indeed, a factory in the woods. Ken might not recognize the enterprise he began sixty years ago—except that he does indeed, since he was part of the long evolution at every step of the way. This operation now has one foot in the family farm tradition and the other in the world of agribusiness.

Bascom Maple Farms, Inc., is a sprawling layout of about fifteen hundred contiguous acres, including half a dozen farmhouses and any number of barns, sheds, toolhouses, and warehouses. The farm is really two separate but connected enterprises. One is a dairy farm with about two hundred milking cows, adjacent to the sugarhouse farm; for although Ken went out of the dairy business in the early 1960s, his son Bruce went back into it a quarter century later by buying a neighboring dairy farm from a relative. The other part of the operation is the maple farm, boiling sap from 40,000 taps and buying, bottling, packaging, and selling tons of syrup and maple sugar in addition. Bascom's is also a major retailer of all kinds of maple equipment. This multiple farm operation occupies several high ridges in the southwestern part of New Hampshire, straddling the town line between Acworth and Charlestown, about a dozen former farms altogether, and along many of the ridges are scenic open fields for corn and hay. Wherever you look from the sugarhouse the views are worth singing about. Stretching beyond the fields and the sugarbush, tier upon tier, are tree-covered hilltops with occasional hay field patches of shining green, and along the horizon itself are the mountain ranges of Vermont and of southern New Hampshire. From the sugarhouse in April, and even early May, as the fields in the foreground are greening up, you can gaze westerly and still pick out the wide white lines of the ski trails on the sides of half a dozen distant Vermont mountains.

Each year on the first weekend in May Bascom Maple Farms, Inc., hosts an Open House, complete with seminars on various aspects of the maple business. Hundreds of maple producers crawl out of the woods to come and learn about and maybe purchase the latest equipment; they come to talk maple with experts, to swap sap house lore from the season just ended, to attend how-to workshops and seminars, and to munch on free hot dogs while they brag a bit if they get an opening or at least tell somebody about their latest technique. In the seminars, whether the topic was hoses or maple candy I found a common subtext: we are making a gourmet product, bacteria are the enemy, cleanliness is next to godliness. The event is not for tourists, although they are welcome; but on such a day you realize more keenly than ever how far the wooden bucket and the old oxcart have been driven into the remote and dreamy past. Reverend Eric Bascom Sr., who peddled syrup from these trees door-to-door in the 1930s, might not even understand such a gathering, everyone intent on learning the latest procedures from an expert. He might have wondered what a sugaring expert could have been an expert *in*. Didn't everyone who did it—like his father and grandfathers—know everything there was to know about it? At the 2002 Open House I attended a seminar on vacuum tubing and gravity systems, also (though only *very* briefly) one led by a factory engineer addressing the finer points of cleaning a reverse osmosis machine.

I slip out of that seminar to walk in the sugarbush. Soon I find a woods trail leading from the sugarhouse up into the trees, and I follow it to the top of a high hill to gaze about me at the countryside. Everywhere are handsome maple trees, not yet leafed out, and miles and miles of plastic tubing, and nothing else. How easy to marvel at these vast groves of wild and stately trees, many specimens over a hundred years old, a randomly growing and richly producing crop which nobody planted, which nobody watered or fertilized, trees whose ancestors were here just like these, thriving on the rocky hillsides for thousands and thousands of years, trees whose mysterious harvest of sweetness was literally taught to us knowing moderns by Stone Age people living in bark huts. For these brief moments at least, as between the marvels of sugarhouse technology and the marvelous maple tree, I choose the tree.

### The Marvelous Maple

The sugar maple tree (*Acer saccharum*), though so commonplace in the Northeast as to be completely taken for granted and seen everywhere, is actually a unique marvel of nature, rightly celebrated for its foliage, its syrup, and its wood. No other tree has been so much enjoyed for its spectacular autumn beauty as it turns to red and gold on a thousand hillsides; and no other tree has been put to use in so cunning a way, its natural sap systematically extracted to produce so delightful a delicacy in so many forms. The sugar maple is also known as rock maple or hard maple, and justly so, for the wood is tough and hard and heavy, and certain specimens have a curly grain that is famously attractive and much sought by cabinetmakers. Maple wood has found a thousand uses in construction and in furniture making, and not least as first-rate firewood. Indeed, the copious benefits, economic and aesthetic, of this one species of tree are hard to exaggerate. From colonial days, before cane sugar was widely or cheaply available, until well into the twentieth century, the annual production of maple sugar was a mainstay of New England's rural economy. Much of New England's soil is poor and hilly and often rocky, but there was always plenty of wood and sap for the taking; so there was maple sugar, a relatively reliable annual cash crop. For hundreds of years and for thousands of farmers, it was the maple trees that paid the annual taxes on the family farm. A wonder of nature and a rare gift to humankind is the sweet sugar maple tree.

The sugar maple's range is limited largely to the northeastern corner of North America, heaviest in the broad swath that flanks the Great Lakes and the Saint Lawrence Valley, but extending here and there as far as Georgia and Kansas. In many of these regions the sugar maple is the most common and conspicuous hardwood tree, especially in the autumn when its colors add their drama and grace notes to the countryside. It is a resolutely North American tree; although it has been tried in Europe frequently since the eighteenth century, it has never been widely successful there. Small wonder that Canadians chose the maple leaf as their national symbol, and that half a dozen American states have chosen the sugar maple as the official state tree, including Wisconsin, which was first, and Vermont, where they say that every fourth wild tree is a sugar maple. (The sugar maple has a poor relative, a swamp cousin, in the red maple, *Acer rubrum*, a smaller and weaker tree, which likes soggy soil, and whose wood is not so hard and dense as sugar maple. The red maple yields a modest amount of sap, its leaves turn bright red in early autumn, and, best of all, it has lovely tiny red blossoms in early spring, beloved of honeybees and other connoisseurs of early springtime.)

Sugar maples are slow growing and long-lived. They are thirty or forty years old before they are ready to be tapped (Yankee proverb: "Don't tap a tree that's smaller in diameter than the bucket you put to it"), but under good conditions they may produce sap for the next couple of hundred years. Some few of the maple monsters still alive may have been growing already when the first Europeans settled here nearly four hundred years ago. The largest sugar maple on record is in Norwich, Connecticut, twenty-three feet around and well over three hundred years old.

The maple tree has many mysterious habits. For one thing, it gets its juices going earlier in the season than any other tree, and it does some very weird things as it makes, stores, and moves its sap around in late winter and early spring. When the visitor asks at the sugarhouse, "Which way is the sap flowing in the tree, up or down, when it gets tapped?" he may be told, "It's going down." But at the next sugarhouse she may be told, "It's going up." Who's right? Maybe both; maybe neither. It depends. Upon lots of things. Experiments with injecting dye into tapped trees indicate the very varied sap movement—which may be up or down, and also sideways, but much less so—but do not tell us the whys and wherefores.

The basic plot of the story is something like this. Under the right conditions for a sap flow—a sunny day of fifty degrees or so after a snappy cold night well below frost—the sap in the maple tree, unlike the sap in the neighboring ash tree, comes under various changing and shifting pressures. Therefore it will move where it can go, and especially out any leak in the bark, such as a tap hole. *Why* it is under pressures, and where the shifting vacuum and pressure points are within the tree, is an extremely complex matter, not completely understood. It has to do partly with gravity, with the carbon dioxide generated last night deep within the tree, also with the frost that penetrated the fibers, and with osmotic pressure, since the tree was simultaneously mixing sugar, water, and various amino acids to make up a good batch of sap, and pulling in liquid through its roots for that purpose. That was last night while we slept, the tree preparing for today's sap run—which probably stopped in the late afternoon as the pressures within the tree were finally exhausted. Tonight again, as the tree freezes, twigs first, then inward from the bark, the gas in the spaces among the wood fibers will readjust in response to the expansions of the spreading frost and will move the sap upward and inward as it is manufactured. Tomorrow, as the morning sun smites the tree once more, it will start thawing in stages, twigs first again, and start building up pressures to leak more sap for us.

That's a simplification of the very mysterious maple tree hydraulics, omitting several variables, but most folks are satisfied to know that other trees do not do anything nearly so interesting as what happens within a maple tree. You can't extract much sap from an ash tree, and you can't find a use for it if you do. It is almost as if the maple tree alone were specially designed to *invite* us to draw off a bit of its lifeblood and put it to use. Maples with the largest crowns produce the most sap—the more limbs, branches, and twigs the better. This is one of the reasons the wide-open spreading specimens along the stone wall on the edges of fields are usually tapped, for they are much better producers than the trees in the forest.

This thing all started long, long ago with the Native Americans, and with maple trees and stone hatchets, and the lucky discovery—back there in the mists of some forgotten springtime, hundreds and hundreds of years ago and maybe longer than that—that the sap which stirred in these March-awakened trees was sweet. Not terribly sweet: about 2 percent sugar on the average, which is discernible but not much more than that. Maple sap is a perfectly fine and healthy beverage to use in place of water, although many find, as I do, that they are soon cloyed by it. Maple sap coffee is a beverage sometimes available in the roadside sugarhouses that cater to the public. The sap itself, quaffed in large quantities, is a "spring tonic"—or that's what old-timers will tell you the old-timers told them.

No records exist, but it seems likely that the Native Americans would have noticed that when they let the sap freeze and discarded the ice (which doesn't lock in much sugar), the resulting beverage was somewhat sweeter. To make it still sweeter they had but to freeze it again and discard more ice. When freezing was no longer possible, the next step was to drive off more of the water as steam by heating it in earthen pots. Eventually they arrived at syrup and, with still more heating and evaporating, a sticky sugar. Lack of metal containers made such production extremely laborious. Still, long before the arrival of Europeans they had the system fully in hand, and the Native American collective sweet tooth was probably thriving. It has been noted that people can survive for a very long time on nothing but maple sugar and water. Sugar from trees! Here was a striking novelty for the settlers from across the sea, and it proved to be just one of many stories of New World marvels brought back to Europe and promptly grossly exaggerated there. However, when the Native Americans had traded their sugar for the iron kettles of the Europeans, they had the essentials for a technological leap forward and were ready for serious business.

It appears that the French more than the English early adopted the sugarmaking practices of the Native Americans. The English came to fish and settle, to worship God, to open the wilderness, and eventually to farm: they chopped down trees, maples and all, they sent lumber to England, they made potash of the firewood, and they took up farming. The French, many of whom came to this continent to save souls or garner pelts, were initially more receptive of the lifestyle of the natives, and they learned about the merits of the maple tree very early. French records dating back before 1600, well before any permanent European settlements, refer to the sap of the maple tree as a source of a drink of "surpassing excellence." Much later, Alexander Henry wrote of his travels in Canada during 1776: "We hunted and fished, yet sugar was our principal food during the whole month of April. On the mountain we ate nothing but our sugar . . . each man consumed a pound a day, desired no other food, and was visibly nourished by it."[56]

Although maple sugar quickly became important for settled New England farmers, by the eighteenth century it was famous in other regions too. George Washington was so impressed by it that he tried to establish a maple sugar orchard at Mount Vernon, and Thomas Jefferson, after a visit to Vermont, promptly ordered sixty maple saplings for planting at Monticello.

Neither of these early research efforts amounted to much, and certainly not in their lifetimes: that region of Virginia generally lacks the northern climate's spring season of cold nights and warm days, as is required for a good sap run. The last of Jefferson's trees, planted in 1798, died just recently, nearly two hundred years old. But it was during the lifetime of Washington and Jefferson that a new technological advance was made. Round spiles, usually made from elderberry saplings inserted into holes drilled with augers, replaced the old wasteful way of slashing the bark with an ax to let the sap out.

Near the middle of the next century other technological developments appeared: metal spiles were patented in 1860 and began to replace wooden ones. Then metal pails started to supplant wooden buckets, and the old iron kettles were replaced by flat and shallow evaporator pans. With these technological novelties the production of maple sugar reached its historic peak in 1860; but inevitably it had then to compete with West Indies cane sugar, soon to be relieved of the moral burden of being slave produced. Remarkably, as maple sugar started to lose its market to cane sugar, maple syrup began finding one. So the tapping of maple trees continued unabated.

*The Sugarhouse*

Bruce Bascom, eldest son of Ken Bascom, is now the principal owner and manager of the scenic little maple empire atop the southwestern New Hampshire hills. The Bascoms are a tough Yankee tribe, long-lived (typically lasting into their nineties) and numerous: sons, cousins, nephews, second cousins, in-laws, and other relatives are frequently on the farm payroll. One supposes there are Bascoms enough in these regions to manage the operation in the next generation, whether or not Bruce's son Keith chooses to be one of them. As a young man Bruce went off to the University of New Hampshire's Whittemore School of Business, not expecting to return to the farm, but while there he did enough maple research to convince himself that there might be a future in it for him. When he graduated in 1973 his father Ken proposed a partnership in the farm and, not incidentally, a chance to apply the learning he had acquired.

Borrow carefully and expand judiciously—that sums up the most conspicuous application of what Bruce had learned, and the farm has been expanding judiciously for the last twenty-five years, taking on more land, more cattle, more trees, more sap, more markets, and sometimes more debt. Bruce, who is now a chunky and friendly man of about fifty, full of restless energy which he expends as much on the phone as in the field, invites me to join him in his sugarhouse office. I ask him to sketch the general landscape of the maple business.

"There are," he suggests, "perhaps three tiers of operators in this business. On the ground floor are the innumerable small operators scattered throughout the woods of the Northeast." He speculates that they still produce the lion's share of the syrup in the Northeast and probably in other states. "At the other extreme," he says, "are the really big, very professional operations, most of which are in Quebec, some in Maine, and a few in Vermont." And these folks are in business seriously, he tells me, ever on the prowl for wholesale outlets, "and it is cutthroat competition all the way. They are used to doing what they have to do. Corporate America at its finest!" Is that heavy irony in his smile? "And then there are the folks in between these extremes," he says, "the middling to large operations—like ours." Bruce now thinks of his operation as being near the upper echelon of the middling maple producers.

My mind flits over momentarily to the evaporator in the next room, which, at this very moment, is rolling out a gallon of syrup for every single minute of our conversation. It seems like a major operation to me. But of course every day is not like today, and each day does not produce a good sap run. Some days the evaporator is idle: the weather is too cold, or has been warm without a hard frost for too long, and so on. The year 1999 was a poor one for the Bascoms, only about eight thousand gallons (still, more than a tenth of the entire production of New Hampshire); 2000 was a good year, a short season but nearly eleven thousand gallons; 2001 was a strange year, with mountains of snow in March, but the sap shut down before the snow was gone, one of the worst years for production ever; 2002 was a record year.

We are now on a walking tour of the sugarhouse. Near the evaporator, the reverse osmosis machines (known as ROs) are churning away in their own little room off to the side, pouring out a thick stream of extracted water that runs copiously down the drain. "These babies do quite an amazing job," Bruce says, and he is undoubtedly right about that. All they do is take water out of sap, but it is still amazing. Bruce taps the machine with obvious affection and tells me how it works. ROs are complicated networks of pipes and tubes and dials and gauges and handles and hisses and grumbles and buzzes; and if you didn't know, you could never tell by looking at them what on earth they do, for they do it out of sight. They depend upon one very simple scientific fact: a sugar molecule is much larger than a water molecule. This is what they do: take in raw sap at about 2 percent sugar content and force it through a set of membranes too fine even to accommodate sugar molecules. That is a very fine mesh indeed. It takes pressure to force water through such a mesh, and it takes some engineering to keep such meshes from getting clogged; but the pure water that goes through is expelled, and the sweetened sap stays behind, now five or six times as concentrated, as high as 10 or 12 percent sugar. Bruce smiles a warm smile at this kind of high technology.

Here, the sweetened sap is piped automatically into the evaporator, which is not large, say twelve by four feet, and doesn't have to be, because the sap it starts with is so sweet and the syrup is made at record speed. The evaporator is heated neither by wood nor by oil (the old-fashioned way and the modern way) but by steam pipes running through the bottom of the pan (the postmodern way). It takes only seven or eight gallons of this sweetened juice to make a gallon of syrup, instead of the small operators' forty or more gallons of raw sap. Automatically the syrup is tested for readiness with a hydrometer, drawn off at the right moment, filtered, and piped into storage containers. Naturally the question arises, Why go only partway with RO? Why not invent a new machine to squeeze out the rest of the water and leave only the syrup? And naturally there is a good answer to that. Boiling is essential for the chemistry of syrup making. Sap from the tree is not just diluted syrup but a different substance entirely, requiring cooking to develop and mature its maple flavor.

At the Bascoms' sugarhouse you see at a glance the evolution of one kind of farming into a business. It has its own logic and laws and economics, and at every point along the production line there is the quest for improvement: tapping trees, installing tubing, collecting sap, processing by reverse osmosis, boiling, filtering, canning, purchasing, storing, marketing, shipping—every stage is on the lookout for new efficiencies that will help the business remain competitive. This maple products enterprise might be called a vertically integrated (farming-producing-packaging-distributing) system. Along the walls of this sugarhouse much of the space is occupied by boxes being readied for shipping, and everywhere else the place is piled high with thirty-gallon barrels and five-gallon jugs of recently made maple syrup, plus boxes of maple sugar. I gaze about at the stacked merchandise, I hear the clatter of barrels and jugs and the buzz and hum of machines, and I am reminded of a factory and its warehouse. Is this farming?

The farm is hundreds and hundreds of acres of maple trees, and the market is everywhere. Bruce tells me that "only a tiny percentage of the syrup we now sell is consumed within fifty miles of the sugarhouse." Two things are exciting at Bascom's: producing the commodity and finding good markets for it, which means striking interesting deals. The syrup and sugar not only goes far and wide; now more and more of it goes abroad, and Bruce is clearly intrigued by this entrepreneurial aspect of the game. It appears that he will cheerfully spend a whole day on the phone, wheeling and dealing with syrup processors, wholesalers, and other customers all over the world.

Just now he is called to the phone, and in the interim I glance at the bills of lading attached to some of the readied shipments. This first pile goes to Florida; this next pile, which looks like it contains boxes of sugar as well as a lot of syrup, is going to Spain, that one to Oklahoma, and that entire pallet load of boxed maple sugar is going to another foreign country. When Bruce returns I ask if it is more fun to deal with this global market than to just sell syrup retail, as his neighbors do. Is there satisfaction in being big? He doesn't think of his operation as very big. "There are a dozen or more that are bigger than we are, and some of those are *really* big. We are about at the maximum of what is feasible here: we have about fifteen thousand taps in our own sugarbush and we tap and buy sap from about a dozen other sugarbushes within a ten-mile radius or so, in all close to forty thousand taps perhaps. That is most of what is available at a feasible distance. There are producers in the Saint Lawrence Valley that have a hundred thousand taps coming into one sugarhouse!"

There is something new every year, and in 2001 it was a shipping container. Normally, large quantities of syrup are stored and shipped in fifty-gallon steel barrels. But the barrels are a big headache: expensive to return, a nuisance to handle, difficult to sterilize, no place to junk them. Now there is a shipping container designed for moving 220 gallons or even 330 gallons at a time. It is a thick octagonal cardboard box, five feet in diameter and four or (for the economy size) five feet high. Inside is a triple-layered plastic bag, to be filled with hot syrup and sealed. The cardboard box is banded with three steel straps and fitted with a cover like a giant hatbox. It rests on a plastic pad and is handled only with a forklift. When full it weighs well over a ton, and when emptied the plastic liner can be discarded and the box recycled. Not for your neighborhood grocery store, but great for shipping a ton of syrup to a Chicago processor.

Bruce is telling me about the many new configurations of the market.

"Some packagers concentrate on just one thin slice of the market, sometimes buying in tankerloads of syrup, or now in these boxes with plastic liners; they package and deliver it to central chain grocery warehouses. And, the packager, in turn, may itself be owned by a holding company for packagers of other kinds of products. All of this squeezes the fat out of the system. A packager you never heard of may buy a million small syrup jugs, more than all of New Hampshire uses in years, fill them with Canadian maple syrup, and deliver them to Sam's Club by the trailerload, who will retail them at a bargain, even if nobody in the system would know a maple tree if they met one." Bruce smiles at all this: he is like a farmer who likes farming and enjoys his farm, and has a chivalrous regard for strong competition. Moreover, he believes the potential market for maple syrup is so huge and varied that he is prepared to bypass some markets. "Because we are vertically integrated, right from the taphole up, we can be pretty flexible, and can actually work with many different kinds of markets—a wholesaler in Spain, a small grocery chain in Oregon, a neighbor producer, a foodstuffs manufacturer in Japan who wants large quantities of maple sugar."

An observant shopper today will notice that although maple syrup remains a specialty item, increasingly it gets more shelf space in quality groceries, and Bruce tells me that that is a crucial market indicator. By a very small but increasing fraction of shoppers, maple syrup is coming to be considered a staple. Moreover, the health food market has large potential for maple syrup—it's a natural product—and only now is that potential being seriously explored. At Bascom's, at least, they are optimistic about the long-term maple market, which they see as a global market.

Bruce's wife Elizabeth, or Liz, is a full partner in this maple business, and she works in the office every weekday. While Bruce is an amiable conversationalist, usually with time to chat about some new or interesting angle on some aspect of the business, Liz is businesslike, tall and slim, very efficient. She walks swiftly from one job to the next, probably does a tremendous amount of work each day, and is always early at her station the next day for more. When I join her to chat one day in the spring of 2002 the racket from construction is loud enough so that we leave her office and sit under a maple tree. Both the warehouse and office space are being enlarged—the warehouse for still more maple equipment and its basement for more syrup storage tanks, and the office to process still more orders. I sense that Bruce is exhilarated about all this and that Liz is merely cheerful about it.

Liz tells me that when she and Bruce met at the University of New Hampshire, "I had had no experience at all at farming." And as for maple syrup, "I supposed it was some exotic Vermont product." Even now she says that Bruce actually likes maple syrup more than she does, and she suspects that "those who really have a passion for it are those who were brought up on it." But she warms to the subject considerably as she tells me about using maple sugar in her green tomato mincemeat. In fact, it turns out that she uses maple sugar in any recipe calling for brown sugar, such as apple crisp, and I cannot think of any objection to that. The Bascoms produce and sell more maple sugar every year—"now that we have finally worked all the bugs out of our system," Liz adds. It appears that the Bascoms had to teach themselves, by trial and error, how to make and handle quality maple sugar in large quantities, and do it efficiently.

As we walk through the warehouse I ask Liz about the varied labels on many of the bottles of syrup being packed for shipment. Because they have the facilities, the Bascoms often take in syrup by the barrel, then process, bottle, label, package, box, and ship it for others, including even some Vermont producers. Indeed, I noticed a "Family Farm" label from Vermont, for example, where the syrup originated; but it was bottled and shipped from Acworth, New Hampshire. Vermont is very persnickety about the use of its name, as well it might be, but other states are less so. Much syrup is bought and sold and mixed from several eastern states, including New York, New Hampshire, and Maine, and simply labeled "New England," but Vermont is protective of its name. It is widely understood, however, that there is no discernible difference in taste or quality of syrup throughout the entire East Coast, and Liz confirms this. Cleanliness, bacteria, seasonality, and other things can affect taste, but not locale or state of origin. That holds, at least, for the eastern states and Quebec; there is a less settled opinion as to whether midwestern syrup typically differs slightly in taste from eastern. Liz is one of those who believes, for example, that Ohio syrup is identifiably different. There is a like dispute, incidentally, throughout the industry, as to whether syrup made from RO-processed sap typically has a lighter taste, due to a shorter boiling time.

Driving home, I pass several sugarhouses by the roadside, traditional operations that do things as they have been done for a hundred years. Some of these have a modest tubing system in the sugarbush, but many pick up the sap from buckets, often at the roadside, and these farmers fire their evaporators with wood, which is in copious supply in a sugarbush. They check the boiling syrup for readiness by temperature (seven degrees above the boiling point of water) or more commonly by hydrometer: too thin and the syrup may spoil, too thick and it may crystallize in the container. They draw the syrup off the evaporator into a bucket, pour or pump it through a filter, and fill the plastic or glass bottles by hand. They retail their syrup at or near the price recommended by the New Hampshire Maple Producers' Association: a higher price would adversely affect their market and a lower one would insult the neighbors and themselves. They sell syrup at their dooryards, or through a mail-order list of customers, or from their website, or from grocery and specialty stores that take it on consignment. Their maple world seems relatively uncomplicated.

Yet it occurs to me that the Bascoms, with their heavy wholesaling, have a kind of control over their marketing that harks back to their own family tradition, though now on a vastly different scale. Long ago, Bruce's grandfather peddled maple syrup for what he could get at Concord, New Hampshire, dooryards ($2.50 a gallon was a good price in the late 1930s); and his father Ken once raised potatoes and poultry on the farm and sold them to whom he wished at a price and time he negotiated. So too with other farm produce of those generations. The Bascoms' selling of their maple products, sugar and syrup, is like that: a market of their own making, far-flung though it be. The Bascoms' dairy farm, in contrast, has none of this flexibility: they sell milk for the going price, with no choice, and that is probably one of the reasons Bruce just doesn't find his dairy farm all that exciting. As wholesalers, the Bascoms have a market flexibility the retailing neighbors in the sugarhouses along the road don't really have. The Bascoms' entrepreneurial strategies enable them to appropriate some of the old farm freedom to operate on their own, creating their own markets for their own products—a very modern and very old-fashioned enterprise.

### The Sugarbush

Maple trees vary in the sweetness of their sap. Occasionally a tree turns up randomly with sap of twice or, more rarely, three or four times the normal sugar content. This interesting oddity doesn't appear to depend upon weather or soil or location but upon the inner mysteries of the tree itself: some trees, it seems, are like some people, just naturally sweet. If a variety of such sweet maples could be intentionally developed, the making of syrup might be vastly easier and more convenient. And, indeed, selecting sweet trees and propagating their offspring is a serious enterprise at several research institutions. At the Cornell University field station at Lake Placid, New York, researchers are cloning sweet trees by rooting scions from sweet maples and planting them for future testing, while other researchers are raising young trees from the seeds of sweet maples, and from their clones. These projects have a long time frame, and no doubt the pancakes will be cold by the time the results are in and the syrup from the new sweet trees is ready and hot. Would it be economically feasible? wise? noble? symbolically beautiful? to plant a sugarbush of sweet maples and wait a couple of generations to begin the harvest? A tree well cared for may be expected to produce for a hundred or two hundred years—so that's a consideration. But the planter of trees will not be around to appreciate the trees' mature years. That kind of farming presupposes that several generations will be in on the project—a brand new argument for the old idea of the family farm. Anyway, such prospects give a new framework to questions of feasibility and cost-effectiveness, and serve also as a timely reminder that farming, which depends upon the earth and the land and the weather, deals in long-term assets.

Meanwhile, the maple community broods under a constant and nagging worry about the health of the maple trees. It is clear that there are a lot of unhealthy or dying trees out there, and everyone knows about it, is worried about it, and most sugar makers have a theory or two about it. There is probably another theory at the next sugarhouse down the road. And there is no lack of possible causes. Insects constitute one: periodically there are severe infestations of gypsy moth larvae, saddled prominent caterpillars, or pear thrips, or all three, which defoliate the trees in midsummer. One summer's leaf loss will not normally kill a tree, but it will weaken it badly, especially a marginally healthy tree, and make it less resistant to other attackers. Severe weather conditions are another: a snowless winter exposes tree roots to dangerous degrees of frost, and summer drought puts intense stress on a tree. Acid rain and other airborne pollutants chiefly from the industrial Midwest consitute another major suspect. Road salt kills some trees and hurts many more. Also, a stressed or injured tree is very susceptible to the entry of fungus, which may easily kill a mature tree. Put all these factors together in the picture, frame it with a roadside row of favorite but thinning and apparently dying old maples, and you have something to fret about.

Yet, a half dozen worries may be more tolerable than just one big worry. The background specter here consists of two tragic episodes, still alive in the memory of old-timers. The first was the American chestnut blight, which totally wiped out that magnificent and valuable tree species during the 1920s and 1930s; and the second was Dutch elm disease, which even more recently utterly destroyed the most beloved shade tree species in the Western Hemisphere. These events were economic and aesthetic catastrophes. The dread in the maple community is this: is our forest stalked by a new maple tree nemesis, which will eventually simply destroy the maple trees as were the elms and the chestnuts? During the last decade a major research effort, the North American Maple Project, set out to measure the health of sugar maple trees and concluded, among other things, that there was not *one* single culprit responsible for the sickly condition of some maple trees—no one dread and efficient maple killer—and that, further, the general health of maple trees may be better than often reported.

Sometimes even qualified good news is hard to accept, or to put into a useful context, and not every maple man and woman found it reassuring to be told that many maple trees were in fairly good health. For they knew many that certainly were not, including many of their own. It is a consensus of scientists and researchers that airborne pollution, and the acids that fall in rain, though seldom direct and sole killers of trees, constitute a very important stress factor, perhaps the chief one. But no one can calculate the proportion of unhealth due to this source. So there is good news and bad news: most maple trees still suffer and eventually die from multiple assaults, air pollution high among them.


Bruce invites me into his pickup to look at "some of the interesting things we have been doing in the woods." We drive along one of the high scenic ridges of the farm to a newly cleared hillside sugarbush, where the Bascoms have recently installed a new tubing system. They have been using tubing for years, but new installation techniques and new products crop up all the time, and this new one is now state-of-the-art. In maple country you will often see whole hillsides of maple trees laced up in a crisscross, seemingly random pattern of plastic tubing of different sizes and colors: small tubes attached to trees, these running into larger tubes, and these into larger ones, zigzag down the hillside, carrying the sap to bulky containers, barrels, tubs, or tanks parked in the snow at the roadside. From there it will be drained or pumped into a tank on the back of a truck and carried to a sugarhouse for boiling. The trees, tubes wrapped around them and across them and sticking into them, look as if they are on an elaborate life-support system; in fact it's just the opposite: their life sap is being drained away from them. But a healthy tree, like a healthy person, has fluid to spare or will make more as needed: drawing ten gallons or so from a tree to make a quart of syrup (which is about average) will not hurt the tree. The sugar not drained away, which is most of it, will be transformed into starch to feed the leaves of the the tree.

Maple syrup production slumped in the 1970s, and the market sagged, but new technologies came to the rescue. Reverse osmosis was the new thing for large operators, but for small or middle-size producers plastic tubing was the big news. Tubing was not new, but it was much improved and much less expensive and could be made to work much better than formerly. No doubt about it, plastic tubing is not very romantic in the woods, and it is not especially handsome: almost anyone would rather look at a hillside sugarbush hung with buckets, maybe even wooden buckets, maybe with a curving trail through the snow for the oxen and the sled. We like our nostalgia. But sap gathering is labor-intensive in the extreme, and the ability to make sap run from hundreds of trees directly into a central container is a quantum leap in efficiency.

In *Sweet Maple*, authors Lawrence and Martin quote Vermont sugar maker Robert Howrigan. Like many, he has installed tubing, and like many, he has had problems with it. He still enjoys gathering some of his sap the old-fashioned way, namely, from buckets with a team of horses and a sled: horses, he says, "don't tear up the soil like a tractor will. They'll paddle through and you'll never know they been there. And you can remote control them; you'll speak to them and they'll move and stop while you dump the buckets and move from one tree to the next. A good team is a pleasure to work with." Howrigan acknowledges that this kind of work is not for everybody: "I've had young fellows who were stars on the football team, but they were a washout when it came to gathering sap. . . . If you gathered any lard in the winter, you could get rid it at sugaring time."[57]

The oldest way to remove lard is carrying the sap by hand to the sugarhouse. This is great fun for a short while, and you are likely to be properly impressed with every bucketful the trees produce. An old-fashioned wooden carved yoke over the shoulders may be used for this purpose: they are sometimes still available in antique shops. (Personally, that's as far as I ever got into high technology with sap delivery, as I was able to fight the tapping habit to a final standoff at something near a hundred buckets.) From hand carrying, the sequence went to using oxen and a sled, then horses, then tractors, and today many use a pickup truck, gathering the sap from plastic roadside tubs. With tubing, however, the sap is not only protected from debris and rain but is often fresher. And the fresher and colder the sap, the less bacterial action within it and the better the eventual syrup; so sap asks to be gathered often and boiled soon. (Bacteria convert the sap's natural sucrose to fructose and glucose, which darken with boiling.) Fancy syrup, which is of lightest color and brings the best price, can seldom be made from sap more than a day out of the tree. Plastic tubing is undoubtedly here to stay.

We are walking through a splendid hillside sugarbush, where the brush has been carefully cleared and neatly piled and the maple trees with their thick trunks and full tops look straight and handsome and healthy. "Actually, my dad did this," says Bruce. "He's over seventy-five, but he really enjoyed working here." And this reminds me that farmers often take pleasure in simple things—straight rows of healthy growing corn, a neat woodpile, an apple orchard pruned and cleared and ready to bloom, a trim maple forest, the understory cleared and the brush piled and the acres of tree stems standing proud. This sugarbush is satisfying just to look at, and we walk among the trees and tubing for a close-up of the new system. Bruce remarks that by now it has been two months since they started tapping, and the bacteria are starting to close off taps, even though the trees are still producing good sap. We conclude that this is the year when those who tapped late may be better off; they could even get a good run yet, if the weather is right, because their taps are still fresh. Bruce smiles and observes that "there is a right time to tap every season, but you never know when it is until the season is over."

The installation of tubing, which a generation ago was a pretty simple and direct matter of getting the sap to the bottom of the hill by gravity instead of emptying buckets and carrying it down, has evolved into a much more sophisticated exercise in engineering. There are reasons for that. First came the discovery that trees not only release sap in the spring, but under certain conditions they also drink it! Sap coming down the tube from one tree may be sucked up and absorbed by the next tree in the line, for a maple tree at high sap season is a complex of intense pressures and vacuums, responding to the weather, to the sun, and to inside dynamics of the tree. Second, and just as interesting, was the discovery that putting vacuum on the hoses will actually suck sap from the trees, stop them from drinking it, and generally increase production. This, in turn, makes it possible to drill a smaller taphole ($^{19}/_{64}$ is now the recommended standard, about the diameter of a pencil) and so do less damage to the tree. Maple farmers are extremely conscious that their trees are their resource, and tree health is of paramount concern. A smaller hole heals faster and fends off disease better. What's more, a vacuum system also makes it possible to install tubes in a sugarbush that is more on less on the level, with no gravity flow. All this bespeaks another major technological step forward, but it is not simple. It turns out that the hydraulics of sap flow in vacuum tubes of different sizes over long distances at shifting temperatures on slopes of varying pitches— well, it's very complicated, and you've got to understand the variables and get it right and without leaks or vacuum pockets, or you will have problems. The Bascoms have been installing tubing for decades, but before putting in this new vacuum system a team of them went to a special installation seminar in Maine. . . . On this farm the days of the old wooden bucket are now *long* gone.

Bruce Bascom appears to me to have a restlessness about him, and I think it is unlikely that he would be content, as many maple people are, just to do what he did his previous year, perhaps streamlining it a little, tapping the same maple trees, selling syrup to the same customers. His last year was probably not exciting enough to repeat it; he needs a new machine or two, some bright new piece of technology, another sugarbush maybe, a bigger warehouse, a new market in Bermuda, certainly some new storage tanks, perhaps a milking parlor—some improvement, or new challenge at least.

Now it is a warm afternoon in May of 2002 and I am standing with Bruce's father, Ken Bascom, in his backyard, on a bluff overlooking the Bascom sugarhouse. Bruce and Liz live in the original early-nineteenth-century stone house west of the sugarhouse, and Ken and his wife live high on the east side. Ken built this house for his retirement years on a bluff overlooking the broad and rolling meadows to the south and the sugarhouse to the west, and it is a splendid spot. He has just showed me, near the edge of the woods, a clutch of wild lady's slipper orchids. He watches for them each spring.

At this elevation he and I now have a perfect vantage point overlooking the new construction at the sugarhouse. Bruce needs more space, more equipment, some better facilities. It is a noisy buzz and confusion down there: a long-armed excavator, a cement truck, a mason or two, carpenters, various laborers, some pounding and calling—the clatter and bang of . . . what? Is it progress? Yonder is Ken's nephew, Kevin Bascom, smiling, waving to us, a roll of blueprints under his arm.

Ken looks up from the lady's slippers and silently takes in the panoramic scene—the maple hillsides whose every square inch he must know by heart, the farm buildings and the far hills, the noise and bustle and building at our feet. In some sense, it is he who sponsored it all, and for him this entire scene must be heavy with meaning. I know what I see when I look, but what does he see? And is it exciting, or inscrutable, or what? Ken takes it all in slowly and without words; he smiles and shakes his head. Eventually he says, "I'm going on seventy-seven—and I've seen some changes." He does not seem melancholy or solemn. Something like sheer wonder is what I think I see in his face and hear in his mellow chuckle.

I could wish to get his complete take on all this in a sentence, a paragraph, but such a sentence does not exist. This is Ken's life. He moved here as a boy sixty-five years ago, fell in love with it, farmed it all his life, passed it to his son Bruce. What Bruce is doing, Ken knows, is developing its potential along lines that Ken, perhaps unknowingly, himself set. Somehow, all this expansion and construction goes back to the decision Ken himself made forty years ago—to sell the cows and go with maple. And Bruce's maple operation: how do you compare 1939's six hundred buckets with today's forty thousand taps on tubes? Or relate it to this present noise and bustle? What is the measure of progress? Is this progress?

As we step back from the bluff, the shrubbery and the young trees quickly and effectively soak up the noise of construction. A few steps farther back, and the sugarhouse itself seems to sink slowly away beneath the lady's slippers. Any day, Ken can walk to the edge of his bluff and hear and gaze upon the future, and marvel at it if he wishes; or he can withdraw a few rods, and then he doesn't have to rejoice or fret over it at all.

## The Sweet Good-bye

The sugar season is short and sweet, and it winds down every spring about the time the bluebirds show up, when the last snow has hardened and hunkered down to dirty pockets in ravines and the brooks are singing out loud. It is April then, and different movements are astir under the tree bark, as the tree mixes up a new batch of ingredients, under less pressure, to feed the swelling buds at its twig tips; and the bacteria stimulated by the warmer weather start to seal off the wound of the taphole. No more sap until next February, and it's hard to regret it.

There are strange and strangely pleasing ironies in maple farming. Take sap. It is so fundamental and natural, so basic and utterly simple, that we learned about it from Stone Age Americans; yet we now subject its harvest to a vast and ever expanding array of engineering tricks and technologies in order to yield, finally, something almost as simple, namely, syrup—which is boiled sap minus water. Surely, it's an unusual kind of farming, and sometimes not thought of as farming at all. We blithely accept the trees as just being there. We did not plant them. It may seem that therefore we do not farm them. But it is a mode of farming, and it exacts the same tough virtues as any other: the tending of fragile growing things, patience and stewardship and responsibility, and the ready acceptance of strenuous labors. It demands as well an everlasting wariness and humility before the great natural facts, sun and frost and wind and rain, over which we mere humans have no control at all. And of course it tests our cultural preconceptions. Mentally, we have left behind the oaken buckets and the iron kettles over open fires, but we may not feel aesthetically prepared for vacuum tubing and reverse osmosis machines.

But some rural labors, some pleasing sights or fragrances, such as apple blossoms in May or new hay in June or a loaded apple tree in brisk autumn, remind farmers ever and again why they do what they do and why they love their calling. For some, the best and most suggestive of these sensual pleasures is a billow of steam and the sweet and smoky aroma of the working sugarhouse with the evaporator bubbling full tilt. It is an enormous amount of work to gather sap and make syrup, and it yields an equal amount of immediate satisfaction; yet it is difficult to put a precise finger on the deep and undeniable appeal of making it each spring. Maybe it is just the bright and warm sun shining on a cold winter's leftover snow; maybe the beloved taste of syrup or the good cheer of a sweet good-bye to winter; maybe it's the prospect of the pleasure the syrup will create, or the simplicity of the thing, the fact that the sap is sheer gift, mysteriously given; or perhaps it is the sugarhouse camaraderie, or the promise of a new season. If you question, as I did, the practitioners of this craft in one sugarhouse after another as to why they do it, why they have done it for generations and intend to keep at it and still like it, then you too may eventually tease out the definitive answer, which is this: "There's just something about it."

# Chapter 5

# Got Milk? Eccardt Farm, Inc.

Fortunate is the son who works in the shadow of his father's experience and knowledge. And doubly fortunate is the father who is associated with the reflected glory of his sons' achievements.                    —Quoted in *Successful Farming*, October 2002, p. 38

## *Farm Family*

It is tangy early October: the pumpkins are orange and hard, the sky is brilliant blue, and the fleecy drifting clouds are soft as new white lambs. We are nearing the peak of fall color season, and already the hillsides are beyond description.

I have stopped by the Eccardt Farm today, as I do now and then, to see what is going on or perhaps to find someone to chat with about farming. We are in Washington, New Hampshire, the town where I live, and the farm is tucked into a scenic little valley up against the eastern edge of Lovell Mountain. Occasionally, I will find that someone else, a nonfarmer like me, has also stopped in, for it's that kind of farm. Some of these other visitors were just driving by and may have been lured in by the welcoming reputation of the place, or by the sight of interesting livestock penned near the road: a couple of implausible emus, a friendly burro or two, some llamas, a couple of goats, a few swans in the little fishpond, ducks of various kinds and colors squatting on the edge, other exotic birds hard to identify, white pigeons overhead, hens here, rabbits over there, pigs yonder, cats and dogs about—a whole welcoming menagerie. In the background is an extended collection of old and older farm machinery on permanent display, a private farm museum.

These attractions, the quixotic livestock and the exotic machinery, are chiefly the hobbies of Hans Eccard, who is also alleged to be trying to retire from farming after more than fifty years but suffers chronic relapses. Through the old tools and animal menagerie Hans adds a celebratory and whimsical note to the life of the farm, and to the life of his grandchildren, and also provides interest for visiting children and welcome for neighbors and strangers. Other visitors who have stopped by today would not know that I am here with a purpose, for I seem to be doing exactly as they are — just hanging around, perhaps kicking an old mower wheel now and then, and shooting the breeze. Actually, I am really hard at work, although I'm not tending crops or livestock, and I call this kind of work research, though only to myself. I carry no tools, and I wear the easy disguise of an idle neighbor.

Today I shall be appointed Inspector of Grass-Cutting and Bunker-Filling Operations, a self-appointment, as it happens, but before I launch that effort I elect to linger about the house and farmyard to savor what is going on. This day, this hour, this collection of scenes and activities, is not at all untypical on this farm, and it might have been cobbled together — as it certainly was not — by someone trying hard to imagine a typical family dairy farm. It is midafternoon (I tend to start work late), and I learn that Hans and his son George are cutting grass at the King place. I learn this from Hans's wife, Julia Eccard, who is just now planting crocus bulbs in front of the house and casting an occasional eye toward her grandsons, tossing a ball in the yard to the east.

Julia is a lean and muscular woman who grew up on a farm in Switzerland within a tradition where women commonly did farmwork, especially milking. Accordingly, she was up extremely early this morning, as she is six days a week, to start the milking. She has been a regular milker here for more than forty years, and she has overseen the steady growth of the dairy herd from just a few cows to fifty, then to a hundred, then to nearly two hundred. While talking to Julia I wave to Margaretha Eccardt, the venerable matriarch of this farmstead and household, who served the family breakfast this morning, as she does every morning; she is now pulling up leeks in her garden. Her labors do not surprise me, because whenever I see her at home she is working — in the house, in the garden, in the henhouse, sometimes in the rabbit warren or the dovecote. The younger generations of Eccards know her affectionately as "Gram." At her most recent birthday Margaretha Eccardt was ninety-six. That is not a misprint — that is just one remarkable woman.

Years and years ago Margaretha Eccardt and her husband, both of German descent, took a young relative, Hans Eccard, under their wing, and after they had settled in New Hampshire, Hans joined them from Germany. (His branch of the family had dropped the final *t* from their name, but the farm's official and corporate name retains it.) Margaretha's husband has since died, but when they bought the farm in the early 1950s it was a two-thousand-bird chicken farm. Hans had a Swiss girlfriend, Julia, and eventually he persuaded her to join him on the farm in this country. Both had had European farming experience in their youth, and that is how they proposed to make their way here. Margaretha Eccardt said to me: "We had no children, my husband and I, so Hans and Julia became our children."

When the senior Eccardts took over this place in the 1950s they started to shift the chicken farm toward dairy—more rapidly as Hans and Julia became a part of the action—and the Holstein dairy herd has been growing ever since. Although the Eccardt Farm always has a few large Brown Swiss cows for traditional and sentimental reasons (and for chocolate milk, one of the grandchildren reported), the main herd is purebred Holstein. Like the Brown Swiss, and probably for reasons that have to do with the origin of the breed, the Holsteins seem to have no difficulty with the German accent they often hear on this farm.

John Eccard drives up in a dump truck loaded with freshly chopped grass, which he empties in front of the bunker (a horizontal silo), then jumps onto a tractor and starts shoving the grass up into the bunker. John, who is also chief of the Washington Volunteer Fire Department, and his older brother George are the sons of Hans and Julia Eccard. Now approaching their forties, they were raised on this farm, and never seriously contemplated any career but farming. Hans tells me with genuine passion how extremely fortunate he is that his two sons decided to stay here and take up farming with him. When they married they each built a house within sight of the family homestead, and their wives joined in the farm enterprise. A bit farther down the road Hans and Julia's daughter Marianne lives with her husband and family. George's wife Sandra (who has just driven up and gone into the milk house to get the latest data to take home to her computer) takes care of the farm books, and John's wife Becca sometimes tends the horses and the calves or joins the milking team, and both take care of the youngest Eccard children, perhaps the future stewards of this place. Four generations are actively involved on this farm; they all live within a radius of one mile, and today I spot one or more from each generation in a single glance from the front yard.

I hurry off to the neighbor's field to get in on the grass cutting. Most of the Eccard corn crop has already been chopped and packed into the bunkers, so it is time for another layer of grass before the final layer of corn. The Eccards cut grass from the fields of more than a dozen landowners within a broad arc extending about twelve miles eastward, former farms that once had their own cows, and they chop up the grass and haul it to their bunkers in dump trucks—a reminder how much this one farm does to keep our fields open, scenic islands of green encircled by wave upon wave of predatory forests. Indeed, most of the landscapes we treasure in New England are working landscapes, and for a hundred years these regions have been losing open farmland to forests. But for the farmers among us we would be swiftly losing still more. Everywhere, the beloved landscapes of New England pay scenic tribute to its family farms.

*Grass for the Bunker*

Farmers have a lingo that seems natural to them but not to everybody: silage is feed (not food) that comes out of a silo, which is a big vertical tube, or out of a bunker, which is a large horizontal plastic-covered trench. Silage is composed of chopped and naturally fermented green grass (including clover and alfalfa) and/or chopped cornstalks (including the ears). Although corn silage has been standard dairy cow feed for over a hundred years, putting grass into a bunker or silo for winter feed is a relatively new idea: I believe it was unheard of fifty years ago in the farming community where I grew up. Hay has long been the standard winter feed for cows (their meat and potatoes, as it were), and corn silage, when it became available in the nineteenth century, was often regarded as a kind of nutritious and tastier fresh vegetable dish on the side. Today a mixture of grass and corn silage is a staple of dairy feeding.

When I arrive at the field I see that Hans and his son George are following each other in circles around the field, tractor and mower followed by tractor, chopper, and trailer. The chopper picks up the freshly cut grass, hacks it into shorter pieces, and blows it into a trailer which it hauls along behind, a kind of deep dumpster on wheels. George hails me with a cheery wave, stops, and invites me to ride with him on the chopper tractor, and I gladly accept the invitation to do so. He throttles down a few notches from his usual speed, to make my ride a bit less jarring and to enable me to pepper him with questions. I am perched high up over the left wheel, with a good view, and since I am inside the aluminum and plastic tractor cab I feel perfectly safe. I recall that fifty years ago I first learned to drive a tractor by observing from a more precarious perch, namely, seated on an open fender of a Ford tractor. It was a smaller tractor, and its fenders were not designed for sitting; they were, nevertheless, universally used for that, uncomfortable and unsafe though they were. The rider just hung on with both hands. Every farm boy and girl did it then, a favorite form of farm entertainment: riding on tractor fenders or, alternatively, standing on the rear drawbar. This is somewhat scary to contemplate now, and there were sometimes serious accidents, although I was never part of one. I take it that safety consciousness has a higher priority on farms than it once did.

George is quick to point out that this is not by any means high-quality grass we are harvesting today. Until recently it was a dry summer: after the June cutting the second crop grew up, but in August much of died on its feet in the summer drought; then hurricane-driven rains came abundantly and new shoots grew very fast for three weeks in September. It is a mixture of standing dead stalks and late short growth that we are cutting. No farmer really enjoys harvesting a poor-quality crop, but they learn to make the best of it. "It will all mix in," says George optimistically.

Mix in. The cows are fed what is called a Total Mixed Ration (TMR), which is carefully calculated specifically for each herd. On this farm it means that the bunker forage is periodically tested for fiber quality and nutritional content, and on the basis of that the appropriate supplements (grains, minerals, etc.) are calculated so as to provide the best diet (the best TMR) for these specific cows. A milking cow's ideal requirements for each of twenty or thirty nutrients are known, and this ideal can be approximated by any of many combinations of feeds—if all *their* components are known. The goal (never completely achievable, of course) is to give every cow the perfect milk-producing and health-preserving diet. All kinds of by-products of other enterprises—by-products whose exact nutritional and fiber content is measured, and which can therefore be mixed with other products to achieve a particular dietary goal—are used in dairy cow supplements: sugar beet residue, citrus pulp, stale baked goods, whey from cheese making, brewery malt, potatoes, fish meal, cottonseed residue, and a dozen more. So today's marginal-quality grass ("It will make good fiber, anyway," I hear said above the tractor's hum) will be nicely compensated for by various purchased supplements: perhaps it will be potato peelings and stale muffins. George has that and many more possibilities in mind when he says, "It will all mix in."

We are going routinely round and round the field, so I have plenty of opportunity to quiz my chauffeur about the many other wrinkles in this feeding story. Sheer quantity of milk is not always the sole aim, he points out, for farmers are also paid in terms of butterfat and protein content of the milk, and these are affected by the cows' diet. On the other hand, he tells me, the grain or supplement price may sometimes be so high and the milk price so low that it may not pay to push for more production, even if you could get it.

While George is chatting off the top of his head, I am getting a cram course in dairying and trying to remember it all. He quickly comes to his next point: "Perhaps you could maintain production by switching to another product that has all the needed supplements and is cheaper. But making the diet switch may stress the cows, which may affect production; so is it worth it?" Judgment calls everywhere. Some dairy farmers work hard at attaching accurate numbers to every one of these variables, with the aim of reducing a judgment call as far as possible to a careful cost-benefit calculation. George reminds me also that the forage in the bunker is periodically tested for nutrition and that forage testing is a service offered free by various feed companies, who are in competition with each other, and who make recommendations as to which kinds and how much of the supplements are required. "They are the ones who sell you the stuff; and, of course, they all want your business," says George.

As I watch the new mown grass slip up smoothly into the chopper, I think of the steps in the long sequence from grass to milk in a glass: into the chopper, the wagon, the truck, the bunker (where it cooks for a month or two), into the loader and feed mixer, where the supplements are stirred in, into the manger, finally into the cow's stomach, where the real milk making begins. The chopper cuts the grass into four- to six-inch lengths; the cow's first chewing breaks it up into smaller bits and sends it to the first department of her stomach, the rumen. There acids soften it further and stomach muscles automatically package it into tennis ball–size wads that are sent up again for further chewing as cud, then sent down again to another stomach department for further processing.

A cow may take in forty or more pounds of forage a day, and as much water, and if left undisturbed will thoughtfully chew her cud for about ten hours a day. Eating, sleeping, and being milked make up the rest of the cow's exciting day. They like things calm, these big dim-witted and amiable creatures, and they are usually content to have the same breakfast and dinner every day, year in year out. A good uninterrupted cud-chewing day is a good day for a cow. Cud chewing not only grinds up the forage; it stimulates the flow of saliva, which is loaded with bacteria, which do the next processing. A cow's stomach is a wondrously complicated, highly articulated, four-department affair that makes our own stomach seem pretty

modest in its simplicity. But then, we don't have to make milk from cornstalks, either.

What if some foreign matter gets into the cow's feeding routine? I wonder, and when I broach the subject George's face lights up with the big
smile he always has on tap: "Oh yeah! Oh yeah," he says, nodding, and I
know he is on familiar territory. "We grind up a few arrows each year."

He got my attention: "Arrows?"

"Bow hunters, out for deer or turkey; they lose a few arrows—which
often have aluminum points." I wince at the thought of a cow inadvertently swallowing chopped arrowheads, as does George, and I realize how
serious the matter is. "Glass is very dangerous too; and aluminum cans—
often you can spot those before they get into the chopper. Sometimes a
piece of machinery. Last year we picked up a rock and it took teeth out of
the chopper and sent them into the wagon. You just have to hope the cows
don't find that stuff. Sometimes a piece of junk will show up in the bottom
of an empty manger, and you're just glad it was there and not in the bottom of somebody's stomach."

"And what if it is?" I can't help asking. "And how do you detect the problem? And what can you do?"

"You can usually tell from the cow's behavior if she has metal in her
stomach: won't eat, milk way down, doesn't seem to have any other problem. So, if that's what we think it is, we feed her the magnet." Feed her the
magnet? "That comes in the form of a big pill, which is actually designed
to latch onto the piece of metal, pull it to the bottom of the stomach, out
of the range where it can do damage, and it may stay right there for the rest
of the cow's life."

The chopper stops. John pulls the dump truck up alongside and George
manipulates the hydraulic controls in the tractor cabin. The trailer into
which the chopped grass was being collected now rears high on its
hydraulic legs, tips, and empties its load of several tons into the truck. All
this takes less than three minutes, and the truck rumbles off to dump the
load in front of the bunker. There, John on another tractor, this one armed
with a big scoop, will push the grass up into the bunker, spread it around,
and pack it down as tightly as possible by driving over it again and again
with the tractor. Pack it down. Anybody with a grass catcher on a lawn
mower knows that a high pile of fresh damp grass on the compost heap will
heat up and rot down and stink and swiftly turn into a very unpleasant
mess as the first stage on the way to becoming compost. Not the grass in
this bunker. Why not?

The bunker's secret is essentially very simple: pack it down; keep the air out. A layer of grass today, a layer of corn tomorrow; pack it down. Then another layer of grass, again a layer of corn. Pack it down. Cover it up with a heavy black plastic tarp, and weight that down with dozens of old tires. Keep the air out. Now the natural sugars and starches in the corn initiate a fermentation process that uses up the oxygen packed into the silage and creates acids that eventually shut down the fermentation process and preserve the organic material. We have a sealed bunker-oven for gentle natural cooking before serving. The ingredients of the silage layer cake—chopped green grass and chopped green cornstalks—have, ideally, been harvested with just the right amount of moisture, sugars, and starches, and just at the peak of their nutritional value (the legumes in the grass just before bloom and the kernels in the corn ears just beginning to harden). If the ingredients were too dry the oven may get too hot, if too wet it may get moldy. Ideally, it all cooks comfortably in nearly airless natural low heat for weeks and weeks, and then stops and remains unchanged for months and months. It is an entirely natural chemical process, but no less marvelous for all that. Such fermentation prepares the nutrients for release; so it's really the first stage of digestion, anticipating what will later happen in the cow's stomach.

When this method of feed preservation and preparation was discovered in the nineteenth century, the silo was promptly invented, built as an upright cylinder, first of wooden but later ceramic tiles, like a big blue thermos bottle beside the barn—upright so that the sheer weight of the silage would pack it down and exclude the air. In recent decades the bunker silo (just an enormous cement trough, open at one end) has become very common, once it was learned that heavy tractors and heavy plastic can pack and seal the bunker as adequately and completely as is needed.

When the bunker pie is opened, it turns out that properly fermented silage has a very distinctive and pungent odor, slightly sour or tangy, and much more pronounced than that of the freshly cut grass and corn that went in. That robust silage aroma makes good dairymen smile and good cows moo. My informal survey suggests that most nonrural folk do not like the smell of silage and, indeed, if inexperienced in these things, may think they are smelling manure. But I have known city folk and even professors who do like it: they would probably have made good farmers. Perhaps the silage-smell-response is as valid a litmus test for one's farming instincts as any. However, if a farmer can recognize the quality of his silage by its smell, that is not a precise enough test for the cows. They are in the milk-producing business, and the ingredients of their dinner have to be regularly scientifically evaluated in a laboratory so the exact nutritional value can be figured into the formula of the Total Mixed Ration.

## Corn Harvest

Hans Eccard is a stocky and colorful bear of a man, good-humored, verbose, full of large affections and large gestures. He loves farms and harvests, loves to talk and tell stories, often dramatizing them with his face, his hands, his arms, his whole body. When fully animated, which is quite frequently, ideas come boiling out of him wrapped in a thick German accent, ever thicker as the drama rises. Often, as when swapping yarns with the neighbors, he is full of hearty laughter and self-deprecating jokes; but sometimes, as when he holds forth at town meeting, and has an audience of a hundred and is defending some cause lost already decades ago, he can be utterly solemn and melodramatic, elegiac almost, discoursing with long and colorful detours on the plight of the American farmer and his vanishing liberties. So far as I can tell, Hans is everybody's favorite character.

He has a bad back, and three times he has had surgery on it, and frequently he wears a brace for it, and still it gives him pain. And still he drives the tractor, bumping over the rough ground almost daily in planting and harvesting season, though he often takes pain pills to endure it. Endure it? He will tell you with passion that he loves the work, loves especially the harvest, loves—no, demands—to be a full part of it. His enthusiasm is infectious, and it seems that everyone at the farm is pleased to take his own turn driving for the corn chopper. Margaretha is exasperated by Hans's work ethic, doesn't think he should get on a tractor at all. "But you can't tell him anything," she says to me with a resigned sigh, and goes back to work herself.

Hans takes a sensual pleasure in the textures of farming. He has a palpable affection for animals, for soil, for silage, compost, hay, for the very materials of the farm. To him these things are not merely instrumental; they have their own qualities and excellence, and are to be appreciated in and for themselves. You can read all this and more in his manner and his tone, as when he says simply, "Nice compost." Today it is Hans's turn at the corn harvest, and my turn to ride with him as we circle the field with tractor and chopper and trailer, near the end of the corn harvest. The corn is chopped—stalks, ears, leaves—and sent into the trailer just as the grass was, then dumped into a truck, hauled to the bunker, dropped, pushed up with a dozer, and packed down atop the grass, there to ferment for a month or two as it turns into feed. Hans takes a deep and visceral pleasure in just seeing all this happen.

I hope to get him to talk corn, so I venture: "Well, the corn *looks* good this year; is it good?" "Good, but not excellent," says Hans, with conviction, as if the matter had been settled with him and formulated well before I asked. Within the next hour or two, and over and under the roar of the tractor and the chopper, he gives me his careful reading of this cornfield, including the things that keep it from being excellent.

The chopper wades swiftly into the wall of corn, gobbling up two rows at a time. We round the far bend and I see an area in the midst of the field with no corn at all, just weeds: it is a low spot where rainwater settled just after planting and all the kernels rotted. Farther on we come upon another feeble patch with plenty of cornstalks but with no ears on them. Something unknown in the weather or soil caused a miscarriage just as the ears would normally be setting in July. Farming is full of mysteries. Hans points and winces: these plants have failed him, and he takes it personally. He throws up his arms and declares: "Why? Who knows?" As we move on and look closely we can see that everywhere many of the lower corn leaves are dry and broken and ragged: that's from the sudden hailstorm that descended one hot July day, shredding every exposed corn leaf: ten minutes of hard hail and the corn was throttled for ten days. Hans shrugs: "When it finally recovered it grew faster than ever." He smiles: these plants are tough; they have not failed him. We chop them up and send them into the trailer: it will all mix in.

Yonder is another patch of cornless weeds; and that, Hans says, is where a flock of crows marched down the rows just after the corn came up in June and pulled up each new shoot. The memory of it fires him up: "They'll even tip over a plant six inches high to get at that *juicy kernel* at the bottom. *Six inches high*," he repeats, with passion and emphasis. Listening to Hans above the roar of the tractor, I think I can taste that kernel myself! Here we see some places where the weeds among the corn are altogether too healthy, and that's because it was too wet in June for the weed sprayer to get on the fields, and waiting ten days meant that "some weeds were too big—*way too big*—for the spray to kill them." Thinly scattered here and there and everywhere are broken cornstalks that never matured. They are the ones attacked by corn borers: when the borer eggs hatch, the larvae eat their way into the stalk and then eat their way upward inside it—Hans gestures, vigorously, wormlike, with his little finger—and eventually the stalk is weakened enough to keel over.

During the summer as I drove past this field, I often glanced over and saw only a handsome corn crop. Hans too sees a handsome corn crop, and his enthusiasm for this harvest is palpable, but like any serious farmer, he also sees everything that is less than perfect. It's a big field, sixty-five acres, with, yes, lots of ways and places to be vulnerable to many kinds of possible setbacks, big and small. But in most places the corn is superbly healthy and thick and up to nine feet tall and decked out with big, swollen ears. "Good crop," Hans says, as once more we watch the trailer rise on its hydraulic legs, tip, and empty itself into John's dump truck. "Good corn." It might have been excellent but for the many wrinkles that developed over the summer, not one of them a real surprise.

There is one more wrinkle in this cornfield that Hans wants me to appreciate—or deplore. Here along the edge near the road are patches where mature corn was very recently broken down and flattened and the ears chewed up, and this introduces a topic that I sense Hans both loves and loathes. Frequently, and especially when the corn begins to ripen, a black bear or two come down from Lovell Mountain and invite themselves to dinner in the Eccard cornfield. Almost every year the Eccards have some bear damage, and this year is no exception: clearly a bear was here within the last few days. Hans glances around, even now alert for the heroic foe.

Sometimes during corn harvest Hans carries his rifle with him on the tractor, as he does today. I ponder the prospect of seeing a bear as we sweep around and around the big field; and I hope we do, and I hope we don't. A few years ago Hans shot a bear in this very cornfield. That one had hid out in the corn during the day, as it was being cut from the edges of the field inward. Eventually, the remaining rows of corn in the center of the field were so few that the bear had little space left to hide, and when he emerged that day near dusk he seemed curious and totally confused that his familiar corn woods had just utterly evaporated from around him. Hans, as is his talent, made a very good yarn of it, even mimicking the big bear as it barged out from the last dozen rows of corn, stood momentarily in the barren cornfield looking, amazed, all around him, then rose upright and sniffed the air, as if to say (Hans's transcription), "What happened to my woods?" Now Hans mimicked himself as he exited the tractor and stalked his prey, excited man and puzzled bear weaving in and then out of the tall corn fence as dusk was settling upon them. Finally, a good shot. But now it is too dark to follow up—seek out a wounded bear in the semidark of the thick standing corn? Nein, Danke. Next morning they found the bear lying dead in the corn. It was a good story—at least I enjoyed very much his telling of it, even though I take no delight in shooting bears. Hans is a diligent farmer and he loves his crops, and guards them like a parent.

Our day is winding down and Hans is telling me about an article in a recent issue of a farm monthly he subscribes to, concerning a farming partnership in Iowa that involved a father and his two sons. It reminded him of his own family and situation, for the article touched on the sometimes complicated family dynamics of such an arrangement. It is something Hans thinks about these days, as he reaches for perspective on his years on this farm and thinks about his legacy. We have stopped the tractor now. He tells me earnestly: "I never wanted my sons to feel that I was leaning on them too hard; I never wanted them to feel that I had them under my thumb," and Hans jams his thumb hard on the tractor fender for emphasis. I teased, "Oh, surely, George and John must think that they are still pretty much under *your eye* if not your thumb." "Oh, no," he says, shaking his head solemnly, then grows reflective: "Maybe . . . maybe sometimes if I give too much advice, they might tell me to go off and play with the bulldozer somewhere." He laughs out loud.

Then Hans comes quickly back to the main point, which he wants to be sure I understand: to be a farmer in partnership with his two sons is to him an altogether magnificent privilege. He decides to go to the house to retrieve the magazine, because he remembers that he wants to share the article's conclusion, which is along these lines: One of the younger Iowan sons carries in his wallet a card that has been passed to him from his father, who had long carried it, and had originally received it from *his* father. Hans is struck by this little ritualized sequence, confirming a family farming tradition. Standing there in his cornfield, farm magazine in hand, he reads aloud to me that card's inscription: "Fortunate is the son who works in the shadow of his father's experience and knowledge. And doubly fortunate is the father who is associated with the reflected glory of his sons' achievements."

Politically, Hans Eccard the farmer is a good-humored mix of convictions, sometimes at cross-purposes. Although he is an immigrant, he has become Yankier than the rest of us. His brand of local politics might be called New England Contrary: land use ordinances, building codes, permit requirements, conservation commissions, town ordinances, planning boards, indeed, the whole arsenal of bureaucratic tools for guiding growth in rural areas—well, Hans is against them. He will tell you that privately with a smile, or with passion at town meeting. He embodies perfectly the

contrary and independent yeoman whom Victor Hanson (chapter 3) celebrates as essential to democracy, and Hans stands foursquare for the old
values of independence and noninterference. At the same time he under-
stands perfectly well that no modern farm can exist without conforming
to a host of necessary standards concerning worker safety, pesticide use,
sanitation, animal health, manure handling, product purity, water and air
pollution, and so on—and these are values and ideas that he seems to have
fully internalized. If his heart is at war with his head, it is a spirited and
sunny battle. George Eccard, who has a bit of his father's temperament, has
his own take on the situation. He will tell you that the Eccards so hate to
be told what to do that they always try to get ahead of the curve and make
some adjustment before a law, or a selectman, or a bureaucrat, or a policy
regulation tells them they have to.

### In the Milking Parlor

On the eighty-acre farm where I grew up, my father kept his farm records
on the back of a calendar that hung in the kitchen. On New Year's Day,
when we hung the new calendar, he transferred to it all the relevant data—
the sum total of which, I believe, consisted of dates on which the cows and
sows had been bred. Other data he kept in his head. We never had more
than eight cows and three sows, so record keeping on our farm was not a
huge challenge.

Sandra, George Eccard's wife, does the bookkeeping on Eccardt Farm.
She uses a computer, of course, but this is a recent convenience of the
1990s, for until then records were kept by hand in a series of notebooks and
check stubs and, yes, also on a calendar. For thirty years or more before
Sandra and her computer took over this department, her mother-in-law,
Julia Eccard, kept the notebooks with the relevant data on the entire dairy
herd, breeding and feeding, sickness and calving, production and butterfat,
and lots of miscellaneous data. Now, each of the approximately two hundred milking cows has her own computer line.

Once a month the tester comes and takes a milk sample from each cow
and measures by weight that day's milk production. From the monthly
series of such measures throughout the lactation (which is the time after
calving during which a cow produces milk before drying off in preparation
for her next calf, normally about 305 days) it is possible to calculate pretty
exactly the yearly production of milk by each cow. Yearly pounds of milk

produced per cow is one simple and ready measure of a herd's quality, and it is the number that usually confers or withholds bragging rights to the farm or herdsman—though it may not be an adequate measure of farm profitability. The milk sample of each cow goes to the laboratory of the Northeast Dairy Improvement Association in Ithaca, New York, where it is tested for a variety of components, most importantly butterfat and protein. These results, including an updated estimated yearly production for each cow, are sent directly to Sandra's computer for her to enter into her own records: each cow has a complete profile, regularly updated, including sire and mother's records, birth date and weight, health history, production history, the feeding ration, and so on. This is the way dairy farmers select breeding lines, cull their herd, and usually achieve what they all strive for, namely, to improve their average herd production. There is no private life for a dairy cow.

I am about to inspect the herd production, and it is 5:30 in the morning as I enter the Eccards' milking parlor. John and Becca Eccard are taking their milking turn today, and have been here at work for three hours already. My job is to keep my eyes and ears open and try to keep out of the way. Milking the cows is the inescapable task on a dairy farm—twice a day on this farm, three times a day on a few New Hampshire farms. ("When are you going to get serious and go to three milkings a day?" I ask. "Never!" is the chorus from the Eccard milkers.) At Eccardt Farm there are two milkers on the job twice a day, seven days a week, 365 days a year, including Christmas. About seven or eight years of this is the average term for each of these cows, after which they begin a new career with America's favorite fast-food industry.

The Eccards can't do all this milking, so they have to hire milkers. I believe that if you live within driving distance and can develop the relevant skills, and if you have discipline and good staying power, and are extremely conscientious, and have a natural affection for the animals, and have unusual patience, and don't mind a little fresh manure splashing around now and then, and can handle routine work for hours on end, and can take the odd hours and odors, you could probably get a good job here—although I have not tried. Milking 180 cows suggests something of the tedium and drudgery often associated with farm labor, but it's one of the main jobs on a dairy farm, and there probably isn't a good way to think of it as fun. To John and Becca, when I probe, it is just another farm job accepted with casual good humor. "Part of the package," said John. "I think of this as quality time with my husband," said Becca.

Upon entering a modern milking parlor for the first time one is likely to be baffled by the sheer otherworldly strangeness of it. Here is an extremely compact area with people and animals in very close quarters intimately surrounded by pipes and bars and hoses, the air suffused with strange noises and unpleasant odors—altogether a weird and intense mixture of the natural and the industrial. The people milling about in the center are rubber aproned and high booted, and the visible parts of the cows shift and heave behind steel bars, and in the center bright white milk surges and splashes against the insides of huge glass carboys—a surrealist scene out of science fiction.

In fact, however, the milking parlor in a moderate-size dairy farm like this one is of fairly direct and stereotyped design, well suited to its purpose, and no more surreal than a bale of hay. This one accommodates two milkers and handles twelve cows at a time. (Incidentally, if they ever catch the one who first thought of calling this place a *parlor*, dairymen would probably vote to give that person a Nobel prize.) The Holsteins know the ropes, and when the gate opens they saunter into the parlor and arrange themselves, belly to belly in tight parallel position, their butts angled obliquely toward the narrow aisle that runs between the two rows of cows, six on a side, where the milkers work. The milkers' aisle is more than two feet lower than the cows for easier access to the udders. It's much quieter today in the parlor than it was on my earlier visits, and that's because the Eccards— after much family discussion—have installed some new equipment, including a system for offering the cows warm water instead of the grain they used to be fed while being milked. Formerly, the cows made a big deal about the small amount of tasty grain, and competed with one another, and banged noisily on the feeders, and left the parlor only reluctantly.

Some very modern dairies equip cows with a computer chip, which, as the cow enters the milking stall, is read by a computer, which then delivers a prespecified amount of feed, an individualized dietary supplement to each cow at each milking. Such extremely sophisticated and fancy technology is, according to the Eccards, by no means worth the cost and trouble, at least for them. On the whole, the Eccards appear to be a conservative lot, not making a major change easily, and only after chewing on it over many a morning breakfast table, where five or six people may wade in on the discussion. One senses that there is always an unspoken and unanimously shared premise for all such discussions, namely, that this family is far more dedicated to a certain way of life than to the absolute maximum of profits or production.

Today I get to talk about milk with the milkers, and I learn that average production of the Eccardt herd increases steadily year by year. John tells me that they achieve this "without the use of growth hormones, which we never used anyway." Why not? "That was a decision my father made long ago; he didn't want the milk contaminated, I guess—anyway, didn't want the cows stressed so much." I learn that Hans was never happy about tinkering with natural processes, that it even took him some time to become reconciled to artificial insemination, that he wanted milk naturally produced, by cows that were improved by natural processes. "So we never used it," says John. During the last decade, what is popularly known as BST (bovine somatotropin), a laboratory-produced protein that is a growth hormone, has been widely given to milking cows. To be sure, all cows naturally produce some BST, which facilitates protein metabolism and regulates milk production; so when more is artificially administered, and more protein added to the feed, this tends to increase milk production— however unnatural this is for the cow, or however hard it is to detect this in the milk. "Now, fortunately, there's a payoff for not using it," says John. The distributor that handles Eccardt's milk has elected to identify and market milk free of BST, and promises to pay extra to those farmers who oblige, which is easy for the Eccards and satisfying as well. John tells me that this happy outcome resulted from a market decision, not a bureaucratic regulation, and I sense that pleases him too. He smiles and says, "Sometimes doing what you think is the right thing even pays off." In most European countries, the use of BST is banned by law, and many American dairymen now believe that the market success of BST-free milk will eventually drive the hormone from the market.

A large dairy farm often has one person who is designated "herdsman," but, as in most other respects, things are a little different at Eccardt's: this is a family farm. It would appear to me that the herdsman is a combination of Julia Eccard and her sons John and George. Julia has a kind of matriarchal oversight of the entire herd, an attitude as much as a set of actions, but I believe that little of importance happens to any cow without her involvement. Becca assured me that "Mom knows every cow as she comes into the milking parlor"—her age, ancestry, general record, recent history. Julia will not admit to this, but it is easy to believe. "Mom will milk till the day she dies," Becca tells me; but Julia simply says that she has risen at 2:00 A.M. to go to the milking parlor for so many years that her body finds it utterly natural. In the milking parlor she can keep a close eye on the entire herd. Despite her sixty-some years, she does this six days a week; and it happens that she is telling me this at about 6:30 A.M., in the milking parlor, on her day off. Since Margaretha, as always, is doing the morning cleaning and preparing breakfast for the family and the occasional visitor, Julia ambles out to see if anybody has a problem needing help.

John and Becca go systematically, effortlessly, through the familiar routines: they brush the udders, they apply a disinfectant, wipe the teats with a sterilized damp cloth, wipe the teat cups, apply them smoothly to the cow, where suction snugs them into place, and go on to the next one. The milking process itself has not changed drastically since milking machines became widespread during the middle of the twentieth century, although in those earlier days one would lug the milking machine from cow to cow as they stood in their stalls. Working for a neighbor, I did this often when in high school. We emptied the milk into ten-gallon cans, then lifted the eighty-pound cans into a water cooler, and each day the milkman lifted out the cans and trucked them to a nearby processing plant. Today's milking parlor, where the milkers have a fixed working area and the cows come and go, represents a huge logistical advance on that old arrangement. Here, everything is within easy reach, nothing has to be lifted or carried, the teat cups usually automatically remove themselves and swing out of the way after finishing, the cow herself is confined by her neighbors so she can hardly move, and the milk is never exposed to the air. It is piped first into a glass holding tank (for visual inspection), then through a cold-water radiator for cooling, and then sent into the large refrigerated storage tank, from which it is picked up each day in a tanker. All this is *logistically* significant and, indeed, absolutely necessary with a large number of cows; but the *technology* involved is itself, surprisingly, only a very moderate advance on that of fifty years ago. The milking machine, which successfully simulates the complex hand pressures of milking (which simulates the natural pressures of a calf suckling), was *the* significant breakthrough in dairying technology; and that happened a long time ago. No wonder technicians are focused on the next breakthrough, namely, putting a robot in the parlor.

To imagine a dairy farm of a thousand cows or more (there are many) is to imagine a way to automate everything here. It's been done: the robot has invaded some large milking parlors, though none in New Hampshire or Vermont. Such computerized devices are extremely expensive to install, so they are not on the Eccard's wish list. Perhaps the most complicated individual tasks John and Becca are performing here are washing the cow's udders and installing the teat cups, and one can imagine these maneuvers being isolated and accomplished on well-trained cows by extremely sophisticated robots. But cows are not machines, and robots are not farmers. In fact, John and Becca are also doing a host of other more nuanced things, including observing each cow as she comes into the parlor, as she stands, as she behaves, as she leaves, watching for anything unusual, anything that needs attention. A farmer's eye does this all the time and often unconsciously, and at every milking session things turn up that need more in response than a robot can offer.

On the wall in the Eccard kitchen, on a nearby shelf, and in the hall are clusters of farm and dairy awards and plaques, including a few silver bowls and a silver pitcher—soil and conservation awards, magazine awards, agricultural fair prizes, farm association awards. High among the Eccard favorites of these is the New England Green Pastures top award, which they garnered in 1990 at the Eastern States Exposition in Springfield, Massachusetts: it honors farm appearance, accessibility, and general presentation. But the family is proudest, it appears, of a handsome walnut and bronze plaque received from the Northeast Dairy Herd Improvement Association. It is based solely upon somatic cell count of the farm milk, a measure both of the milk's quality and the cows' health. Every monthly test of every cow's milk is entered into the totals on which the award is based, and the one farm with the best yearlong numbers in the entire region is singled out for top honors. Eccardt Farm is often high on the competing list, but for that one year at least, their milk was rated the best and purest in New England. Some of the other plaques and bowls may have gathered dust or tarnish, but not this one.

During the 1990s, Douglas Harper, a professor at Duquesne University in Pittsburgh, spent time in dairy country in upstate New York documenting the changes there in farming practices during the last half century. The results were published in 2001 in *Changing Works: Visions of a Lost Agriculture*. As a part of his project the author looked closely at about fifty present-day dairy farms in northern New York. He came to see these dairy farms as embodying two different types, two distinct cultures, which he called the *craft mode* and the *factory mode* of dairy farming.

These are idealized conceptions, of course, but very useful, and they illuminate the neighboring regions of New England as well. "The factory farmers," he said, "epitomize the American ideal of rationality, efficiency, and profit maximization, embracing expansion and modernization as the twin pillars of their professional identity." Of the factory-mode farmers he studied, the author found that many had become farmers as adults and had come from outside the region. They farm, he said, "to make a profit rather than participate in a lifestyle. . . . The craft farmer, by contrast, extended traditions that may have been many generations old."[58]

In his survey, dairy farms in the craft mode were generally smaller, so their owners were more personally attentive to the animals, and they were far less concerned with finding the perfect feed formula, or with the highest possible efficiencies, or the very latest equipment, or the greatest profit. Most were good farmers who loved farming as a way of life, and not all of them were convinced that they would be better if they could be bigger. Some still pastured their cows. Most of these farms had evolved carefully, buying into new technologies step by step. As I read this book, it seemed to me that the author could have been describing Eccardt Farm and, perhaps, many New Hampshire farms; for I, at least, would have described Eccardt Farm in these craft farm terms. I find it significant that this author believed, in 2001, that most or all of the New York craft farms he had studied were economically viable as they stood. That means that in his judgment these farmers had no strong economic need to take on the burdens and vulnerabilities of becoming a megadairy—but he realized that that did not necessarily mean that they would not.

Factory-mode farms, in contrast, usually had larger herds, which they culled oftener and more ruthlessly, and they usually had higher production—and more stress—per cow; they made more use of technology and machinery, and had a very specialized and rationalized division of farm labor. Theirs was a business perspective: cows are replaceable parts in a production machine. And what the author found significant was that many of the New York craft farmers felt and expressed the powerful attraction of this factory farm model. Despite the apparent reasonableness of their own craft mode of dairy farming, several craft farmers, when asked "what farmer in the neighborhood they admired the most, cited the largest in the neighborhood, then milking 268 cows. The sprawling cow factory seemed like an extraordinary new possibility to a farmer making do with craft ways and a herd of fifty to eighty milkers." Harper found these craft farmers keenly aware of current trends, and he concluded that many of them do see their future, for good or ill, as somehow linked to ever larger dairies. "There is spirited criticism of these trends by some farmers, resigned acceptance by others, and by some an enthusiastic endorsement that growth, even as represented by the megadairies, must be a good thing."[59]

In 1987, New York State had no dairy farms of one thousand cows, but now it has more than twenty. Such is the trend throughout the Northeast: in the last fifteen years, roughly twice the number of "megadairies" and half the number of small dairy farms. Many New Hampshire dairy farmers, most of whom would be called craft farmers, look at these practices next door, these numbers, and shake their head. George Eccard snorted: "A thousand cows! That's not a farm; that's a factory." Concerning factory farms, Harper cites a few of the issues he saw crop up or seriously intensify in the ten-year span of his survey: problems of labor turnover, groundwater pollution and the general offensiveness of the standard liquid manure systems, neighborhood changes where megadairies concentrated, and the sheer vulnerability of the farmers, many with million-dollar debt loads.

The author of *Changing Works* is a professor, not a farmer, but in the end he could not persuade himself of the benefit of the rapid changes he saw taking place in Northeast dairy farms. The megadairies "threaten the very rural culture that they are coming to dominate." He notes that, ironically, we happily accept many benefits of mass production even as we lament the decline of the craft era. But he remains confident that "milk does not have to be made in a factory. In fact there are no benefits in doing it this way, and there are enormous costs. The costs are experienced by the animals, the land, and non farm neighbors, but they are also shared by the farmers I met who had become harried and driven by the demands of an incredibly complicated system. The pleasure had gone out of farming."[60]

It is not just the size of the herds that has changed drastically. So too has the average yearly production of each dairy cow. And these two factors interact in profound ways that change almost all the terms of reference. Fifty years ago the average New Hampshire dairy cow produced about six thousand pounds of milk per year; today it is three times that, about eighteen thousand pounds. That's a quantum jump in production, such as was not really foreseeable a couple of generations ago. It was achieved by selective breeding, especially through artificial insemination, and by careful culling, by scientifically derived feeding formulas, by closer attention to the health and general well-being of the cows, by consistent year-round feeding schedules, and by several other factors. As compared with forty years ago, New Hampshire today has only a fifth as many dairy farms and less than a third as many cows. Yet total milk production in the state is not far behind what it was then. However, this is not all good news.

Milk production is not a problem; milk prices are. In 2003 prices are so low that almost all New Hampshire dairy farmers are losing money on every gallon of milk they produce, which means that the largest and most productive farms are hurting the most. The worst milk price depression he has seen in twenty years, says the agriculture commissioner. Sometimes several things gang up on dairy farmers: processors are few and large and can manipulate wholesale prices; farmers' buying cooperatives are too weak to bargain for better prices; consumption has not increased, perhaps due to retail prices; and competition from the American Southwest, where overhead is inexpensive (animal housing easy, Mexican help cheap, irrigation water subsidized), gets ever stronger. So prices are down and dairy farms are hurting. And beyond this there lurks a broader and systemic problem, one of the things that drives dairy farms to expand. Precisely because of the newer efficiencies and technologies and the resulting increased production, the farmers' wholesale price, compared to feed costs, is systematically held down (regardless of other factors), with the eventual result that the consumer has come to take for granted comparatively lower prices for milk products at the grocery. Although it was the farmer who created and paid for the efficiencies that made this possible, it is the consumer and the processor, rather than the farmer, who reap the benefits. The ultimate irony is that dairy farms, by becoming more productive, have become more precarious.

### Butter's Golden Age

The traditional diversified family farm of half a century ago often had a certain indefinable and complex *texture*, made up of many different strands and ingredients: tastes, smells, sights, objects, foods, expectations. Follow out the tracks of one of these ingredients, and it may eventually connect you with most of the rest. Butter is a good example, and one whose recent history may very well serve as a significant and many-faceted metaphor for some features of modern farming. For ages and ages keepers of dairy cows have made butter from cream that was separated from milk by the simplest of methods: let it sit for a day or two until the lighter cream rises to the top to be skimmed off. (Hence our familiar word *skim* milk—in earlier days, *skimmed* milk.) Margaretha Eccardt still does it that way at Eccardt Farm: she skims the cream, saves it, and when she has accumulated a week's worth she makes homemade butter, a practice that goes back to her Europe of generations ago. She appears to endorse the simple belief that when you live on a dairy farm it is unacceptable to buy butter from the grocery store.

Because separating cream from skim milk was always slow and awkward, and not readily open to mechanization or mass production, butter making long remained a very local cottage industry: for hundreds of years milk was skimmed and butter made on nearly every farm, first for copious use by the farm family, then to be traded at the village store or packed into tubs and sent to the city market. Americans liked butter, and tinkerers and inventors had long played with the beguiling idea that cream, being lighter than skim milk, could somehow be separated out much more quickly and efficiently than by nature's slow way.

The successful trick turned out to be finding a way to spin the raw milk at very high speed through a complicated mechanism, forcing the lighter cream eventually to slide off at a slightly different trajectory from that of the heavier skim milk and so be captured in a separate container. Gustav DeLaval patented the most compact and successful design in 1878, and thereafter the cream separator became a fixture on many farms. Many, not all, farms; for of course the new machines were expensive. Didn't the farmer need more cows to justify buying a separator? Yesterday and today, and forever and ever it seems, a similar question recurs in similar form for every farmer with respect to every new implement that could lessen his work or improve his production. The clever but lowly cream separator was much more potent than it first appeared—a simple hand-operated machine, doing easily and efficiently what almost every farmer with cows needed to do, but implicitly revolutionary. Here is the irony: it didn't make farming easier; it made farms bigger. At that time many a farmer chose to adjust his farming style by enlarging his herd, to sell cream to the new town butter-making factory, to feed skim milk to veal calves and to pigs. The separator forced farmers to face the following questions: Do I expand to justify more efficient equipment? Or do I work harder with the old equipment in order to compete with the more mechanized, more efficient farms down the road?

And this perplexity is already the seedbed of agribusiness. For it is likely that another revolutionary piece of equipment, raising the very same questions, is on the horizon. The cream separator is just one of a hundred devices, every one of which raises the same questions.

In the late nineteenth century, when it became possible to separate cream from milk in efficient ways, many new butter-making factories, known as creameries, sprang up like mushrooms in farming communities, each with its own separators. Then the farmer who had not invested in a separator could sell milk to the creamery by weight or by measure (the ten-gallon milk can became standard); but since there was still no accurate way to measure how much butterfat (the principle and valuable ingredient of milk and so of butter) was in a given quantity of milk, an old problem showed up again—watered milk. There even exist reports showing that farmers sometimes discussed discreetly among themselves just how much water it was permissible to add to milk before it was sold—whether to the creamery or to the neighbors. That this was an old problem is indicated by a jaunty remark of Thoreau: "Some circumstantial evidence is pretty compelling; as when there is a trout in the milk."

It was little more than a hundred years ago that an accurate way of measuring the butterfat content of milk was invented: Stephen Babcock of the University of Wisconsin designed the method in 1890, another revolutionary development for the dairy industry. Not surprisingly, creameries all over the land eventually adopted the new method of testing for butterfat content, which eventually dammed that particular flow of watered milk. Indeed, the governor of Wisconsin confidently declared that "the Babcock Test has made more dairymen honest than the Bible." Moreover, the ability to test the butterfat content of milk was destined to change the outlook of dairy farmers. It had long been observed but hard to prove definitively that some cows just give better milk than others; the dairy herd could now be studied more scientifically, and more careful breeding programs developed.

Which brings us back to butter. Since the making of butter is as ancient as milking cows, as making yogurt and cheese, it is the more remarkable that all those centuries of inventing and churning should have finally culminated in our own time in that bland little butter pad on cardboard that we find on our local restaurant tables. Most Americans appear to be serenely unaware that butter at the beginning of the twenty-first century is not at all what it was—not in taste, tang, character, or even social standing. Most commercial American butter now looks and tastes pretty much the same, whatever the reason, the season, the brand, the region, or origin of its ingredients. Such a remarkable technological achievement! What if they succeeded in doing that with wines?

On my desk as I write is a copy of *The Book of Butter*, dating from 1923, one of the Macmillan Rural Text-Book Series edited by Liberty Hyde Bailey. (The series also included *The Book of Ice-Cream* and *The Book of Cheese*.) This was a time when large grocery stores devoted an entire counter to butter, like a meat counter at a butcher's shop today; the book pictures butter counters and discusses their preferred arrangements. Aspiring agriculture students in those days took college courses in, yes, butter. Here are three hundred pages of textbook butter facts and details, references and charts, pictures and graphs, advice and warnings on making, storing, pasteurizing, displaying, eating; on cream keeping, ripening, churning; and much more. A twenty-page chapter is called "Flavors of Butter." It acknowledges that "the public in general prefers butter that has a quick acid flavor" but goes on to say that "since it has been discovered that butter made from cream with a low acidity keeps better than the high acid cream product, there has been a change in the methods of manufacturing. *In time the public will be trained away from its present preference, which is a snappy high acid flavor.*"[61] Those are my italics, but they are the author's words and prediction. In a fully candid world that statement might be seen as pointing to a culinary conspiracy, now fully implemented. Alas, the author knew whereof he spoke in 1923: the time is long since upon us when the public has indeed been trained away from its ancient preference for a "snappy high acid flavor" in its butter. Butter has been successfully industrialized and thoroughly blandified. With further progress in the dairy industry we may look forward to other triumphs—in cheeses, say—a time when, for example, the public will be trained away from its present quirky preference for many and varied cheeses, from soft and silky cheeses, smooth or tangy, to rich textured cheeses redolent of long national and regional traditions, old-world cheese of goat's or sheep's milk, cottage cheeses, to a multitude of aged cheeses, acid or mellow or snappy or seriously sharp. Maybe all cheeses, every last one, in a bold triumph of industrial efficiency, will eventually achieve the taste and texture of American processed cheese.

On the traditional farm of half a century ago butter often still had its ancient and honored place, part of the flavor of the farms of that era, with a significant role in their cookery and diet. There were not then a dozen kinds of nonfat, no-cholesterol, or salty soybean-margarine or no-salt butter substitutes, and there was no health establishment to impugn one's proclivities. In my own family's case, the butter I remember so clearly had an intensely tangy, varied, and richly robust flavor, such that I might have called it, if I had thought if it then, "a snappy high acid flavor"—a flavor that may be improving even now as it recedes into the past. This butter's character was amply and richly transferred to the enormous number of foods that it regularly garnished, including, to name only the most common on the traditional farm of that time, warm homemade bread and strawberry jam. The butter's snappiness differed one time to another depending on things like the cows' diet, the age, ripeness, and richness of the cream, its acidity and temperature, the method of churning it and working it and keeping it, and a half dozen other things. In pallid contrast, the butter we buy today is absolutely predictable; and though it doesn't have much interest or taste, still the health mentors eye it with a cold and steely suspicion. By all this, the very cows may be depressed.

Margaretha Eccardt leads me to the pantry to show me her butter tools. The skimmer she holds up for my appreciation, I am glad to observe, looks like an exact duplicate of the one pictured in my 1923 butter book. Every day she uses it to skim cream from two large shallow bowls of raw cow's milk, and the cream then goes into the refrigerator. I am led to ask about her churn, and I imagine a picturesque ancient wooden tumble tub, or possibly even an antique squarish two-gallon container with a small crank, such as I used as a boy in my own mother's kitchen. Now there are smiles all around, and Margaretha's is the broadest. "I use the Kitchen Aid" she announces in triumph. Well, I am crestfallen; but so be it. I will not cease to rejoice that Margaretha Eccardt, age ninety-six, is still making butter in her kitchen.

*Of Cows and Pastures*

One may wonder, sometimes, driving through the countryside, Where are the cows? They do not appear to be grazing peacefully on a thousand hillsides in the numbers we seem to remember from decades ago. The impression is correct: there are fewer cows and they are not so visible. Beef cattle, yes; but a herd of milking cows in the pasture? It has become an exceedingly rare sight. In fact, most dairy farmers now, whether they like it or not, have to view pasturing milking cows as an outmoded and inefficient means of feeding. Given their preferences, many farmers would probably rather see the cows in the pasture too; but they are trying to make a living in a competitive environment, not creating pleasing scenery for passersby; and so most of them now bring the feed to the cows instead of sending the cows out to get it. In a sense, of course, this represents an incursion of the "factory mode" of dairying into their "craft mode."

The fact is that today's cows are bred and fed simply for efficient production of milk. That means a carefully controlled life and diet: rich feed, lots of it, limited exercise, no stress, the shade of an open barn. Cows eat more and produce more under conditions that vary little or not at all. With pasturing, marginal differences come into significant play, and all the profits are in the margins: fresh grass often has more moisture than is ideal for the modern cow's digestion, and its nutritional content varies some-what unpredictably with weather and season and particular pasture. More-over, it takes the cow time to adjust to pasture in the spring and to be weaned from it in the fall as she goes on to winter forage, so production suffers. Then there are the huge and endless challenges of pastures them-selves: they have to be managed, fenced, fertilized, rotated, kept disease-free, provided with shade and water. In many settings and for large herds this would be a very large problem. The differences add up; the bottom line is that most dairy farmers, even those who would desire for traditional and aesthetic reasons to pasture their cows, find they cannot remain competi-tive that way.

There was a time when the Eccards pastured their milking herd, as they now pasture only their heifers and dry cows; but the herd was smaller then, and the profit margin not so narrow. Hans and Julia had collected large numbers of cowbells, reminiscent of European, especially Swiss, traditions, and many of the cows wore the bells so that the entire valley tinkled and rang all day with the reassuring sounds of the countryside. At that time, too, many of us who live in the neighborhood bought our milk at this farm: once or twice a week we brought our bottles and had them filled at the milk house; we listened to the cowbell music of the valley, sniffed the air, watched the corn grow. We in the neighborhood identified with this place, and many simply referred to it as "the farm," as if they had a stake in it. Which they did and do, although no price can be put upon these intan-gible things. While the tinkling bells are remembered by the neighbors, now the unbelled cows are chewing their cud out of sight, and their milk is no longer regularly sold at the milk house. The Eccards could not possibly pasture their present herd of cows in this very limited space, and these three families could not stay in dairying if they reduced their herd to a size that could be pastured here.

It is partly as an effort to retain some of these more recent traditions of being a family farm embedded in its community that Hans Eccard has assembled his quirky collection of animals and specimen farm machin-ery—to make the place continually interesting, informative, and inviting to visitors; and that is also why the Eccards sometimes declare an Open Barn day, inviting all and sundry to inspect the premises and enjoy free ice cream. Eccardt Farm occupies a comparatively small niche of real estate, tucked up against the eastern side of Lovell Mountain, and is boxed in by firm natural conditions: mountain and sand hill and brook and neighboring rocky and hilly forest, certainly not a natural spot for a large dairy farm. Since the eighteenth century this was a modest and traditional New Hampshire farm, but in the 1950s with the Eccardts it became a dairy farm, and then it thrived and grew. Nobody would have imagined two hundred milking cows here or, for that matter, that this one enterprise would be managed to support three families. A remarkable thing about this family farm is that it prevails despite the severe constraints of physical setting and economic environment. More than might have been expected, it represents one of the small triumphs of Northeast agriculture.

# Chapter 6

# Cornucopia: Eggs and Corn at the Coll Farm

In all our years of farming we have never had any farm subsidies paid to us and we have always operated without any price supports or financial aid from anyone.

—HELEN COLL

## Farming and Farm Standing

If you travel U.S. Route 202 as it winds through the southwestern part of New Hampshire between Peterborough and Jaffrey, you need to keep a sharp lookout if you are to spot a small blue sign at the roadside that points you to Coll's Farm Stand. You turn off to the east on a side road, which slopes downward to a new bridge that crosses the Contoocook River; then you bear left and climb straight up a steep hill to the farm stand, about a third of a mile off the highway. Despite the modest name, you find more than a farm stand when you get there: it is a thriving hilltop produce and small general grocery, located on a farm. This is a retail farm, you might say.

It has been there, retailing farm products and slowly growing, the farm and the farm stand, for almost forty years, ever since it first got going in the Colls' front yard with some boards and sawhorses and a pile of sweet corn. Outside the growing season Archie Coll now has to buy much of his stock on the Boston produce market, where it has been funneled from all over the world. The small farm stand is thus also an open front for the world's agribusiness, but I am sure the customers do not think of it that way. Indeed, many of the essential things at the farm stand, signature items, come straight from this farm, including eggs, maple syrup, and cut flowers, not to mention tons and tons of vegetables. There are often piles of the farm's own corn and squash, and in the autumn the whole landscape is bright orange with pumpkins. But especially the place is known far and wide for its sweet corn, abundant and famous here from July to October, earlier and later than anywhere else in the vicinity. Then there are the fresh eggs, thousands of eggs from "free range" chickens, regular eggs in every size, fertile eggs, organic eggs. In fact, Coll's corn and vegetable farm and farm stand is also a chicken farm, with up to twenty thousand hens in full production, and always thousands more aspiring chicks and pullets.

Helen Van Blarcom was a Jaffrey, New Hampshire, farm girl, and she married Archie Coll, the farmer son of the farmer across the road, and more than forty years ago they bought a farm just down the road from their childhood homes and together set out to be farmers themselves. Such a personal profile was a most familiar American stereotype for a couple of centuries, but it is most rare today. Helen Coll is a strong and sturdy woman with a classic Dutch face and reddish hair and ready smile. Both Helen and Archie were formed in a culture and an era wherein long hours and hard work were simply taken for granted: they always both assumed from childhood on that that is just what farmers do. Archie is a stocky farmer, and he walks with an erect and jaunty spring in his step that suggests he is actually looking forward to a day's challenges. Farming is a package deal, Helen has written, "the farmer and the farm—and at times it is a love/hate package." She knows the irony and the ambivalence: "I love the idea of living on a farm and raising our children here and having the sun shining and the corn growing and hens laying, but I hate it when there hasn't been rain for weeks and storms come and wreck what we have growing and the temperature is 90 in the shade and everything becomes all consuming."


From the Colls' sweet-corn fields and the squash beds, some of which are on the hilltop next to the henhouses behind the farm stand, you can peer past the trees and see against the blue sky the craggy, rocky top of Mount Monadnock, the landmark mountain for all of southern New Hampshire. On a clear day, and if you are in the right place in the cornfield, the mountain spectacle is a splendid distraction. Now it is mid-July, and Archie Coll is showing me the sweet corn, planted in April under layers of plastic and now ready to pick. Involuntarily, my eyes form a line past the corn and over the treetops, and I gesture toward the mountain and offer the obvious comment.

"It must make farming a bit easier with a view like that whenever you look up."

"Yeah," says Archie, without looking up at all, for he is looking at the weeds in the corn and making plans to do something about them. "Helen says we should have our house up here—instead of the henhouses, which are closed. The hens can't even see the view; we could." Now he looks up and smiles.

I have the impression that Archie thinks of the irony here—the lowly hens high on the hill with the best view on the farm, except that their windows are too high for them to look out—as a pale joke, which he is not minded to take at all seriously. What Archie takes seriously is work: he does a lot of it, every day, all day, always has, probably always will. He appreciates the mountain and the sweeping landscape view, which may be one reason why he has stayed right here, in the very neighborhood, indeed, on the same road where he was born and raised. But he does not have a lot of time for just looking. Usually, he is working.

Some things on American farms have not changed much throughout the years, and a chief one is that farming is a great deal of work. It is a distinguishing feature of farm life: you are always confronted with work. Work to do, work undone, work postponed, work you can't get to yet, work you may never get to. Work. Perhaps no farmer ever feels completely caught up, for the season advances swiftly and new work sneaks up on him or her, and new obligations grow like weeds in farmers' footprints. There are two dozen jobs that could be done today, a dozen that should be, five that must be. The farmer may get to four. This world structured by work is implacable, tedious—and often very exhilarating. For generations, most farmers have just accepted it; many have loved it. But some who grew up in this world itch to escape it, and do, and are grateful. And some, such as Archie Coll, take it in as if by osmosis, absorb it into the fiber of their being, and would not have it otherwise. To choose to farm is to be committed to living within a world framed in farmwork to be done, farm chores to be attended to, farm discipline to be internalized—indeed, committed to the intrinsic value of work as an unspoken source of life's dignity.

For a long time Helen Coll too was far too busy to stop working: the family, the farm, the farm stand were ever making demands. But then a few years ago she did pause to look up and to take stock of her own life on the farm. Did she want to do just this and only this for all her life? She later said that farm life requires "dedication to something requiring attention twenty-four hours a day 365 days a year." She meant: such a life can be very draining. And it had drained her. True, the Coll Farm and Farm Stand had become a thriving family business, with a thirty-year tradition of its own, resilient as a tough old harness; her children were grown and nearby, and their son Mark and daughter-in-law Lori were even poised to become partners in the farm operation. Archie was steady and energetic as ever, his favorite form of relaxation still being simply to work at something else on the farm. "But I was just burned out," she says now.

So Helen also decided to work at something else. Since she had not been to college, she would go back to school, she resolved; she would focus on writing, and perhaps eventually compose her personal version of family and the farm life, which she knew so well from the inside out. Her intuition was that every successful farm contains a rich layering of significant stories, the Coll farm no less so. The effort she then undertook required plenty of courage and, like farming rocky soil itself, not a little struggle and dogged persistence, especially for someone who had known only farming and managing a farm stand from her youth up. But she brought it off to the sound of applause: she earned her degree, and her own detailed farm story now rests between the covers of her book, *Cultivating Life: A Story of Earth and Hearth*, published late in 2001.

There the reader finds an account of the simple and almost accidental start-up, in 1965, of what has become this regionally very well known farm stand. It was a day of small beginnings. The Colls supposed that they were in the chicken business, and intended to concentrate on that. But Helen's father, helping out a neighbor, had inadvertently planted much too much sweet corn for himself—would the Colls like to pick some of it and maybe try to sell what they could not eat? Helen writes that she "told Archie about the corn and he agreed to pick some the next day." Then they found an old board and painted "Sweet Corn" on it and set it up near the highway. They placed two sawhorses and several planks across them to form a table in front of the house, and "that was the beginning of the farm stand." Helen recalls discovering that people wanted other things too. "So I stripped my garden and sold everything—which I had not intended to do. . . ." The next year the Colls planted a much larger garden and lots more sweet corn. Almost by accident, the chicken farmers were now in the farm stand business.

Location was an early consideration. The Colls' house and the adjacent farm stand are a third of a mile off the highway and up a steep hill, and at first they often questioned whether the stand should be brought out to the highway. Eventually, as their potential customer base became clear, the question seemed to answer itself. Helen writes that "we have consciously chosen to stay on the farm site and promote farm life in the beautiful setting we have on this hilltop." Being on the highway, they knew, would have made the stand more accessible to travelers, but they were more interested in local people, who would not mind driving to the farm. A farm, after all, is the sort of thing you would expect to have to drive to.

Archie Coll grew up on his father's farm, where, at different times, eggs, hatching eggs, chicks, chickens, roasters, roosters, broilers, fryers, and more eggs were principal crops, and he has enthusiastically continued that line of work—or, rather, continued whatever strand in that line seemed viable. There never was a time in Archie's life when he was not involved in the chicken business, and it appears there never was a time when he was not pretty serious about it. Archie's father had begun his chicken enterprises in 1930, and for more than thirty years the elder Coll ran a large hatchery business, shipping over a million day-old chicks every year. Sometimes the chicks were sold to New Hampshire farmers, many of them part-timers, on a contract basis, the Colls supplying the newly hatched chicks and agreeing to take the birds back at a set price and market them when they were about twelve weeks old. In 1938 New England played host to a furious hurricane, which lifted the roof off the senior Coll's eighty-foot brooder house. Since the market was good Coll thought about his situation for a week, then added two more stories to the house, then put the roof back on. Thus the business expanded. For many years Archie delivered his live birds to the New York market, as his father had done, and Helen's book describes in detail one such 1960s trip to New York. "We went to one of the small, Jewish kosher stores. There our live chickens were chosen by the customers from wooden crates, then blessed by a rabbi and butchered." However, by the 1970s the market for live broilers in New York and elsewhere had diminished and transportation costs drained the profits, so the Colls made adjustments again. Today they buy newly hatched chicks, and they sell eggs—organic, natural, fertile—from about twenty thousand of their own birds, plus many more eggs that are produced especially for them on several farms in Pennsylvania and New York.

Sweet corn is the other big deal at the Coll Farm and Farm Stand. Corn, of course, is more American than apple pie, and native to this hemisphere. It was a source of dietary sugar for Americans for thousands of years before Europeans arrived here—probably before maple syrup, before honey, or sugarcane. By Columbus's time corn had long since been brought north from South America and had adapted itself, through careful cultivation and selection by Native Americans, to colder climates, and resolved itself throughout North America into hundreds of varieties. Corn was the food that saved the lives of the very earliest colonists. Despite initial prejudice learned in Europe, most of the new Americans were reasonably quick to adopt and grow corn, but eating it fresh and green and boiled was slow to catch on. Thomas Jefferson recorded "shriveled corn" at Monticello, probably sweet corn, and in the early nineteenth century Timothy Dwight noted that shriveled corn "when in the milk" is the "most delicious of culinary vegetables." However, Betty Fussell, in the well-researched *The Story of Corn*, says that eating sweet corn became common only late in the nineteenth century, and didn't become a passion until about a hundred years ago, and then first and mainly in the Northeast. The year 1902 was pivotal, for that is when Burpee introduced Golden Bantam, which was to become a national favorite. Supersweet hybrids started to appear in the 1960s, derived from a mutant with a recessive gene that prevents the full conversion of sugar into starch that occurs in other types of corn. It's the sugar instead of starch in the kernel that makes it shrivel when mature and dry. Today, when there are more varieties of supersweet supercorns than you can shake a stalk at, it seems to be everybody's business to be up-to-date on sweet corn, or at least to have firm opinions about which is best.

The shift of emphasis at the Coll farm to add more sweet corn, first as a sideline and gradually as a major crop, was fitted in smoothly with the chicken business. Chickens do well on corn: corn requires a lot of nitrogen, chicken manure is higher in nitrogen than any natural fertilizer—it's a tight little symbiotic circle. When the Colls began to get serious about raising sweet corn they soon meant business, and business meant having lots of freshly picked quality corn, early, midway, and late in the season. Archie figured out how to do that, and he achieves it now by planting in April, under clear plastic, and planting every five days thereafter throughout May and June and into July. To meet the demand he has created through pricing, quality, and freshness, he also rents land for corn in a neighboring town, and trucks chicken manure there, and also leases a sweet-corn growing operation farther south in Massachusetts. As a result, he may be the only farmer in New Hampshire who, in early July, is both selling fresh corn on the cob and still planting corn in his fields. Hens for eggs and fertilizer, and sweet corn for a large portion of southwestern New Hampshire—on this farm they are naturally adapted to each other.

*Hens and Eggs*

Hens at the Coll farm start out as day-old chicks which are housed in small indoor cages, with water and feed automatically available. As the pullets grow they are given more room, but not more light, and not much liberty. We are inspecting the pullet house, and when I ask about the semidarkness, I learn it is quite intentional: pullets grow to full size more readily in dim light. At the chosen moment, which is about twenty weeks, they are put on a new diet, and into a new building, and into sunlight, and given room to walk free with thousands of others. It is a sudden coming-of-age for the young birds. They are so stimulated by the light and exhilarated by the good food and fresh air and like-minded company and space to roam that they promptly embark upon their life's mission: they start laying eggs, and moreover the eggs are full size. Under wholly natural conditions, new-laying pullets start slowly and produce small eggs for some weeks or months; they need practice. Later I checked the eggs for sale at the farm stand and found packages labeled Super Jumbo, Jumbo, Extra Large, Large, Medium. The modern henhouse produces few small eggs, and the category is actually falling into disuse.

Now Archie invites me to step with him gently in among the hens in the free roaming building, where thousands and thousands of birds on two floors cluck and strut and eat and drink and preen and lay eggs and cackle about it for a living. They are extremely handsome red feathered birds, and their particular variety has a fancy scientific name, but to the layman they are New Hampshire Reds, and derive from the famous Rhode Island Red stock. They lay brown eggs, which are traditional and much preferred in this part of New England, although everywhere else in the country white eggs predominate. Many New Englanders just don't like the looks of a white egg—though they have long since forgotten why. Life here would appear to be pretty good for a hen; they seem entirely content with it, and the background buzz and hum of thousands of healthy cluckings tells you as much. (Personally, I found the fine dust in the air from the feathered bodies of all those thousands of birds, and perhaps also the ammonia from the manure, mildly unpleasant.) For the birds, though, feed and water are always right in front of them, fresh air is always available, and there are abundant darkened nests to encourage egg laying, and thousands of abso-lutely identical red birds for reliable company. I heard no complaints.

I can see that this henhouse is almost fully automated: the windows open and close as dictated by a thermostat; the manure drops through the plastic or wooden slats on which the birds walk and falls onto a platform below, from which it is automatically swept twice a day. The eggs are automatically removed by padded conveyor belt, and an ingenious device assures that water is always clean and available. Everywhere are little spigots, outlets from a piping system, just above the birds' heads, so a thirsty hen has but to reach up, peck at the spigot, and lo, a little trickle of clean water is promptly delivered right into her mouth. At first this manner of watering hens seems odd and unnatural—which, of course, it is. Since chickens, like most birds and unlike most animals, cannot swallow with their head down, their normal habit is to take a brief sip from a puddle, say, and quickly tilt their head back to allow the fluid to run down their throat. Here, where everything is designed to make life easy for the birds, they can just reach up and have an automatic nip whenever they wish.

As I watch this red sea of birds in this automated setting, the cackle of the hens involuntarily pulls me back a half century to the chicken coop on my father's farm. Suddenly I am scattering wheat and cracked corn for the hens to hunt down and scratch up and devour. Then and there I can hardly imagine that producing eggs could ever be much more usefully efficient than the way we did it. And we did as everyone else did. Yes, it would have been possible to imagine that perhaps feeding and watering might be automated; but these tasks took so little effort for us that we would not even have considered it. So where would modernization, automation, streamlining, come in? Where was there need for it? How might we even have conceived it as a value? The one firm truth we did not imagine was the one lodged within the modern cliché "economy of scale." We would not have thought of having thousands of hens, for nothing in our rural culture of a half century ago allowed for such vulnerability. We had at most two hundred hens, more often about a hundred. Housing those birds required some planning, but caring for them on a daily basis was easy. A farmer with a child or two to join in the light work—feeding, watering, egg gathering—knew a simple truth, namely, being more efficient at these minor tasks simply did not matter, *it had no value.*

So I am brought to mind of two things: first, that to understand traditional farming is to understand a world where very often being more efficient gained you absolutely nothing; and, second, that to contemporary ears cocked in a certain way this sounds almost perverse, for is not efficiency, productivity, among the greater goods? The supreme value, in fact, our economy preens itself on? It is not that we then neglected or failed to notice or acknowledge its value; it is that in farmyard things as basic and essential as caring for chickens, efficiency simply had no value at all. It was like, say, efficiency at eating dinner: you *could* grind it up all together and shovel it in quickly with a spoon. But what would be the point? Only when the units are very numerous, and there is a very heavy dependence on the profitability of these many units, is efficiency of any value. As, for example, in the henhouse before me. One difference between traditional agriculture and that of the present day is the essential difference between this henhouse and ours. This one *has* to be efficient or it is dead; ours was not even judged in those terms.

When Helen or Archie or another worker enters the henhouse and walks in among the birds, the loud background hum created by thousands of individual clucks simmers down and grows noticeably quieter, and all the hens are heads up and on alert. When I walk in with one of my hosts, the birds seem to recognize a stranger in their midst, and they quiet down even more; and as I enter they are on very high alert, every one of them looking at me with a sidelong glance, not caring to speak to this stranger, or even about him. Eventually, they figure out that since I move slowly I mean them no harm, and they will turn away from me, peck at the water spigot with practiced and professional nonchalance, and start gossiping among themselves; but they don't go back to full-volume chatter until I leave.

Now we go to the upper floor to see the hens that produce organic eggs, and they seem to me to be on the highest alert of all. Perhaps these feel under more pressure, since theirs is a special mission in life and, indeed, their dinner is specially designed and prepared. Archie feeds these hens a mixture of organic corn and organic soybeans, ground and mixed with other dietary supplements, and all of it delivered to the birds automatically. If they do seem a bit tense at my presence, perhaps it is just that they are eager to have us leave quickly so they can get right back to the serious business of making very high quality eggs. New regulations for organic products, which went into effect in October 2002, now require that to bear the organic label eggs must come from hens that have been feed only organic food from the time they were baby chicks (not just for the most recent thirty days, as hitherto). The Colls sell some organic eggs at the farm stand, but organic production on this scale requires a serious niche market, and this is just the sort of challenge Archie likes and is good at. He points out to me that when a major grocery chain of several hundred stores decides, for its own marketing reasons, to add a new item to its line—such as organic eggs, or fertile eggs—a large market possibility suddenly opens up. Archie smiles, knowing that over the years he has built up a reputation that will usually put him at the head of the line when such opportunities appear.

A generation ago, putting laying hens into cages was widely touted as the modern and efficient way to industrialize egg production, and the Colls, forever willing to experiment, actually tried that too. Helen writes in her book that their operation has continuously evolved: "We started with chickens free-roaming on the floor, went to cage buildings, and now are back to free roaming floor chickens once again. Cage buildings have individual cages that hold four chickens, and are stacked three high and end to end in long rows for automation of feed, water and egg collection." Their experiment did not last long. A chief reason for abandoning it was that they saw it as a miserable and unhealthy life for a hen, requiring copious antibiotics; and a second reason was that they saw the possibility of developing a niche market for eggs that could be advertised as from "free range" or "free roaming" or "free running" chickens. (The phrases all essentially mean "uncaged," not that the birds are running loose outside.) The idea worked; they uncaged the birds, junked the cages, and Helen now speaks dismissively of the cage method as running an "egg factory." The Colls advertise natural eggs, from free-range birds that dine on pure grains, without animal fats or by-products or antibiotics. Perhaps a further step will be required for their organic eggs: Archie is studying ways to make his buildings comply with regulations that may eventually require that these hens have "free access to the outdoors."

Americans eat far fewer eggs than they did a generation ago. Consumption has dropped by almost one-third in thirty years, and is less each year. Why? It is not the price: eggs are cheaper than ever. I remember a time—though it was a half century ago, just after the Second World War—when farmers worked for, say, four or five dollars a day and sold fresh eggs for up to fifty cents a dozen. A day's work for a mere ten dozen eggs. Not any more. A day's work will now fetch you a pickup truck load of eggs—which is exactly why the grocery shopper today is far better off than formerly and the farmer is worse off. If, as compared with fifty years ago, most food today is cheap, eggs, by the same comparison, are cheaper still. You'd think we would be eating lots of them, but instead we eat fewer. Eggs have had some public relations problems in the last generation. First it was cholesterol, then they became rather unfashionable, then it was salmonella.

A few decades ago the reports that eggs might increase heart problems were big bad news, especially down on the farm. Within a few years everybody had mastered a brand-new word, "cholesterol," and very swiftly it became conventional wisdom that a fondness for eggs was probably not a good habit to cultivate: fewer is better. Eventually we all ate fewer. Almost unnoticed, many a chicken farmer quietly went out of business: no living to be made in this climate. But in 1999 the Harvard Medical School published results of a study of over 100,000 egg-eating citizens that showed "no overall significant association between egg consumption (up to one a day) and risk of chronic heart disease or stroke." Too late; sorry, farmers; we had already changed our habits. We are now down to 225 eggs per person per year. Consequently, the entire state of New Hampshire is down to about 140,000 laying hens.

If there were a conspiracy to maintain egglessness at breakfast it would appear to be well orchestrated, for the worry that eggs might be unhealthy was no sooner refuted than it was promptly replaced by the suspicion that they might be poisonous. "Salmonella" was a word we had heard and associated with chickens, not eggs; but that too changed, as the media spread the alarm that some investigators believed the eggs themselves might carry it. (Salmonella is a dangerous bacterium that circulates up and down and sideways throughout the food chain, through animals and feed, and it is not clear how it might get into eggs or, indeed, even if it has significantly.) Since 1985 there has been an average of just five salmonella deaths per year in the United States (lightning is ten times as likely to get you) and an unknown number of infections, but it is unclear that any of these are attributable to eggs. Like many another bacterium, salmonella waxes and wanes in its general prominence—and thereby in its public relations—and it is not known exactly what causes this. At the moment there seems to be a firm professional consensus that eating raw eggs is not a good idea, but the consensus goes little further. Meanwhile, the egg business is not exactly thriving, and there are ever fewer places like the Coll farm.

*Attracted to Chickens*

The Coll chicken enterprise and those like it are actually within a very long tradition of very distinguished farming efforts. The chicken and the egg—they may appear at first glance to be the simplest, the most banal and lowly of farm products, cocks and hens among the least interesting of barnyard creatures. But, historically speaking, theirs is a long and wonderfully varied saga, very ancient, very modern, extremely rich in the lore of food and ritual and religion and magic and irony. Chickens pop up everywhere in story and song and art, and from Chanticleer to Chicken Little they are alive and aflutter in legend, folklore, literature: ornamental chickens, pet chickens, cockfighter chickens, chickens and eggs as culinary delicacies, chicken taboos, chickens or eggs in magic and divination, chickens in medicine, chickens grown for their soft or colorful feathers, chickens for religious sacrifice, here a cock as herald of the dawn, there one as barnyard despot, there a cock as religious symbol, allied with Saint Peter, everywhere a cock as sex symbol, cultural symbol, national symbol—chickens fluttering every which way through all the pages of history.

Some years ago the historian Page Smith and the biologist Charles Daniel taught a course called "The Chicken" at the University of California, Santa Cruz, and they later published a book on their researches, *The Chicken Book*. Many of the historical data in this and the next paragraphs are gleaned from this book. Domestic chickens, for meat and eggs, and for ornament and cockfighting, and probably for religion and medicine, go back to prehistory in Asia. There are very early records of chickens in India and China, and before 2000 B.C. the Egyptians, astonishingly, had developed brick incubators for hatching eggs by the thousands. What for? Presumably their principal purpose was chickens for meat and eggs, but perhaps not only that. Sometime thereafter Persia learned the dubious pleasures of cockfighting from India and it soon spread to the Greeks and eventually to the Romans; indeed, it spread throughout the world. In the modern world laws have retarded it, but they have not stamped it out.

The Greeks used chickens for religious sacrifice, for fighting, and for eggs and meat and, in Aristotle's case at least, for systematic research: he opened a series of incubating eggs as they developed to study and report upon the growth of embryos. Later, Greeks from Delos were regarded as decadent by some Romans: the fastidious Pliny, for instance, writing in the first century, said that these folks actually fattened up their hens, "whence arose the revolting practice of devouring fat birds basted in their own gravy."

Nevertheless, in Rome, where the economy was based on agriculture, chicken culture was enormously important. Smith and Daniel comment that among the Romans "as food, as a sacred bird, as medicine, as the subject of philosophical inquiry, the chicken had no serious rival." And it was the Roman Publius who gave us the splendid put-down "A cock has great influence—on his own dunghill." It turns out that all the Roman agriculture writers held forth at length on chickens, and all of them highly recommended chicken farming, and included lots of advice, some of it good, on how to succeed at it. They also offered tips on fattening the birds (bread soaked in wine was one favorite), no matter how revolting Pliny might have found that. The Romans, whose banquets often began with a course of eggs, called the chicken *Gallus domesticus*. When their armies under Caesar got to England, taking chickens with them, they found chickens already there, and Caesar wrote that the populace there did not "feed upon hares, pullets, and geese, yet they breed them up for their diversion and pleasures." It would appear that "diversions," such as cockfighting and keeping ornamental and religious birds (somewhat like bull sports), are extremely ancient phenomena, and so too the study of chicken entrails and other body parts for purposes of divination. Indeed, within the Romance cultures down to the present day the centrality of the cock, as bird and symbol, derives primarily from the high and many-faceted esteem accorded to the chicken by the Romans.

Attitudes throughout the modern world toward chickens and eggs are also extremely diverse, and apparently always have been. Many taboos regarding chickens are based on the idea that the bird is sacred. According to Smith and Daniel, in many parts of the world, especially Africa, tribes living in proximity to each other may have entirely different customs in regard to eating chickens or eggs. "Since the keeping of chickens for sacred rituals and/or for food is almost universal, a natural assumption is that certain archetypal attitudes toward the chicken have existed since earliest times. That the hen with her eggs and the cock with his insatiable sexual appetite should be highly potent sexual symbols is hardly surprising." Many Orthodox Hindus avoid close contact with chickens, though many of them also enjoy cockfighting. The lamas of Tibet are forbidden to eat chickens, but in most of Southeast Asia chickens and eggs are commonly eaten. In some of these regions the preference is to eat eggs with half-developed embryos—which would probably be a taboo in most places. Yet, in other regions, fertilized but fresh eggs are desired by a minority. Among some Orthodox Jews the second day prior to Yom Kippur, the day of *kapparah*, or atonement, has long involved the ritual slaughtering of a chicken, which may then be consumed by the family or given to the poor. In much of the Arab world eggs are regarded by the well-to-do as a low-class food for the poor, and in various parts of Africa chickens are kept for their feathers, or for divination, but not eaten.

And in America at the present time, where health food stores are common and the natural food aisle in the typical grocery store is being enlarged, there is an active and growing market not just for organic eggs but for fertile eggs for consumption, whether organic or not. Indeed, the Colls now process large numbers of fertile eggs, which they purchase from Amish farmers in Pennsylvania. These farmers have many cocks running with the hens, and that creates a different social dynamic in the henhouse. Some customers apparently regard such fertilized eggs as more natural, and it is not always clear whether this is a regard for the hen's social life or a regard for the eggs, or both. Similarly, others find organic eggs more natural, even though most organic hens' diet is *severely restricted* from what the naturally omnivorous and undiscriminating hen would chose for herself. And still others find the eggs more natural if the hens are running loose and allowed to scratch in the barnyard, pick through dried manure, as is their natural inclination, and fight over grasshoppers and beetles for their snacks. Widely differing desires and taboos and doctrines regarding chickens and eggs are, in fact, worldwide. And very near home.

Meek and lowly as the farmyard chicken may seem, it would be hard to name any other domestic creature at all that is kept and valued by more different human groups and cultures, is more widely distributed throughout the world and throughout history, is put to more varied uses, and is surrounded with more diverse attitudes than the banal dooryard chicken. It is hardly a wonder that some farmers are just naturally attracted to chickens.

Archie Coll has always been attracted to chickens. He was an aspiring farmer in 1949 when his father, who had lots of chickens and kept getting more, designed, built, and installed a novel egg-gathering machine. It was called an *automatic egg picker,* and it did its work in a three-story state-of-the-art henhouse that still stands, unused, on the original Coll farm, which Archie now owns. The egg picker was a complicated but also commonsensical device for gathering the eggs from three floors of nests and bringing them carefully, on a system of padded conveyor belts and egg elevators, to one central packing place. Helen Coll is telling me about this invention ("At the time it was a big forward step—when you have thousands of hens.") and summarizing the several stages in their own subsequent experiments with various forms of henhouse automation: watering and feeding and ventilation systems, and then the elaborate and clever devices for sorting, grading, and packing eggs. Later, when Archie is showing me the current modern free-range henhouses, I ask him about his father's invention. He is modest about everything, and quietly matter-of-fact about most, saying his father's invention was really just an early version of his present system. The idea, he says, has always been to remove the eggs as soon and efficiently as possible. "You can't do it by hand with this many birds."

I understand that the chickens—at least if they have a choice in the matter—usually go into the nest box only when they have an egg to lay, and that occurs most often in the morning. I remember from my own days on the farm that if a hen were to find a comfortable nest there with multiple eggs already in it, she will be tempted to linger over the laying process, and that might give her the notion of trying to hatch the eggs. That, after all, would seem to be her deepest instinct, to hatch a clutch of young chicks; so the farmer really has to trick her out of it. He does this simply by taking away the eggs as they are laid, for the hen is, fortunately, not programmed to try to hatch a single egg. Somehow she knows that would be a poor way to perpetuate her kind. But the instinct to hatch is still there, safely dormant, and I remember from the hens on my father's farm that sometimes one became "broody" despite our efforts. I saw no broody hens at the Colls' farm; all the thousands of them seemed intent on the business of eating and drinking and making eggs, and forever clucking about it with the neighbors. I recall that a broody hen is a sullen and unfriendly bird, as well she might be; she wants only to warm some eggs, but not lay any, to resist all efforts to urge her off, and to cluck sulkily in a broody tone of voice. (Broodiness, it is now known, is induced by the presence of a protein hormone, usually called *prolactin*, which is regulated by the pituitary, and it has the same effect, namely, inducing behavior and chemical changes associated with motherhood, throughout all vertebrates, including ourselves. Injected into a hen, it will produce broodiness within a few hours; injected into cows it will induce estrus, and so facilitate artificial insemination.)

In a modern henhouse the newly laid egg rolls away on the slanted nest floor and disappears down a slight incline to be eventually captured gently by the padded conveyor belt, which takes it smoothly to the central gathering place—which is a pretty simple idea really; but it was Archie's father who mechanized and capitalized on it a half century ago. With no eggs in sight or underfoot, and with her own most recent offering slipped out of reach, the hen is the more inclined to rush out of the nest to brag to her friends at a hen party and cackle cheerily with the other girls and eat more protein to make more eggs. (This activity appears to inhibit the pituitary's production of prolactin.) Meanwhile, twice a day the Colls' conveyor belt system is activated, and it slowly brings eggs by the thousands and from two floors to one gathering place where two workers rapidly pack them into trays for transport to the packing room. This is handwork, and it is one of the few things not automated here.

The packing and grading room resembles an assembly line where many different operations happen in smooth and uninterrupted sequence, almost all the work being done by machines: suction cups gently pick up the eggs and place them on a belt that sends them to the wash, then to one that candles them (shines a bright light through each egg to identify slight cracks in the shell or blood clots inside the egg), then to one that sorts them for size, using individual weight as the measure, then to one that puts them carefully into boxes of a dozen, which are then packed into larger cartons. These processes require attentiveness, but 99 percent of the actual work is done by the clever and gentle machines; and I didn't see them break any eggs.

The machines are complicated and insatiable, and so is the market at the other end of the machines. When the Colls learned that Amish farmers were producing more eggs than they had a market for, Archie began making regular trips to Pennsylvania to purchase their eggs and soon established regular leasing arrangements with half a dozen farmers. These eggs he also feeds to his grading and packing machines: he has a good market for more eggs than he can produce. His own market, which was traditionally mostly directed to groceries and not wholesalers, is strong because he is temperamentally aggressive about high quality and service. A satisfied customer is what satisfies Archie Coll. But he now has other markets that he services through a New York distributor, and Coll eggs now go to more than a dozen states. It may happen that some eggs were laid in Pennsylvania, processed at Coll's farm, sent to a New York distributor, then shipped to Georgia for retail. Moreover, some of these eggs may even take a slight detour before he gets them. For some Amish farmers it is not permitted that they have business dealings with the outside world, though they may deal with certain Mennonites. Most Mennonites in turn are permitted to deal with the rest of the world; so they transmit Amish eggs to Archie, and he brings them back to New Hampshire for processing.

More than most farm operations, the Coll farm remains a work in progress, never static. Over the years Helen and Archie have explored every aspect of the sweet corn business, and every aspect of the chicken business too. Some years ago they even tried "contract" farming, raising "roosters for roasters" at so much per head for a wholesaler. They found it a good way to take on major risks and a poor way to make a living, and they abandoned it. Retailing too has evolved continuously: what was initially a farm stand has become a full farm store, now open year-round, carrying a line of groceries and much produce as well as the farm's eggs and, in the summer and autumn, the huge quantities of the farm's own corn and produce. Two things especially, the Colls believe, are important in their particular farm venture. The first is diversification, and the second is direct marketing. "The farm stand and the egg production complement each other and ease the burden of relying solely on one form of agriculture," Helen wrote; and as for direct marketing, it "requires a lot of time and commitment but is essential to the survival of agriculture on the family farm." At least they found it to be essential for them. An observer would say that theirs are strategies that both require and reward flexibility, that is, the willingness and skill to design continuous adjustments.

For the Colls, finding and keeping reliable help has always been a challenge, and it is not getting easier. Prompt her slightly and Helen can amusingly mimic the familiar litanies she has often heard: don't want to work weekends, or late evenings; find the work too hard; don't like the smell; the work is dreary or lonely or boring; don't like the heat or cold. These are not complaints to make to Colls, or to any farmer, for that matter. Fifty years ago Louis Bromfield denounced a similar fecklessness in the upcoming generation. No doubt our great-grandfathers said or heard the same. Young people who don't join in these litanies will be among the few destined to become the next generation of farmers. The Colls' grandson Joshua, born in 1990, thinks all the farmwork is exciting and fun. At one time or another all the Colls' four children, and later their spouses as well, and some of their grandchildren, have been involved in the work of the farm and farm stand. But it is their son Mark and his wife Lori who seemed to enjoy it the most and were always the most deeply involved. Mark started a small maple syrup operation while still in high school, and he has tended and enlarged it year by year, so that maple syrup is now a major item among the stand's line of farm products. Mark and Lori and their son Joshua are the ones destined to carry on this particular family farm, and recently the Colls began the process of transferring ownership to them.

When asked about the future Archie says: "I would hope that Mark and Lori would be able to continue successfully, basically along the present lines, with chickens and sweet corn and the farm stand—at least for the next ten years or so, without big changes. Beyond that, who knows?"

## The Reputation of Hens and Cocks

"Farmers should go to bed with the hens and rise with the cocks"—that's an ancient country maxim, and it pays tribute to both the farmer and the chickens. Beyond that, however, there is something in our common discourse about chickens that is not at all complimentary to the bird. Could it even be that we casually, though unwittingly, disparage chickens? Here is a paradox. On the one hand, a cock is frequently strident—the cock of the walk, for example—and often famously brave, as witness the long centuries of cockfighting, which are often battles to the death; and recall, too, that a hen can be aggressively protective of her nest and her young, and even fierce in defending them—giving rise to the observation that both cocks and hens can be, well, cocky. But, on the other hand, there is the casual slur upon these birds whenever we castigate a fainthearted person as "chicken." Since Shakespeare, at least, the term "chicken" has been used to describe a coward, and "chickenhearted" is almost as old an epithet. A similar one is "chicken-livered," an insult of uncertain lineage and scarcely any intelligible explanation. For all of its unfairness to the bird, for all its lack of ready rationale, this use of chickens for one form or another of disparagement seems entrenched in our language, perhaps in our habits of thought.

As for language: from classical Greek times forward poor handwriting was known dismissively as "hen scratching," and even the ancient rule not to count your chicks before they are hatched (recorded centuries ago) may slight the hen doing the hatching. But our language is actually much more intense and specific than that: you can be cruelly dismissive of an annoying person by telling him to go suck eggs (whatever that would achieve), which, indeed, you might be inclined to say if he is insufferable or running around like a chicken with its head cut off. For untold generations chattering women have been labeled a hen party, and certain kinds of men are said to be henpecked by their wives. Elderly women who are disliked, or at least can no longer be regarded as spring chickens, may be dismissed as old biddies—especially by adolescents, who will egg each other on. Commit a social blunder and you have laid an egg. Small change is chicken feed. If this use of language maligns chickens, or if it makes you angry, someone may think you mad as a wet hen. Alas, it would take an egghead to sort out everything that inspires this abuse of chickens.

There are some few linguistic examples on the other side of the ledger, that is to say, complimentary uses of chicken idiom. Creating a nest egg might be a case in point, but generally such examples are scarce as hens' teeth. One familiar but now fading example is the use of "chick" for an attractive young woman; however, spokespersons for political correctness, who now own a high place in the social pecking order, have impugned the reputation of that word. To question whether this is progress requires something like walking on eggs.

What are we to make of these uses and abuses?

Cocks, who began life as cockerels, may not have been so quickly disparaged as hens, but they have been linguistically manipulated in other ways. Clearly no one is complimented by being described as cocksure, or of going off half-cocked, and it is worse if his ideas are thought to be cock-eyed. It may be a dubious honor that the lingo of working-class Londoners is known as Cockney, either through an insulting reference to cock eggs or because cockfighting was long the chief sport of these folks. However, cocks have more interesting linguistic challenges than that, chiefly the historic and certainly intentionally salacious ambiguity of that word itself. "Cock" is a very old four-letter Anglo-Saxon word that has cheerfully lived its double life for fifteen hundred and more years. It is no accident at all that throughout those centuries the strident and crowing cock has almost everywhere been, among other things, a potent masculine sex symbol. And the word in its secondary sense, says the *Oxford English Dictionary* (*OED*), "though the current name among the people . . . is not admissible in polite speech or literature." (The book you hold in your hand, dear reader, is polite literature all the way.)

It appears, however, that many languages other than English have a very similar sounding word for the same things, applicable both to the bird and to the organ, with the same bold ambiguity, many going back to the Sanskrit, *kukkula,* to the Latin *cucurio* and *coccus,* or to the Old Teutonic *kok,* Old French *coq,* Old Norse *kokk,* or Old English *kokke, cocc,* and *cock,* or the Middle English *cok.* Moreover, scholars think the words "cock" and "chicken" (not to mention "cluck") are probably etymologically related, perhaps inbred and crossbred in the dim light of the Dark Ages, and possibly being linguistic echoes of the clucks of the birds themselves—which, incidentally, Chaucer renders as *coc coc coc.* Well, most of this and much more can be painstakingly extracted from the *OED,* but trying to get it all straight is somewhat like unscrambling eggs.

One thing you don't find, however, in this great *OED* treasure-house of linguistic detail is a similarly long and trailing history for the word "rooster." That is a very modern word, chiefly American, it turns out, but exquisitely Victorian in inspiration and rationale, and it derives from the nineteenth century, only yesterday as these things go. Apparently, the secondary and sexual use of "cock" was becoming too dominant, and the political correctors of the day, joining forces with the tribes of those concerned with the state of polite speech and literature, demanded an entirely new word to stanch the bawdy breach in linguistic etiquette. So in America the chaste word "rooster" was deliberately and successfully conscripted for this purpose. Now no one cocks an eye anymore at that once weird word, rooster.

But not so in Merrie Olde England, which for centuries had been a hotbed of the sport of cockfighting, with scores of famous public cockpits in London and likewise throughout the British Empire, where cockfighting thrived in a dozen colonies. There was no likelihood whatever that gentlemen and ladies would now purify their patter and start chatting chastely about "rooster fighting." And it didn't happen. In the *Oxford English Dictionary* rooster-talk was firmly exiled and bracketed as a piece of American dialect, while in England it is still the jaunty cock that crows and fights and there he still, so to speak, rules the roost.

### *Boston Produce Market*

"What are you doing here?" A bright flashlight full in my face gets my attention and wakens me. Groggily, I slide down the car window and pick out the outline of a policeman's uniform behind the sharp light. I sneak a quick and worried glance at my wristwatch: it is 2:15 A.M., so I have just dozed off. I seem to recall vaguely that I am in the parking lot of Coll's Farm Stand. Let's see . . . the question was about . . . what I'm doing here? I am just awake enough to resort to the unvarnished truth.

"I'm waiting for Archie Coll. We are leaving together shortly for the Boston Market." The officer accepts my story, implausible as it must seem, and I am free to wake up. This already promises to be a somewhat unusual day. It began for me at 1:00 A.M. when I got up, then drove to Jaffrey over absolutely carless roads, and got here early. I had suspected that when Archie said to meet him here at 2:30 A.M. he did not mean *about* 2:30.

At exactly 2:30 Archie appears out of the darkness; we greet each other and he gestures toward the Peterbilt ten-wheeler we will take to Boston. He will fill this huge refrigerated box with fresh produce, lug it back to the farm stand for retailing, and within three or four days he will do the same thing again. We climb up into the cab, where we ride high above the traffic, and I marvel at the casual way Archie guides the huge truck around the countryside curves. It is a misty morning, but driving a truck is as easy as breathing to him. How many hundreds of thousands of miles has he covered over these roads? For almost fifty years Archie Coll has pounded New Hampshire highways, trying to make a living as a farmer's son, a farmer, and a businessman. As a young man he worked with his father, and they hatched chicks and trucked them, day-old, all over New England. He raised broilers and delivered them, live, everywhere in New England and brought them by the truckload to New York City. Over the years he delivered hundreds of thousands of chickens, broilers, old hens, young chicks, and now each year hundreds of thousands more of eggs to New Hampshire and Massachusetts and New York markets. This farmer has always been on the road, moving chicks, chickens, eggs, produce, always using a truck to help his farm. A couple of million miles or more, I suppose.

I glance over and notice that while I am belted in, Archie is not. Should I have asked about this? Too late. I did. "Just never formed the habit, when I drive," he says. Archie is a man of settled habits, or a settled lack of them. "When Helen drives, I usually buckle up," he adds.

Soon I am concentrating on food and farming, and I can pepper Archie with questions all through the wee hours to Boston. The wholesale market toward which we are heading, known formally as the New England Produce Center, is just outside Boston in Chelsea, Massachusetts, near Logan Airport, near a clutch of railroad sidetracks, not far from Boston Harbor. It has been active here for more than thirty years, and before that it was part of the famous Boston Quincy Market (now retail), near Fanueil Hall. The center, I realize when we get there, is enormous, and it occupies probably fifty times the space of the Quincy Market and handles probably a hundred or more times the business it did in downtown Boston. That itself testifies to a total revolution in New England eating habits since I myself became a New Englander a generation ago: fresh fruits and vegetables have come to be regarded as a year-round necessity. If that is a boon for family health, as it may be, it is not a boon for the family farm. The produce distributed here comes from intensely competitive corporate farms all over the world, the only ones with the quantities and capital to be part of this vast marketing network. A small portion of the produce, like Archie's truckload, will go to farm stands associated with New England family farms. More of it will go to restaurant distribution companies, and much of the rest will go, directly or through a distributor, to grocery stores. Large chain groceries, which have their own private distribution centers, and to which much produce is shipped directly from a boat dock or corporate farm, are also here to fill in their niches.

It is a wondrously intricate and far-flung distribution web that binds agribusiness to the dining table, and here in Chelsea we are heading toward the nexus, the place where it all gathers, from which it all departs. There is a sense, surely, in which every small vegetable producer like Archie is in competition with the enormous network and concentration of economic power represented here; but I do not think that proposition interests Archie. It certainly does not intimidate him. There will be sweet corn here, but it will not get his attention.

It is misty and mostly dark when we arrive at 4:30, but already in the dim morning fog I can discern a great hithering and thithering of activity which appears to involve legions of long trucks and long docks and long warehouses. To my eyes the heavy mist makes everything a little more mystifying and mysterious as Archie and I climb down out of the truck and then up again to the dock to join the growing confusion among the mountains of crates and boxes and bags. Fresh produce is everywhere—tons and tons of it. Archie is about to begin what will be up to five hours of shopping. He will spend whatever time it takes to load his truck with only the best and freshest things at the best prices. Whereas the produce department in many a local chain grocery sells what is shipped to them, Archie sells only what he has personally selected for his customers—the next best thing to growing it himself.

Suddenly a juggernaut bursts through a door, corners sharply, and careens past us down the dock. It is a heavy electric-powered forklift—two great prongs and a motor and a tongue to steer by—this one ballasted with a pallet piled with a ton of onions, deftly steered by a driver standing on one foot on its narrow platform. He stops, turns, backs to the wall, drops the loaded pallet, and wheels away. The dock is not wide and the produce is soon piling up, coming out of coolers, off trucks, out of boxcars, being carted into other trucks. Shortly it seems that there are electric forklifts everywhere, each a giant Go-cart, fast and powerful, lugging heavy pallets of produce in every direction. Nothing—not one bag, not one crate—will be handled here by hand. Forklifts move every strawberry and celery stalk, a half ton of them or more at a stroke, from van or boxcar or cooler or warehouse to dock or waiting truck. I remind myself that this is just one more piece of mechanization that makes our food ultimately cheaper, just as it puts one more bit of pressure on the family farmer who handles his sacks of onions by hand. It is not easy to see at first glance just what is going on here, only that there is a great deal of it going on. I am peering into a strange and confusing netherworld, a complex and bustling network of high-piled and swiftly moving produce and intricate business dealings, surreal when concentrated like this but altogether the inevitable supporting underside to that clean and crisp produce section in a thousand grocery stores.

I walk the docks and enter the bays, where boxed produce is piled or displayed everywhere and everywhere men are standing at high wooden desks and yakking away. It occurs to me that I may be a slightly out-of-place specimen in this strange world. Piles of boxes loaded with asparagus. Crates and crates of strawberries. Tomatoes everywhere. More and more apples. Everyone seems to be at some task—talking, bargaining, shouting, telling jokes in a foreign language, smoking, selling, driving a Go-cart forklift with high speed and great skill—but what am I doing? I am staring at a twenty-foot stack of sacks of garlic and a row of tubs loaded with fresh and sweet-smelling cantaloupes. I am counting dozens of crates of clementines. Archie rode off on his own Go-cart, returned with two enormous tubs, each twice the size of my desk, full of Georgia watermelons, and then wheeled off again. Perhaps I am a little too well dressed to be in this place. Look at those radishes! In fact . . . am I here, or am I in a foggy dream? Did I really get out of bed? Is this night or misty day?

I should have brought a clipboard, which would serve as a pretty fair disguise. I appoint myself inspector, and take out a pen and a bit of paper. Make that Inspector of Produce. I peer at box labels, move on, peer at others, make a few notes, move on. Most of this stuff comes to New England from thousands of miles away, some of it from halfway around the world. Nobody stops me. This is a weird and wacky world: luscious produce is everywhere, tons and tons of it; Texas is feeding New England, the air is thick and noisy and smells of garlic, and heavy laden Go-carts are tearing around like crazy, and they may run me down if I don't watch out. Everything is strange here. Am I being watched? I amble along the dock, where there is always another bay, dozens and dozens of them, full of produce, where I can continue my serious work as Inspector. Here, side by side, are boxes and boxes of apples—from Chile, New Zealand, South Africa, Washington State, California; here, pears from Argentina and from Florida; next are boxes of tomatoes from Mexico stacked and plainly labeled "vine ripened," and all are green as green grass.

The Boston Market (like the two larger markets in New York and in

Los Angeles) is a wonderfully vivid symbol, at once stirring and grotesque, of that passionate and troubling marriage of farming and corporate capitalism—a booming, clangorous relationship, this, growing tighter every year, sweeping everything in its path, and decorated anew each day with ten thousand crates and boxes and bags of vegetables and fruits, the daily offerings brought to this Boston altar from more than a dozen countries and two dozen states. Here it all funnels together, arriving wholesale, departing for retail outlets, and eventually trickling to the plates and palates of thirty million New Englanders. Triumphalism is rampant here, for this place smiles at continental distances, and negates the seasons. Come here *any* time, America; name *any* fresh fruit or vegetable you want! It's here— or it will be tomorrow, carried to you fresh from Peru or Israel, or maybe Maine. Later, at home, I was able to locate some interesting statistics provided by the Northeast Sustainable Agriculture Working Group. Examples: the average shipping distance per pound of fresh produce handled at this Boston terminal in 1995 was 2,374 miles; the Northeast's share of fresh produce distributed here declined from 20.2 percent in 1980 to 11.6 percent in 1995; foreign producers increased their share of the total fresh produce from 9.2 percent in 1980 to 22.6 percent in 1997; the Northeast's market share of the apples handled here decreased from 50 percent in 1980, to 25 percent in 1995.[62]

What helps to create this system and make it irresistible is a collection of little pressures that push every farm, every shipper, toward greater efficiencies, toward larger production with less labor, for each seller requires a competitive edge. Archie and Helen's retail prices for produce are a direct function, adjusted weekly or oftener, of what he pays for that produce right here. And what he pays in Boston is a negotiated price and always subject to competition from the product in the very next bay on the dock— though the produce in the next bay is less and less likely to originate in the Northeast. In any case, if the shipper can find a way to sustain profits and undersell his neighbor and so enlarge his niche, of course he will. It is the way of capitalism. It is very good for Archie's customers. It is not very good for neighboring New England farms.

Once the logic of machined efficiencies and economies of scale are let loose in this tightly integrated network, it becomes a ruthless story, wonderful and terrible: retail food prices go down, and small food producers, such as family farmers and their communities, even local farmers' markets, are in jeopardy. The capitalist logic that drives down food prices for the consumer is the very same logic that for recent generations has driven farmers to "get bigger or get out." The carrots in the grocery probably came from a thousand-acre field in Texas: never touched by laboring hands, they were refrigerated almost from the time a machine lifted, topped, washed, and packaged them, and they are reasonably tasty and so cheap that nobody raising a few acres of carrots in New England can compete. As it happens, the tomatoes, too, were machine harvested and packaged and machine sorted by color, and they are not tasty at all and they are about as hard as the carrots. They are not for Archie's customers: most will go to restaurants, where there is a mechanical slicer perfectly designed for producing very thin slices of very firm and faintly red tomatoes. You can hide the slices in a hamburger or a salad. A truly ripe and juicy tomato would never survive the machine that harvested these, nor the machine that packaged them, nor the machine that sorted them, nor the truck that transported them, nor the machine that will slice them. The stock of the agricorporation that produces these firm carrots and hard tomatoes trades well on Wall Street. Such too is farming.

By 1:00 P.M. we are back in Jaffrey, and hungry, and the produce is still ice cold. In a few days Archie will be back to the market to fetch another load. Next week, same thing, for he has hundreds of customers who depend on him for quality produce, and he tends to their wishes like a pastor to his parish. He is well beyond the days when his produce shelf was a broad plank, two sawhorses, a handmade sign, and spare corn from the field. The appetites he still stimulates with his own produce he can now fully satisfy only by these regular forage trips to the Boston Market.

When you leave Coll's Farm Stand to return to Highway 202, you face down a steep hill, which gives you a wide panoramic view of the rural countryside of southwestern New Hampshire. You can look straight west across the valley through which the highway and the river run and see the fields and rolling farmscapes beyond—a beguiling scene. Should these farms fail and vanish, so too eventually would these patterned landscapes, and many of the scenic amenities that now stretch out toward Mount Monadnock. A road winds up yonder hill, and beside it you can see the farmstead where Archie was born and grew up and learned farming from his father, and learned business entrepreneurship as well; and across the road from it you can see another farmstead, which is where Helen came to live as a little girl. Archie Coll and Helen Van Blarcom—their parents were farmers, and they were farm youths and neighbors, and they met and married and bought a nearby farm. They took up farming together, and they are still at it, and so are some of their children; they are still changing with the times whenever they have to, still adapting, and still prefer to see themselves as farmers, and they have children and children's children who look forward to more of the same.

# Chapter 7

# Apples: The Glow of Autumn at Gould Hill

Conversation with a hired apple picker in Gould Hill Orchards in October 2001: **Q.** "I'm doing a book on farming; . . . apple growing is a form of farming, isn't it?" **A.** "More like a form of gambling, I'd say."

The apple tree has been celebrated by the Hebrews, Greeks, Romans, and Scandinavians. Some have thought that the first human pair were tempted by its fruit. Goddesses are fabled to have contended for it, dragons were set to watch it, and heroes were employed to pluck it.
—H. D. THOREAU, "Wild Apples"

*Apples of Desire*

There are two moments each year when apple farming seems glorious beyond singing. One comes in early May when the trees, entire hillsides of them, explode into luscious, virginal bloom, when the air is warm at last and the blossoms sweet and the hum of a million bees mingles with the snowy drift of delicate white petals. The other moment arrives with October, when another glow is on the trees, and all their stretched-out and bent-down limbs are pregnant with luscious fruit, red and russet and burgundy and golden, and the air is brisk at last, and you can almost inhale the smell and taste of apples by the wonder of your gaze. Two glorious moments. For the farmer-grower himself, there may be another blessed moment, perhaps in bleary November, when the entire crop is safely tucked away in cold storage.

The rest of the year is somewhat less exhilarating. Today's apple grower is often thinking about pests, about the weather, about markets. About scab and fungus. About planting more trees, about cutting down trees. Maybe, about chaos and red ink. It was just about blossom time last year when Agriculture Commissioner Steve Taylor began his column of news and farm comment this way: "Will consolidation and shrinking of the New England apple industry bring order and profitability instead of the chaos and red ink that have prevailed for the past several years?"

One can easily get the impression that the news for New England apple farmers is not particularly good as we enter a new century. Commissioner Taylor wrote: "A prolonged period of tough times for wholesale apple producers is precipitating major change. While many operators are simply giving up the business and selling out to developers, others are rapidly getting rid of their full-size trees and replacing them with dwarf types in new varieties." He went on to cite shifts in the retail food sector that favor large suppliers "capable of providing the latest in packaging and logistical services." Here is a recent example: a major Massachusets apple wholesaler recently absorbed his largest counterpart in Vermont. This new firm will handle about 40 percent of all New England commercial apples, and will dominate the market for McIntosh exports to the United Kingdom, where Macs are much desired.

Erick Leadbeater of Gould Hill Orchards is one committed apple grower who is never pleased with negative publicity for orchards—even if it is true. "When people are told the apple crop or the apple business is bad they will think of something else to do instead of coming to the orchard. It's good news that means good customers." He referred to a recent (September 2002) story in a New Hampshire daily, which began this way: "The toughest weather conditions in decades—including cold spells, drought, hail, a heat wave, more drought—produced an apple crop 40 to 50 percent smaller than previous years, growers say."

Well, *some* growers said that; but that won't bring in customers, said Leadbeater, and that wasn't the story at Gould Hill Orchards, which had an excellent crop. But good news doesn't always make good news stories. "We can make do without the doom stories," Leadbeater says cheerfully, "I learned long ago that we don't make any money from sympathy."

Almost by definition, apples themselves are good news. Apples are the fruit of passion—of myth and legend and folklore and allegory. "Comfort me with apples," pleads the singer in the Song of Songs. Apples have pleased and gratified humankind since long before records were kept, and carbonated remains of apples have been dug up in prehistoric sites in Switzerland. Most scholars believe that our apples ultimately derive from a cross, many thousands of years ago, of wild native Asian and European crab apples (which still exist), and were first cultivated in the Caucasus. Homer in the *Odyssey* mentions apples, using the word *malon,* which sometimes refers to the fruit of any tree. About two thousand years ago the Greek historian Plutarch noted that the best sensual qualities were combined in the apple: smooth and silky and seductive to the touch, imparting warm fragrance to the hand, sensuous in shape, colorful and pleasing to the eye, sweet and satisfying to the taste. Even earlier, many ancient writers had taken to referring to female breasts as apples; and by a natural extension an apple tree loaded with fruit early came to signify a fertile and fruitful woman, the seed-filled apple came to be compared to pregnancy, and so on. Throughout ancient history and literature apples are often associated with many of the rites and rituals of marriage and also with the gift of immortal life.

The sensual qualities of apples, their shape and fragrance and feel, may be one reason why ancient mythologies, and many mythologies the world over, are full of apples, and why they have such a powerful symbolic presence. In many traditions apples have oracular powers of divination, in others life-giving qualities—and, indeed, King Arthur in Avalon is supposed to be sustained by magic apples. A favorite ancient association is with the Greek love goddess Aphrodite, often portrayed as distributing apples as tokens of love or immortality, or both. In one myth, the judgment of Paris, the goddess Discord tosses into the midst of assembled gods and goddesses a golden apple inscribed "For the fairest one." Goddesses Hera, Aphrodite, and Athena all immediately claim it, but they finally agree to let Paris, prince of Troy, decide the beauty contest and award the golden apple. In turn they disrobe and display to him their charms, but each also proffers a bribe. Aphrodite's bribe is to offer as wife to Paris the beautiful Helen, who is married to the king of Sparta. (As a goddess, she can do this.) Paris accepts the bribe, awards the apple to Aphrodite, and runs off to Troy with Helen. The Spartan king, enraged by his wife's abduction, rallies a coalition of Greek cites and descends upon Troy, besieges it, and eventually wreaks revenge. And that is how Aphrodite, goddess of love—and all for the desiring of an apple—was responsible for starting the Trojan War, the war that was the major cultural reference point for Greek civilization.

In the biblical story of Adam and Eve in the Book of Genesis, the Tree of Knowledge stands in the midst of the original Garden. Its luscious and forbidden fruit is highly recommended by the sly and subtle serpent. "And when the woman saw that the tree was good for food, and that it was pleasant to the eyes, and a tree to be desired to make one wise, she took of the fruit thereof and did eat; and gave also unto her husband with her; and he did eat. And the eyes of them both were opened, and they knew that they were naked." From the woman's first glance, the sensuality of the scene and the narrative is unmistakable. True, no apple there. But it is also no surprise at all—indeed, was it not inevitable?—that religious art and experience and the impulse of Greek myth have long ago placed the apple there in the midst of the Garden of Eden. This most sensuous and desirable of fruits has been consistently in Eden since the Middle Ages. Lust for the apple as token of forbidden desire. The passion fruit.

And there is a splendidly banal reason why apples have been cherished time out of mind. It is that they come to us in such prodigious, almost reckless, richness and variety—colors, textures, tastes, sizes, densities, fragrances, uses, cider qualities, seasons of ripening, adaptations to soil and climate, responses to storage, resistance to diseases and insects, style of tree, hardihood. Does any other fruit arrive in such an extravagance of habits, forms, and beloved varieties, more of them unfolding all the time? Nearly two thousand years ago the Roman Columella described twenty-four varieties of apples. In 1588, a Frenchman, Julien de Paulmier, published a list of eighty-eight different named apple varieties. In 1872, an American scholar, Charles Downing, listed over a thousand named apple varieties in American orchards—every last one of them with its own unique characteristics, its own color and tang and taste and local partisans. And there are, of course, unnumbered unnamed crosses, hybrids, sports, spurs, and mutants—the mysterious sources of ever more new and distinct varieties. Indeed, every apple tree grown from seed is unique, though the great majority of these will bear only fruit that is scarcely edible: they tend to revert to their ancestral prehistoric crabs. Nursery apple trees of a given named variety and grown for production are all botanically the same, the result of scions, or cuttings, from that variety of tree grafted individually onto different apple rootstock. The resulting tree is a clone, genetically identical to that from which the scion came, and is the only way that particular variety can be propagated; for, except in rare cases, the seed will not do it. Nevertheless, the vast and extravagant variety preserved in our apple heritage is a luxury to give pause and bring joy, as it has since Roman times, since Greek and biblical times.

Many of the thousand varieties once known and named and loved have subsequently vanished, of course, and many other nearly forgotten varieties are probably even today still bearing and dying slowly to oblivion in the back row of some forgotten orchard that was long ago abandoned but never hacked down. Meanwhile others, though fewer in number, have been developed or discovered to take their place. And new ones come from abroad: Braeburn from New Zealand, Mutsu and Fuji from Japan. Varieties were created and named voluminously in the nineteenth century but many disappeared in the twentieth, with the attacks on cider drinking, the disappearance of old farm orchards, the movement of people to cities, and the imperatives of commercial markets. Today, despite the immense variety once and still available (if there remain three hundred apple varieties, do we need a thousand?), the overwhelming majority of apples sold commercially in the country are of just a few kinds that have predictable sales: Golden Delicious, McIntosh, Jonathan, Granny Smith, Jonagold, Cortland, Red Delicious, and a small basket of others.

The career of Baldwin apples typifies much of the story. Baldwins were long famed not only for eating and cider but especially for baking and for their long-lived natural storage capacity. A great all-round New England apple, deep red on the sunny side but otherwise not notably handsome to look at. But less cider is now made than formerly, few people now bake apples, and no one depends on natural storage. Farewell, Baldwin. Enter Red Delicious, which often now heads the best-seller list. The distinctive profile of the Red Delicious and its fire engine color certainly make it as conspicuous and attractive as Eden's apples, but its remarkable success suggests that many people live their apple lives more by sight than by other values. (One gentle critic told me that those who buy Red Delicious may not plan to eat them but only to offer them, like Eve, to others.) From all that rich and savory historical array of apple varieties, one might wonder how we could have been reduced to this peculiar triumph of apple style over apple quality. Popular but controversial, one book says of the Red Delicious, pointing out that it ships well (as do potatoes, incidentally). In my book it would be better just to be candid: this is an inferior apple. The flesh is often insipid, reminiscent of cheap perfume, the skin is tough and betimes bitter, and the apple flaunts a seductive exterior even after the inside, often mealy, has turned to mush. As a cider apple, a nonstarter. All in all, lack of character seems indicated. Fortunately, one can easily bite into many, many apple varieties of an entirely different stripe. Baldwin and Northern Spy were favorite apples in the northern states already a century ago, while the York Imperial topped the list farther south. Then came the ascendancy of the McIntosh and the Jonathan. One can do worse.

Not to be too solemn about it, but the curious triumph of Red Delicious may be connected with other things, such as the naming of new apples, where beige and vanilla tend to prevail. Time was when apples were named things like Duchess of Oldenburg, Red Gravenstein, Wolf River, Esopus Spitzenburg (favorite of Thomas Jefferson), Newton Pippin (favorite of George Washington), Granniwinkle, Belle de Boskoop, Black Gilliflower, Stembridge Cluster, Boxwood Foxwhelp. Recent names of apples are Idared, Gala, Jonagold, Pink Lady, Easygro. Something seems to be missing, *gravitas* perhaps.

Today, at Gould Hill Orchards in Hopkinton, New Hampshire, there are over eighty named apple varieties, old and new, including Red Delicious. There are at least fifteen kinds of peaches, making about a hundred different fruit varieties in all. Two of the apples, Kearsarge and Hampshire, were discovered and named here, and Hampshire bears a Gould Hill patent.


*Goulds and Leadbeaters*


The road to Gould Hill Orchards seems a bit out of the way, but then you realize that most farms are out of the way in New Hampshire. You may suppose you are driving through an offbeat suburban development when the houses suddenly give way to broad vistas and apple trees. This has been a family farm for nearly 250 years, and an apple farm for the last 100 years. The farmstead, a big rambling, nondescript hundred-year-old barn that needs paint and an older attached house that looks comfortable, squats right on the very edge of the road. But up here you don't think about the buildings; you think about the view.

The roots of Gould Hill Orchards go straight back to colonial days. About 1750 Moses Gould acquired a piece of unsettled hillside wilderness that his father had already owned for twenty-five years and began converting it into a farm. Four successive generations of Goulds then farmed here, weathering as best they could the downs and ups and downs of New Hampshire hill town agriculture for 175 years. The last of this tribe, Robert Gould, appears to be the most resourceful and interesting farmer of this family. In the 1880s, when New Hampshire upland farms were being abandoned left and right, he created a viable dairy herd, very large for the time, with twenty-five head. Thus equipped, he successfully marketed his milk and his farm-made butter in nearby Concord. It must have been good butter, for it was manufactured in an era and for a clientele that knew its butter. At the Columbia Exposition World's Fair in Chicago in 1893, New Hampshire took the highest prizes for butter, and Robert Gould came home with a bronze medal for his.

There is a local tradition that in 1901 Robert Gould pruned and manured his few dozen apple trees and found himself nearly overwhelmed the next year with over four hundred bushels of apples—and a good market for them. Came the thought: maybe this is better than milking and churning. He promptly set out a hundred new trees, mostly Baldwins, and so added serious apple farming to his dairy operation. The die had been cast, and Gould Hill was on its way to becoming a significant fruit farm. Each year, cows were fewer but apple plantings increased, including a large planting of McIntosh in 1912, probably the first major stake for this variety in New Hampshire. By 1926 he had few cows but over two thousand apple trees, half of them Baldwins, and was producing three thousand barrels of apples annually. Most of the apples went to Boston, and from there many went directly to England. Robert Gould, first with his dairy and then with his apple farming, represented the crest of successful New Hampshire farming in his era, and he probably did as much as anyone to turn the English palate toward McIntosh apples. But he had no son to succeed him on the farm, and in the late 1930s he began to look around for a buyer.

Edward Leadbeater had spent the summers of his youth in these regions and couldn't get the New Hampshire hills out of his system. Although he had become a city man, working on Wall Street in New York, he took a correspondence course in pomology from Cornell University. That tipped the balance: he went shopping for an apple orchard in New Hampshire, and his dream came to earth at Gould Hill. He often spoke afterward of "the privilege of living in God's country atop Gould Hill here in the midst of bearing apple trees." It was 1939, and Edward Leadbeater and his wife Lucille were now resident farmers in Hopkinton, New Hampshire, ten miles from Concord, with vistas to the northwest that spread past Mount Kearsarge over rippling hills toward Vermont and panoramic views to the north and northeast all the way to the White Mountains.

Sixty years ago, and three years after the Leadbeaters arrived, their son Erick was born; so apple growing is the farming he has known all his life. When he was young the farm started its cider operation, successful ever since, and long known for its careful blending of sweet and tart apples. Shortly thereafter, the farm opened its modest autumn retail business: peaches, apples, vegetables, and other farm products. By the time Erick went off to Bowdoin College, as his father had before him, the farm was producing up to thirty thousand bushels of fruit a year, including twenty varieties of apples. After college Erick entered military service, then went off to be a sailor and see the world. ("Farming is much like sailing," he told me. "Everything absolutely depends on the weather.") When the wandering sailor returned to the farm to rejoin his father thirty years ago he was a bit uncertain that there was a solid future in this kind of apple farming, but Gould Hill seemed like a great place to raise a family. He plunged in and eventually led the effort to modernize the whole operation, open it wider to the public (pick your own, seasonal store in the barn, wagon tours, organized visits for school kids, and so on), develop modern pest control techniques, move the orchard toward dwarf trees, eventually build a modern storage facility, and more.

Erick is wiry, a whip of a man, much used to hard work, like all farmers. He has studied apples, apple trees, apple farmers, apple markets, apple customers, apple enemies, apple lore with quiet intensity for more than half a lifetime, and some of his knowledge of this business is distilled into dry epigrams. He has learned to think like an apple tree. And he is a little uncertain about the future still. Or again. Is this the right size apple operation to be continuously successful in the twenty-first century? Should it be about half as large? Or perhaps three times as large? At this stage the Leadbeaters are not about to embark on a big expansion program to compete with the largest orchards, although they have the farm acreage for it. Even some major commodity farmers have become, almost by default, niche farmers. At present, Erick and his wife Susan are carefully slimming down the operation: more trees on fewer acres. Almost every year they take out some old trees, but they plant many new ones too; and, of course, that represents more overhead for some years into the future. But Erick has his reasons: "Old trees grow wood and leaves; young trees grow apples." The Leadbeaters have built themselves a splendid new house out of old materials at the very top of Gould Hill, with panoramic vistas and completely surrounded with apple orchards. Orchard manager Steve Gatcombe and his family occupy the original house by the road.

The challenge of determining the right scale of operations, which every farmer faces, is much more acute for an orchard farm than for almost any other kind of farming; and the reason is the time frame of an orchard. With this line of work, you are in business for the long haul, and you don't plant apple trees unless you are pretty sure you have a market for the apples ten years down the line. You can reduce your dairy herd by one-third next year, or your flock of hens, but how do you reduce your orchard by one-third—except by destroying it? You can't quickly double your size either.

In 1989 the *Concord Monitor* heralded a milestone in the long traditions of Gould Hill. First, the five successive generations of ownership by the

Gould family, stretching back to the middle of the eighteenth century; and this year, said the newspaper, "the Gould Hill Orchard in Contoocook celebrates its 50th year of Leadbeater family stewardship." The paper was saluting an old family apple farm on a craggy New England hilltop, and the underlying theme was simple and a bit too familiar: there are not many of these institutions left anymore. "Passed from father to son," said the paper, "the orchard is the epitome of a family farm, and Gould Hill itself the epitome of New England." A decade later, in 1999 and the sixtieth year of their stewardship, the Leadbeaters' Gould Hill Orchards was honored as a New Hampshire Farm of Distinction. The citation said that "the honor recognizes farms which present an image of quality and careful stewardship of the land."

### Dwarfs and Pests

Once upon a time, a typical orchard on a typical American family farm consisted of a few dozen trees of a dozen or more varieties, always carefully planted on a grid pattern in the flatlands of the Midwest, but in New England sometimes haphazardly scattered, wherever space and soil permitted. Such trees typically just grew larger and larger each year, for more than half a century, until, far along in life and often not well taken care of, they started to get smaller: old gnarled and unkempt limbs began to peel off and branches broke, perhaps the trunk hollowed out, and the tree entered a fifty-year period of slow death, piece by piece, limb by limb, but still pouring down apples. Such are the trees I grew up with on my family's farm. They are all well over a hundred years old now, though more than half the originals are gone completely and the ones still standing have lost not only huge limbs but entire halves. They are not growing but they are still living, though they have been dying steadily too for many decades, and most of them are still stubbornly bearing apples, year after year. Such too are the abandoned orchards one still sees here and there across the countryside: aged trees, weirdly warped and gnarled and misshapen, huge jagged limbs pointing high and far and to the four winds. They don't make them like that anymore.

Indeed they don't, and there are reasons. It is not just that it takes a lot of time to make a big apple tree. The fact is that those who depend on apple trees for a living don't really want those old bony trees that some remember so fondly. In commercial orchards they are being cut down and bulldozed out, making way for small trees and close planting. Although it is the root-stock that determines the eventual size of the mature tree, yet, miraculously, this has no effect upon the size or quality of the apples. At Gould Hill some of the trees newly set out this spring are on sixteen-foot rows, and the trees are as little as six feet apart—which puts as many as 450 trees on a single acre. Many of the dwarf trees planted in recent years are supported by stakes or trellises, somewhat like grapevines, for the vigorous young trees are capable of bearing more fruit than their slim branches can support.

So why dwarf trees? I talked with Erick Leadbeater about this one day, and I learned how a fruit farmer thinks about these things. For one thing, dwarf trees come into fruiting much younger, so growers can plan their operations within a shorter time frame, and respond more quickly to a shifting and volatile market. Also, a smaller tree is easier to check for pests and easier to cover adequately with pesticide, sometimes on an individual basis, without unnecessary waste and spilling. For aesthetic reasons we may like to see big apple trees around the yard, but that is not the apple farmer's model. For him, appearance is a matter of apples, not trees. Erick points out that a small tree generally exposes a larger percentage of its fruit to the sun; and more sun makes better-colored and better-tasting apples. He smiles and adds that "picking apples from a small tree is easier and safer: you can keep both feet on the ground."

I wondered whether an orchard of large apple trees would produce more apples than the same-size orchard of dwarf trees. Erick guessed it would, since there would be more total tree surface, but he also believed that the apples would not be up to the same average quality. The question prompted him to make another point: "All that wood in the large tree is wasted energy, wasted nutrients. We're in the fruit business, not the wood business." None of this leaves much room for sentiment, although sentiment may help save some of the great old trees at Gould Hill. There is a handsome orchard section of veteran trees, planted by Robert Gould, all still bearing well. One splendid and spreading giant McIntosh among them is fondly known as "The Wedding Tree." Apples are love tokens, after all, and under the spring leaves and blossoms of this old and lordly tree two Leadbeater daughters have spoken their marriage vows, and perhaps that benign setting conveyed a blessing that may bear fruit in future generations of family apple farmers.

Dwarf trees are also easier to control and prune. During winter months a fruit grower has a brief respite from daily farming concerns, such as a dairy or chicken farmer does not, but he still spends much winter time in the orchard. Pruning trees is a major task, and Erick usually hires some assistance for this. Left to its own strategies an apple tree may smother itself with leaves and small branches, leading to poor fruit and an unhealthy tree. From a tree's perspective, it might be said that pruning, and the wounds that it leaves, alarms the tree into concentrating its energies on producing fruited offspring, rather than more leaves and branches. In the spring of 2001, Erick Leadbeater, having already suffered a heart attack, realized that he could not manage everything, so he hired Steve Gatcombe as orchard manager. Steve brought with him his family and twenty years of apple experience—planting trees, selling apples, spraying and pruning skills—and this arrangement enabled Erick to back off the workload just a bit. At least, that is what he said at the time. Based on what I have observed, here and elsewhere, I'd say that farmers very rarely back off much from the workload that they have accustomed themselves to.

Erick keeps experimenting in his new plantings with different varieties on different kinds of dwarfing stock—that is, the root upon which the new young tree is grafted. Different rootstocks have different growth habits and response to soil conditions, and they impose different restrictions on the eventual size of the tree. But always the orchardist is working with an absolute law of nature: the rootstock determines the potential maximum size of the tree, and the scion grafted to that root determines the variety of apple tree. Erick is always looking for the best combination of rootstock, apple variety, soil conditions, and the way different combinations respond to his particular hillside and hilltop locations and weather. There are innumerable combinations, and he expects that he may almost understand which combinations for which varieties on which sites are best for Gould Hill at about the time the market shifts and upsets his planning.

Erick and I now walk among new young trees and talk about Integrated Pest Management (IPM), which is the official name for the complex bag of tricks whereby modern orchardists endeavor to keep pests at bay, to keep their orchards healthy, and to minimize spraying. "Farmers dislike spraying much more than customers," he says, because it's environmentally hazardous, it's costly and dangerous, it takes time, and there may be unintended consequences; so every farmer has a major vested interest in minimizing it. Erick was once readying himself to become an organic orchardist, but he became disillusioned with that approach to apple growing, and now he goes so far as to say he thinks it is ecologically irresponsible. It is much too formulaic, he says, "farming with a set recipe—do this, don't do that—rather than with pinpoint scientific judgment." You need sensitivity to a host of changing factors, he says, including the unintended effects. Like everything else in farming, this turns out to be a complicated story, but Erick gave me a simple example: he is proud of the earthworm population in his orchard; they are good for the soil, of course, but are especially essential, he says, for "chewing up the leaf debris that harbors apple scab." Now, sulfur, he tells me, a natural product, is widely used as a fungicide by organic growers, and it is extremely hard on earthworms. Should it be used? Not in his orchards.

Erick uses sprays, some toxic, some benign, in accordance with IPM standards, at different times for any one of many reasons: for insects (when he has documented an outbreak), for scab, for fertilizing, for fruit thinning, and sometimes to hasten ripening to get certain tart apples for early cider. We stop at one of his insect traps, a bright red croquet ball suspended by a string on an apple tree. It is smeared with a sticky flypaper substance, and he counts the maggot flies he has caught. They come out of the ground, where they pupate, usually after a rain, and are attracted by the bright red ball, supposing it to be an apple. Their sole mission in life is to mate, land on an apple, pierce its skin, and lay an egg. The maggot that hatches then eats its way inside the apple. Erick's decision to spray will be made on the basis of how many flies he catches in a specified area within a specified time. Altogether, he estimates that he sprays about one-third as much as his father did, and that he achieves better controls, and with less toxic chemicals. Another New Hampshire apple grower, Elwin Hardy, now in his eighties, told me that in the 1940s they sprayed regularly every week, now only a few times a season. Today's fruit growers are extremely alert to weather conditions, to matters of timing, dosage, side effects, and they also get expert consultant advice, have a larger choice of sprays, and can tune in on a far better understanding of pest life cycles and how to protect pest predators. Certain kinds of spraying remain essential in the Northeast, Erick says, but not everywhere in the country, for the best conditions for growing apples are probably to be found in an irrigated desert. And that is precisely why western Washington State dominates the U.S. apple market. Erick's maxim for pest management: "Keep lots of tools in the toolbox, use them only when you know you have to, and no more than necessary, and very carefully, and consider every one of the known effects of the spray."

*Summer Fruit*

It is May and apple blossoms are in the air. Dozens of hives of bees have been brought to Gould Hill to make honey (as the bees hope) and to massively cross-pollinate four thousand apple trees (as the Leadbeaters hope). Bees are incredibly smart but single-minded and lacking in imagination, often unhelpfully flying right back to the very same tree after unpacking their nectar and pollen in the hive. But with blossoms so prolific they may get careless or indifferent, or drunk or confused, and try another nearby tree, thus accidentally dropping pollen grains on another variety, where they will do their appointed job. These trees are deliberately planted so that, whenever possible, there are at least three varieties within every fifty-foot radius, especially among those varieties which absolutely require cross-pollination; and the orchard is also speckled with crab apple trees, which are notably good pollinators. The strategy here is to induce the bees to do a massive job of cross-pollination of the different varieties, aiming at a fruit set so thick that it will have to be drastically thinned.

Think of a tree, any tree, Erick says, as having the potential for a certain maximum weight of fruit—as determined by its variety, size, condition, the nutrients available, weather, and so on. Now, he says, "assuming the tree is fully pollinated you can have that amount of fruit in small apples, less efficient to handle and with virtually no market, or in fewer but larger and better apples. Timely thinning of the fruit is what makes the difference." He points to several young trees loaded to their tips with marble-sized apples (this is now mid-May): "If all those apples were allowed to develop it would break the branches and probably wreck the tree. And if the tree survived it would not have much fruit next year." I am about to learn a simple and important fact about fruit growing: it is in early June that next year's bearing buds are formed, and if there are too many apples forming this year there are insufficient nutrients for a good crop of next year's buds. That is the heart of the reason why many apple trees left to their own ways tend to bear only on alternate years. Thinning the fruit drastically and in time tricks the tree into bearing again next year—though some varieties are very hard to trick.

At Gould Hill they thin the apples with careful applications of a spray developed for the purpose, hoping to eliminate maybe three-quarters of the newly formed apples before they reach thumbnail size. The peach trees, however, far fewer in number, are still thinned by hand, because no spray does what Erick and Susan regard as a satisfactory job. Their peaches are a late-summer specialty crop, and they know exactly what they want the trees to bear. They are thinned not just once but continually, the fruit monitored carefully for size until well into July. "Thinning fruit is an art, not a science," Erick says. "If you think like a tree, then no matter how tasty an apple or a peach is to us, it's just a tree's way of producing seeds, the more the better; it's just a seed package." The grower aims to coerce the trees into producing fewer seeds but in bigger and better packages.

By late July the peach packages are ripening, and Susan Leadbeater is triumphantly in charge of this retail operation when the store opens for the season. It is obvious that she loves the role, and loves the product, and is proud of it. Not hard. Sixteen varieties of tree-ripened New Hampshire peaches. What can one say? During late summer one finds oneself returning to Gould Hill again and again, and some customers return year after year to do what they and their parents have always done: buy a bushel of peaches for canning. But New Hampshire is not natural peach country. "It's marginal," Susan tells me, adding that they may lose 10 percent of their peach trees each year without knowing exactly why. "So you can blame what you want to"—cold December, wet March, too much snow, too little snow. "We just plant more trees and go on," she says.

When you hang around the store in the summer you sense that many customers approach the peaches as the rare and fragile delicacy they are. The selling and display area in the barn and attachment is a cheerful medley of miscellaneous farm products, craft shop, and museum. In a casual glance around I see peaches, apples, seasonal garden produce, cider, baked goods, an antique pie cupboard full of fresh pies, jams and jellies and mustards, many sorts of crafty things with apple motifs, also a collection of miscellaneous historical fruit-growing paraphernalia, such as apple peelers, long-handled apple pickers, old cider barrels, apple scalers, pictures and clippings on the walls, small cider presses, old stencils for painting the Gould Hill and apple variety name on apple barrels. The environment around here gets richer and thicker as the harvest season advances, and in a few months there will be more than twenty-five varieties of apples to pick from.

Already by the first of August at least a small portion of the public is hungry once more for the juicy crunch of a fresh apple. Summer apples now occupy only a very tiny niche in the northern retail apple market. Erick tells me that people's tastes in apples have changed noticeably even within his own lifetime. And it's not just color and appearance, he says: crispness seems to have superseded both flavor and other textures as a criterion. "Anything that is not very firm and crisp is just not regarded as a decent eating apple," he says. It is early August and we are looking at the Gould Hill display of half a dozen kinds of summer apples. Well, they are very crisp, but they also strike me as too tart and a bit green. Do I misremember all the wonderful mellow summer apples of fifty summers ago? Probably not, but what I am tasting here is one of the commercial dilemmas with summer apples: harvest them at their best, when they are still firm but no longer hard, and they will last but a day or two. A farmer can hardly afford to do that. If the customer expects summer apples to be as crisp as fall apples, they will have to be picked while still hard and a bit green. Trouble is, summer apples, unlike many fall apples, do their best final ripening on the tree, in late July or August, and are at their peak for a very short time, indeed, for only a few days, if not refrigerated. Erick remarks that a Yellow Transparent is at its peak for about six hours!

Only a relatively small number of summer apple varieties are now grown commercially, though researchers keep developing new ones, seeking the right combination of taste and texture and staying power. For good reasons, heirloom varieties still endure, beloved as many still are on some old farmsteads. When planted commercially, these gallant old specimens are usually tucked off in a small corner of a large orchard: Yellow Transparent, Duchess of Oldenberg, Gravenstein, Red Astrachan, Early Harvest, and a few others. Most of these apples, if taken at their prime, make superb sauce, and good pies, and excellent eating.

Erick's remark about crispness calls attention to the fact that today's public—no longer chiefly a rural public—has a taste formed by fall apples and by their naturally crisp texture. Summer apples at their best are a different thing, and have gentler and more subtle textures; coming to appreciate them is a different kind of pleasure, one to which very few people now have adequate access. In the days of many farmers and when most farms had an orchard and probably several large trees of each summer variety, there was usually a surfeit of summer apples, bushels of them to spare, and the extras often went to the pigs to be recycled into pork. Only those apples in prime condition and at perfect ripeness would be used by the family, a tiny fraction of the total crop. That, indeed, was the principal reason for the enormous success and importance of summer apples in generations past. They were not and were never expected to be stored, nor sold nor shipped, but were harvested on a daily basis, very selectively, and used immediately on the farm and by the neighbors.

Many of us believe that an ancient rule still holds: a summer apple is at its prime just before it would naturally fall from the tree—a tree, that is, not sprayed with a fruit drop retardant. For harvesting quantities of them, as for example for sauce, the method used and kept unchanged for a hundred years on my family's Michigan farm, and the method I still use today on my New Hampshire Lodi trees, is very simple: you shake the tree limbs gently, and then collect and immediately use only the prime apples of those that fall, and let the others lie. Shake a little harder, and the falling apples will include slightly tarter ones to add summer zing to the sauce.

### A Rhapsody of Apples

Summer apples, autumn apples, cider apples, winter apples from cellar storage—from earliest colonial days, apples have seemed to symbolize and embody the rich promise of America. Apple growing and cider making had been widely practiced and promoted for centuries in Europe before the colonists left for America, but publicity was directed not to the peasants or working people but to gentlemen, who owned the land and the cider presses. In 1597, just a decade before the Pilgrims left England for a temporary stay in Holland, John Gerarde published his *Herball,* which enthusiastically explored "the vertues" of apples and recommended planting "tame and graffed Apple trees," an idea that he urged on "Gentlemen that have land and living," as he put it. "Forward in the name of God," he advised, "graffe, set, plant and nourish up trees in every corner of your grounds, the labour is small, the cost is nothing, the commoditie is great, your selves shall have plentie. . . . and God shall reward your good mindes and diligence."[63] If the future colonists read things like this, as some might well have, most of them could not *do* anything about it—until they got to the American shores. In America, apple trees were to be one more asset available to almost everyone.

According to a reasonably reliable tradition the first apple orchard planted by European colonists in this country was the work of William Blaxton somewhere near the present intersection of Charles and Beacon Streets at the base of what is now Beacon Hill in Boston. This was about 1625, and well before the beginning of the major colonial settlement in that region. Blaxton went on to what became Providence, Rhode Island, and planted the first orchard there too, perhaps taking scions from Boston. A hundred years later some of his Boston trees were still bearing. In the early decades of the New England colonial settlements apple orchards quickly became common, and it was soon realized that New England provided a good climate for apple trees. One supposes that most of these started as seedling orchards and then the trees with poor fruit, which would have been most of them, were grafted with a better variety, just as Gerarde and several other contemporary authors had recommended.

All the horticulture literature of the time recommended various grafting techniques, and almost all of these had been known for thousands of years. It is therefore strange that the myth persists and is often repeated as fact that early American orchards were composed of seed-grown trees. A book on my desk states that "orchards planted with seed-gown rather than grafted trees were the rule in America until early in the nineteenth century." It seems implausible on the face of it, and many colonial records and diaries refer to grafting as routine. Moreover, grafting is in fact relatively easy to do, and many books available to early Americans describe techniques in detail, going back to the Roman Marcus Cato's book on farming written about 160 B.C. Relatively few seed-grown trees are worth the trouble of caring for them (though some inedible wild apples are excellent ingredients for cider making), but myths and imagination about them are probably more interesting and potent than the facts. Indeed, they have successfully transformed the prosaic John Chapman (1774–1845) of Massachusetts into the poetic Johnny Appleseed of the Midwest, and who is to complain about that?

Not only were apples in this country as soon as the colonists were, they were early and for centuries thereafter being promoted with patriotic zeal. The assumption took hold that an apple orchard or, more generally, a fruit orchard, should be an integral part of every family farm, and this idea spread from New England across all the northern states as farming moved inland. "Our fruit-Trees prosper abundantly," wrote John Josselyn in the middle of the seventeenth century, "the Countrey is replenished with fair and large orchards."[64] The American orchard didn't just grow—it was fertilized with propaganda: apples are not only good for the palate, good for health, but an abundance of fruit orchards is itself good for society, an affirmation of stable values. An orchard and garden, declared one eighteenth-century writer, are "the poetry of common life." Orchards, said another, give country homes "an air of comfort and modest thrift."

Typically, James Thacher declared in *The American Orchardist* (1825) that "in the whole department of rural economy, there is not a more noble, interesting, and beautiful exhibition, than a fruit orchard. . . ."[65] Henry French of Exeter, New Hampshire, wrote in his agriculture report for 1849 of the important stabilizing effects of apple growing: "An influence is much needed in New England to counter-balance the roving propensity of her people," he said. "He who has planted a tree, will he not desire to eat of the fruit thereof? and he whose father has raised it, will he not feel it to be almost sacrilege to give it into the hands of strangers?"[66] Horace Greeley, with typical nineteenth-century verbosity, amplified the rhapsody on orchards: "If I were asked to say what single aspect of our economic condition most strikingly and favorably distinguished the people of our Northern States from those of most if not all other countries which I have traversed, I would point at once to the fruit trees which so generally diversify every little as well as larger farm . . . [and are found] in every village, and in the suburbs and outskirts of every city."[67]

One realizes that all this orchardy sentiment was not only authentic pleading on behalf of the pleasures of apples but sometimes special pleading on behalf of the pleasures of hard cider. Cider had become the national beverage, true, but important symbolism was in play as well. Fruit orchards had historically been associated in Europe primarily with privilege, leisure, and the gentleman's life, and this carried with it the idea of an orchard as a source of inspiration and uplift or, as one historian put it, that cultivating an orchard "offers intellectual, even spiritual benefits befitting an enlightened citizenry." Hence, the orchard as "the poetry of common life." The abundance of American land promised once more that the orchard too would be a great equalizer, that even the poorest American family could have, and so should have, what only the rich had in Europe.

The apple rhapsody naturally lent itself to commercial production of apples for the burgeoning city populace, a trend already evolving two hundred years ago, and accelerating throughout the entire nineteenth century. Marketing possibilities in turn, often local and small, encouraged the discovery, creation, and promotion of one new apple variety after another— it became a great form of advertising—and long before the century's end there were a thousand varieties to be found. Far too many said one blunt grower already in 1886: "Multiplicity of varieties works as great damage to orchards as polygamy does to the Mormons, and you want to avoid it." He suggested that nine varieties was about the right number for most growers.

By this time American apples, tons and tons of them—including apples from Gould's New Hampshire farm—carefully surrounded with ice, were being delivered in shiploads to Europe, and also sent in railroad cars to almost every major American city. Commercial orchards were rapidly multiplying throughout the country, and with them came entirely new competitive market pressures—shipping, advertising, storing, as well as a large consumer base much further removed from the experience of the farm than ever before. Very soon these factors drastically cut down the total number of apple varieties readily available and widely known. Within just one generation around the turn of the twentieth century, the American fruit scene shifted: rather than a large mix of small family farms each selling the surplus from its small orchard, full-time orchardists producing only apples, in large amounts and in limited varieties, came to dominate the apple market. Robert Gould at the newly planted Gould Hill Orchards was one of them. Within thirty years from the time when there had been alleged to be too many varieties, Liberty Hyde Bailey, at the time surely the country's best horticulture spokesman, had this to say in 1915 in his major work, *The Principles of Fruit-Growing*:

It is much to be desired that the fruit-garden shall return to men's minds, with its personal appeal and its collections of many choice varieties, even the names of which are now unknown to the fruit-loving public. . . . The commercial market ideals have come to be controlling, and most fruit-eaters have never eaten a first-class apple or pear or peach, and do not know what such fruits are; and the names of the choice varieties have mostly dropped from the lists of nursery-men. All this is as much to be deplored as a loss of standards of excellence in literature and music, for it is an expression of a lack of resources and failure of sensitiveness.[68]

## Cider's Career

New Hampshire's first historian, Jeremy Belknap, writing late in the eighteenth century, put it simply: "Among husbandmen, cyder is their common drink." It is not clear whether the Reverend Belknap, a clergyman and scholar who owned a farm, thought of himself as a husbandman. Probably. "Cider" meant in colonial days, and in England still means, what we commonly call hard cider, the fermented and mildly alcoholic beverage made from what they called apple juice, and we call cider. Some orchardists today are eager to retain or recapture the original meaning of "cider," and they carefully use the term "sweet cider" for the fresh unprocessed product. At any rate, cider in the original and fermented sense early became America's beverage of choice. Initially, the colonists would have preferred beer, which they had been accustomed to in Europe, and which was why even the *Mayflower* had barley seed aboard. Belknap, who stated that the healthiest beverage of all was water, did appear to regret that "malt liquor is not so frequent as its wholesomeness deserves." But English barley did not thrive in coastal New England (too cold, for one thing, and sandy soil too poor) or Virginia (too hot, for one thing, and sandy soil too poor); so cider became the colonial default beverage, especially in New England, where many apple varieties thrived.

Unfortunately, it took some years to get an orchard into production, so in the absence of beer the first default beverage, especially in the newly founded inland towns where the orchards were still young, was often rum. Belknap was not pleased: "In traveling up the country it affords pleasure to observe the various articles of produce and manufacture coming to market; but in traveling down the country, it is equally disgustful to meet the same teams returning, loaded with casks of rum. . . ." Since moving large amounts of liquid was expensive and troublesome, as the inland towns were settled it fell to hard cider to wean early Americans from rum.

Thus for hundreds of years, almost every New England farm had a sizable orchard of up to several dozen trees or so, and every neighborhood had a cider press, and everyone knew how to ferment the cider, and how to store it away in barrels. At about the time of the American Revolution, according to one scholar's calculation, there was one cider press for every ten New England families. It appears from scattered inventories and diaries of this time that enormous quantities of cider were made and consumed, and often used for barter or for paying debts, as had been done in Europe since the thirteenth century. Cider was cheap and easy to make and keep, and it usually had about the alcoholic content of strong beer, though sometimes honey or maple sugar was added to the fermenting, which raised the eventual alcoholic level. Up to six or ten barrels per family was not unusual, a yearly average of thirty-five to forty gallons for every man, woman, and child, by one careful estimate. John Adams's diary indicates that when he was home in Braintree he had a large tankard of cider every morning, and often in the evening. He sometimes credited his health to it, and he lived to ninety-one. Apple brandy, namely distilled cider, was also a common beverage, one of several favorite "spiritous liquors," applejack, made by freezing cider, being another. Cider making spread easily from the Atlantic Coast to the South and to the Midwest, and by the early nineteenth century it was a solid American rural tradition. Indeed, from the time the young George Washington first ran for public office in 1758 and had his friends pass out cider and other beverages on election day, and for more than a hundred years thereafter, cider was often generously distributed on election day. (Voter turnout was better in those days than today, and politicians have wondered why.)

To the casual observer, cider making appears to be a rather direct and earthy farm task; it is more transparent, perhaps, than some other mechanized farm operations, such as milking cows, or processing eggs, or extracting water from maple sap with a reverse osmosis machine—to pick examples that I have become familiar with. A cider press does a straightforward job, and you can take in the process with a long glance, and, moreover, that glance leaves you quite willing to hang around and sample the end product. Erick pours the selected apples onto a conveyor belt where a series of swiftly moving brushes clean and shine them up, and meanwhile he or an assistant picks out any apple not up to grade as it rolls past. The apples disappear into the maw of a grinder that reduces them to a juicy pulp of raw applesauce, which goes automatically into a large holder. Close at hand is the press itself, and on it another operator, frequently orchard manager Steve Gatcombe, places a wooden frame, about thirty inches square and three inches deep, and lined with a large clean cloth. Handling a large flexible hose, he directs several gallons of soupy sauce (properly known as pomace) into the lined tray and then neatly folds it in; another frame and cloth is placed on top of the first, filled with pomace and folded in, then another filled and folded, and another, and so on—eventually a high stack of juicy frames all loaded with now dripping pomace, but all of which is now completely folded neatly inside the cloths inside the frames. Flick a switch and the press descends upon the whole stack, very slowly, irresistibly, hydraulically powered, pressing, pressing, squeezing, squeezing. The press applies more and more pressure, but patiently, slowly, allowing the juice to ooze through the cloths, run into troughs, and be piped away to the holding tank. There it waits a few minutes, allowing bits of pulp to settle to the bottom, and is then led through a hose to fill plastic jugs, one at a time, which are stacked on a dolly and promptly wheeled into the cooler. Observing all this makes you thirsty, and you start looking around for a glass, a paper cup, anything to grab a taste of this stuff; and you are not disappointed. These were the right apples in the right order!

For centuries, Yankee ingenuity was poured into devising effective systems, with pulleys and gears, to turn the apple grinders and power the presses. Often cider presses used waterpower, available in abundance in grist and lumber mills already established; but sometimes it was animal power on a treadmill or, more commonly, simply a patient horse walking in a large circle pulling a long arm to tighten a screw that pressed the cider. And sometimes too it was just well-contrived hand power, as in the small presses still in use today. But the days of cider by the barrel in nearly every home appear to be history. In the presidential campaign of 1840 the log cabin and cider barrel served as symbols of traditional American values. But times change. Shortly thereafter the temperance movement, led by teetotalers, moved into full stride, and the campaign against alcohol abuse soon extended to cider as well. Indeed, cider was a much more conspicuous symbol than beer or rum or other distilled spirits, and the cider mill on the brook and cider barrel in the basement became fat and easy targets. Thus the fruit of passion and romance and fable, the very gift of the gods, became widely demonized. Before the temperance campaign had spent itself, literally thousands of healthy American apple orchards were sent down the road to neglect and ruin. Indeed, by the beginning of the twentieth century the very word "cider" had been shorn of its original (hard cider) meaning. And now, a century later, the worry is that even sweet cider may also be stripped of its original tang.

One of New Hampshire's largest apple growers, considering the prospect of new cider regulations and the likelihood that large chain groceries will refuse to buy unpasteurized cider, has just installed $100,000 worth of cider pasteurizing equipment. To justify that kind of expense, a cider maker has to deal in very large quantities, which raises two problems from the point of view of cider craftsmen like Erick Leadbeater: one is marketing that much cider, and the other is the difficulty of precisely monitoring the cider "recipe," the mixture and ripeness of apple varieties to produce the best possible cider at each moment of the advancing season—which is where the cider maker's pride in his craft comes in.

I am listening to a discussion on New Hampshire Public Radio; it is cider season, and Erick Leadbeater is being interviewed. In the face of the current pasteurization movement, what is Gould Hill planning to do? the interviewer wishes to know. Erick reports matter-of-factly that his farm has been selling cider since the eighteenth century, and he does not know of any problems with it. Each year over a thousand bushels of his apples go into cider, which is sold at the farm and at a number of local stores. Since he does not use manure in his orchard, there is almost no chance of *E. coli* contamination, several dozen cases of which, from a California orchard, had triggered the pasteurization movement. "There are two ways to deal with the threat of contamination," he says. "One is preventively, by very high standards in your orchard, in the cleaning of apples and equipment, and the making of cider; the other way is to be perhaps less scrupulous about these things and purify the product by pasteurization. We prefer to follow the first way." Gould Hill cider apples are handpicked, not drops, they are all mechanically cleaned, and picked over again before being ground for cider. Afterward, the press is dismantled, and every surface and piece of it is blasted clean with superheated steam.

But what if it becomes illegal to sell raw cider? the interviewer asks. Erick's position is quietly adamant: "To pasteurize the quality cider we make would be a more expensive way to make an inferior product, for which there would be a smaller market. We wouldn't do that." I am guessing that what he is also thinking is, We could not betray the heritage of Gould Hill in that way—rather, drop the cider entirely. Later, the interview turns to broader issues of farming, and I hear Erick say: "Farming is dying out in the urban shadow. Little things are picking away at it, one by one, and slowly killing it. Cider is just one of these."

Cider remains, of course, a much loved beverage, and for those who have the taste for it, all cider is now enhanced with the faint tang of irony: hard cider, long the target of the temperance and prohibition movements, carries only the standardized fine-print alcoholic warning to pregnant women, whereas sweet and unpasteurized cider, even the best and most carefully made with steam-cleaned equipment, is required by federal regulation to bear a conspicuous label declaring to one and all that it may be dangerous to drink.

### Tree to Storage

What do you do with ten or fifteen thousand bushels of apples? That's about enough to take care of nearby Concord, New Hampshire, and surrounding towns for an entire year; but that, of course, is not where most of them will go. The apple market, especially for the grower with both a retail and a wholesale component, is a curious and shifty scene. Next year the folks in Concord, for example, though there are eighty-five varieties raised right next door, will munch apples from six or eight other states besides New Hampshire, and from at least half a dozen foreign countries as well. The price will not be bad, but the quality may vary from excellent to poor. One wrinkle here is that the public today is more attuned than formerly to buying apples at the grocery store, rather than at an orchard, for the stores themselves, typically large chains, now have facilities for keeping and displaying more varieties of apples under better conditions than formerly, and with the effectiveness of modern storage capabilities, apple customers think less seasonally than they once did, seldom packing several bushels into their (probably heated) basement or garage. Another wrinkle is that the stores themselves are now also attuned to the ease and predictability of purchasing from large contractors handling apples from worldwide sources, and may thus entirely bypass local orchards.

Gould Hill Orchards is both a wholesale and a retail enterprise, and the farm store is typically open daily from early August, when the first apples and peaches ripen, to about Thanksgiving Day, when the pumpkins freeze. There are over eighty varieties of apples here, and at the height of the season in October twenty-five to forty are arrayed for sale at one time. Retail business accounts for about a third to a half of the Gould Hill apples, and this includes daily sales at the farm store, pick your own, apples made into cider, sometimes salvage from drops, and so on. The rest are put into storage and sold wholesale sometime during the winter. I find it satisfying to learn that many Gould Hill McIntosh apples eventually end up in Scotland, just as they did a hundred years ago. Today they are known there as McReds.

Apples on a given tree do not all ripen simultaneously, and at least two and sometimes three pickings may be required during the autumn. The right time for picking, which varies with each variety and sometimes with the plan for handling the fruit after picking, is determined by a combination of things, chiefly the calendar, the color of the fruit, and the weather. The Leadbeaters keep three regular pickers busy most of the time for about two months. A good eye is essential, and swift hands and a strong back much to be desired. It is no surprise that a Seattle company is even now working on creating a robotic apple picker. It is envisioned as rolling through the orchards, octopus-like, with sets of swiveling, retractable arms equipped with programmable electric eyes that can detect and respond to the exact color and shape of objects. Do we need it? We shall probably get it.

As I walk through the October orchard with Erick I can't help wondering about all the good-looking and well-formed apples strewn under the trees: drops, they are called, and it seems like a lot of wonderful fruit just wasting in the grass. I ask what will happen to them. "Most years most of them will stay right there for now," he said. "Oh, sometimes some of them will be salvaged." I suspect Erick is taking a deliberately hard-headed approach to my question. This is not a matter of sentiment. Successful farming, I am reminded again, especially farming on a family-sized scale such as this, is often a matter of working carefully on the margins, and with precise calculation. In this case it is a matter of finding a ready market that pays more than the cost of handling the drops, including the cost of finding and hiring laborers to pick up and sort the fallen apples. The best prospect—usually the only one—is the juice market, and Erick tells me that this year his break-even point for juice apples would be at about five or six cents per pound: if he can find a buyer paying more than that, and if he can make the arrangements, and if the weather holds, then he might go for it. In the 1970s, he tells me, such drops often brought ten cents a pound.

I am suddenly aware again of the long arm of the global market. For example, some countries have subsidy programs whereby their governments buy up their growers' surplus and sell it on the world market, which may turn out to be less than a New Hampshire apple farmer's break-even point. Also, in the 1990s China, half a world away, made a major commitment to apple farming, and now has more apple trees than the United States; these orchards are just now entering serious production, and already the Chinese are reported to virtually own the world's apple juice concentrate business. Consequently, trees in New Zealand, Africa, South America, or China are directly linked to the fate of the Northern Spies I see lying under the Leadbeaters' trees. To appreciate this, I select and test one of the fallen Spies. It still has a good snap and is just beginning to mellow out, and to me is even tastier than the last one I had directly from a tree.

Different varieties of apples have different habits of ripening and of responding to different conditions of storage. Usually, an apple is not yet in peak eating condition when it is picked, and in any case it may face months of storage before being eaten. So nice questions arise: precisely what kind of storage environment is best, and for how long, for what variety of apple, and picked and stored at what point in its own normal ripening schedule? Much research goes into these questions. Roughly, this is the apple's natural behavior: as it ripens (whether on the tree or off, but generally faster when off), its starches turn to sugars, its skin loses its green chlorophyll, its acidity drops, its flesh begins to soften. To accomplish this, the apple takes in oxygen through tiny holes in its skin, it emits carbon dioxide (and a sweet fragrance as well), and it also emits ethylene gas, which in turn (somewhat mysteriously) facilitates this whole process. The waxy surface bloom of a mature apple is a skin sealer, part of whose business is to retard these processes.

Since Roman times it has been known that the ripening process is slowed by cold storage and by close confinement. In close confinement the oxygen is used up and carbon dioxide accumulates—though the Romans wouldn't have put it that way. Consequently, apples have been stored in cool caves, buried in the ground, immersed in cold water, covered with sawdust, surrounded with ice, wrapped in paper, and, most commonly until about fifty years ago, packed into closed barrels—all to slow the process. And all such methods work to some extent. Now that most of the various components of ripening are far better known, it has become possible to slow them much more effectively and in some cases virtually stop them entirely for long periods of time. The conventional and historical process of cold storage has been refined, during the last forty years, into what is called simply Controlled Atmosphere, or CA.

Now it is late October, a chill day, and I am about to learn something about apple storage, for I have been recruited for one of the final acts of the growing season, namely, sealing the door of the CA storage chamber. It was twenty years ago that the Leadbeaters built this giant storage shed, which includes a loading, packing, and work area for apples, also a huge cold room where thousands of bushels of apples are kept in a very cold but otherwise uncontrolled atmosphere. Apples give off heat from the chemistry of their ripening process, so no artificial heat is ever needed in this insulated building, even in the dead of New England winter. Within the building are also several smaller chambers, the CA rooms, which can be completely sealed off and made airtight. As he sets about the closing task Erick tells me that no one in New England builds a CA facility anymore, mainly because the apples that come out of CA storage in the spring or summer now face the global assault of fresh-picked apples from the Southern Hemisphere, South America and New Zealand especially. The marketing rules have changed since this state-of-the-art storage facility was built.

Now Steve Gatcombe, Erick's farm manager, joins us to assist in this project, and we peer into the inner chamber: it is a vast and high room completely lined with foam insulation, and chockablock with fifteen-bushel bins of apples, piled eight high, stack after stack, hundreds of bins. We now proceed to line the edges of the chamber's huge door with sealing caulk. The tools we handle are cold to the touch, for this entire building is already refrigerated. Erick then climbs onto the forklift with which all the apple bins are handled in this facility, then lifts the door with its prongs and eases forward, while Steve and I guide the great door gently into place. We bolt it tight. This leaves only a final small window in the center of the door. When that is closed the system will be activated: the temperature inside will be lowered very close to freezing, thirty-three degrees at most, and nitrogen will be pumped in to drive out the oxygen, cutting it from a normal 21 percent to about 3 percent. A sound apple, Erick reminds me, is a living, breathing thing; we want them to hibernate comfortably, but not die. So the oxygen level is crucial, and even in this dark and cold cave the live apples will suck in what little oxygen is allowed and breathe out carbon dioxide. Too much or too little of these gases and the apples may turn to mush or rot.

Since the apple environment will soon be heavy with carbon dioxide, the excess has to be drawn off, so we review the inlets and outlets for gases and water, and I learn that there is even another water-filled burp valve, to let air in or gas out whenever the outdoor atmospheric pressure rises or drops suddenly, which might threaten the whole airtight system with imploding or exploding. This is all routine stuff for Erick and Steve, one of the autumn chores, but I am duly impressed with this complex and delicate arrangement, and I realize that it needs to be carefully monitored each day and often adjusted. I remember that the last time I stored apples I just wrapped them in newspaper, put them in a box, and brought them down cellar.

So we close the center window and bolt it shut and then turn out the light. Tons of apples are safely tucked in for their long winter's night. The wonder is that the relevant variables and needs for each of the different apple varieties are now very well known, and when the CA system works well the apples are put quietly into a deep sleep, to be wakened when the market calls and the seal is broken. They will emerge still dressed in full autumn bloom, still crisp and sweeter than ever, still the passion fruit.

 *Part Three*

# PROSPECTS

# Chapter 8

# The Ironies of Success

Social fashion, delusion, and propaganda have combined to persuade the public that our agriculture is for the best of reasons the envy of the Modern World. . . . What these men are praising . . . is a disaster that is both agricultural and cultural. . . .

—WENDELL BERRY, *The Unsettling of America* (1977)

Abundant crops and a surfeit of inexpensive food. Surely, one might say, that is an American farming success story. But success is a subtle and coy mistress, and easily panders to selective viewing. Farming "success," whether on a local or national scale, has many sides, many implications, many forms, many obscure costs, and many definitions, and the word itself can seldom be safely deployed without the protection of quotation marks.

For the family farm is no longer an isolated and self-sufficient entity. Everywhere farms are more deeply than ever embedded within communities, economies, within the myriad industries that supply them, and within those that process and market the farm's products. The long American withdrawal from eighteenth-century self-sufficient farming has brought us to a point where it is not merely useful but often necessary to think of the farm-and-food enterprise as a single analytical unit. *Farm-and-food*—that's a big waffling abstraction, of course, but our current economy obliges us to think in these terms, for most of the important issues are systemic ones.

The multitude of intimate relationships between food and farming are as complex as they are important, and they are also the source of the most baffling ironies. It is clear that an ethic of production dominates America's farming, and that an ethic of cheap food dominates the food industry. And these are intimately related, feeding each other. In 1950, average Americans spent over 30 percent of their income on food; in 2000, about 10 percent. In 1950, the farmer received over fifty cents of every food dollar spent; today, less than twenty cents. Consumers spend less of their income on food than ever, and farmers receive a smaller percentage of that lesser portion. Small wonder, therefore, that industrialized agriculture has institutionalized the narrow and seductive idea that productive efficiency is, almost alone, the measure of its success.

In order to fully understand some of this, and to judge it for good or ill, it will help to become familiar with some of the abstractions that now cluster around the farm-and-food nexus. I propose three sets of categories for understanding some—emphasis on *some*—of the elements of farm-and-food dynamics. These three ways of looking at farm-food issues are conceptually independent of each other, but they are connected in that they deal with different aspects of some of the same underlying facts. Thus these three simple models are complementary, different ways of trying to grasp the historical tendencies of that complex enterprise, the farm-food system.

### (1) The Logic of the Farm-Food Industry

In one sense, you can sum up recent decades of farm-and-food industry economics in remarkably few words. For starters, about five big words will do it quite nicely. The words come heavily loaded with complex meanings, and they point to exceedingly sophisticated economic processes. But the words themselves have become almost common currency. The words are these: *specialization, consolidation, contracting, integration, globalization.* Bland and bureaucratic words, every one, but representing inescapable organizational and economic trends in the farm-food picture, processes that accelerate year by year. I am reminded that none of these terms was readily applicable to the majority of American farm operations at, say, the end of World War II; indeed, they are not part of the traditional vocabulary of agriculture. But now they lie near the heart of any portrait of the American farm. Individually, the processes represented by these words may seem unthreatening and not even particularly interesting or newsworthy. Collectively, and released into the marketplace, they become far more ominous.

*Specialization* is the oldest concept here and the easiest to grasp, since it has always been with us in some form or other. If at one time almost every farm produced up to a dozen crops for the market and a half dozen more for home consumption, today most farmers raise just one crop, which they produce and market more knowledgeably and more efficiently than ever. Our farmer is indirectly competing, for markets and for efficiency, with every other farmer specializing in that product—a radically altered rural dynamic, just in itself. In the five years between the end of World War II and 1950 my father raised and sold the following products from his eighty-acre farm: cream, eggs, chickens, veal calves, pigs, beans, string beans, strawberries, potatoes, sugar beets; in addition he raised and used the following crops for his animals' feed: wheat, oats, barley, corn, hay—a total of fifteen farm products, and there was nothing unusual about that. The only such farmers today are probably Amish.

*Consolidation* is the benign word for the harsh process whereby the big fish eat the little fish: large farms, or wholesalers, or processors absorb their smaller neighbors or competitors and so develop economies of scale. It too is a process that has been with us for a long time, but never in such impressive dimensions; and it is to be noted that, of course, it is aided and abetted by farm specialization.

Agricultural economists calculate the percentages of total sales of a particular commodity now consolidated under, say, the four largest processors of that commodity. Professor Heffernan of the University of Missouri has named this percentage "the CR4 rating." Beef, for example, in mid-2003 he assigns a rating of eighty-one, meaning that eighty-one percent of all beef in this country is processed by just four firms (Tyson-IBP, ConAgra Beef, Cargill, and Farmland National). In broilers the CR4 is fifty; pork packing is fifty-nine; pork growing is forty-six; and in many other sectors his CR4 rating runs over fifty, and sometimes to the eighties. Some companies, such as Archer-Daniels-Midland, appear as one of the four in several different sectors. All CR4 ratings are moving rapidly upward, largely undeterred by current applications of antitrust laws.

*Contracting* on a serious scale is a relatively new element in the farming picture, but in a modest way it has long been a minor part of the scene. A farmer, for example, contracts individually with a huge meatpacker to raise ten thousand hogs from ten to two hundred pounds in a set time at a set price per head. The farmer is guaranteed a market price for assuming the risks, and the wholesaler is guaranteed a predictable product—essentially a mode of production that rearranges the risks and benefits. In practice, of course, the farmer is always the weaker partner in the bargain. One-third of all U.S. pork, and more every year, is now finished under such production contracts. Such contracting is becoming common practice for many commodities, including many fruits and vegetables, where it streamlines decision making in planting and harvesting for the farmer, and in transportation and sales for the buyer. (Question: who supervises such contracting between unequal partners, and how are disputes resolved?)

These three—specialization, consolidation, contracting—work smoothly together, and each reinforces the others. The most important thing about these arrangements, and the most easily overlooked, is the fact that each strategy facilitates the others. Together they form a whole much more powerful than the sum of parts. And there is more.

*Integration* is the process whereby both producing and processing come under one ownership: the corporation that packages and ships the carrots also owns the carrot farm. A vertically integrated single corporation may include not only the farm that produces but also the harvester, the wholesaler, the processor, the packager, and the distributor as well; and if one facet of this compound business loses money to meet (or, more likely, to overpower) the competition, the loss can often be made up in another facet of the same business. Such a system usually presupposes a farming world of specialization and consolidation, and frequently employs contracting for some portion (harvesting, shipping) of the integrated business. For farming, such integration is a relatively new phenomenon and it is extremely effective in squeezing the small farmer, without access to these economies of scale, completely out of the market. In all this, the law is astonishingly permissive, and the making of laws is astonishingly responsive to lobbying. A proposal to ban meatpacker ownership of livestock, though passed by the U.S. Senate, was quietly slaughtered in conference committee on the 2002 Farm Bill.

*Globalization* is a new term and, indeed, a rather new phenomenon, so far as farming is concerned. Though peoples and then nations have bought and sold products with each other from time immemorial, the present degree to which agricultural prices and profitability are determined by the world market and its cheap oil-powered transportation is entirely unprecedented. As much as manufacturers, American farmers are in competition with producers from numerous other countries. There, workers' wages are typically lower and, in a competitive world, this wage-cost disadvantage rewards every bit of efficiency (e.g., specialization, etc.) that U.S. farmers and agribusiness can extract from the system. More than that, it rewards externalizing every cost (e.g., pollution) that can be contrived.

Each of these five—specialization, consolidation, contracting, integration, globalization—could by itself appear to be a rather uninteresting process, and by itself not an earth-shaking phenomenon. But recent history shows that these processes run in packs; the pack is where the life is, and when the pack is let loose upon American farmland *it represents altogether a revolutionary presence and force.* Each process enables the others.

Each is powerful alone, as a force in the farm economy, but each also combines with the others to create pressures for radical transformation on the farm. The modes of interaction are complex, but not obscure, and interaction within the pack is stimulated, of course, by the lure of profits. Profits normally derive from greater efficiencies, which may derive from technological innovation (see next section), both on the farm and on every level of transfer of farm products to the dining table.

This network of processes is likely to coil itself slowly around any commodity farmer. The Eccardt Farm (chapter 5), for example, is *specialized*—for them, it's milk or nothing—and they are *consolidated*, three families on one farm, farming neighboring farms. Their milk goes to one of the two processors (fifteen years ago there were ten) that together handle about 80 percent of Northeast milk. No real options there, because for a decade the processor has been *consolidating*, absorbing smaller companies, and vertically *integrating*, by buying out cheese and yogurt factories and fresh milk distributors. (If it loses money on yogurt distribution, it can make it up by paying less for the Eccards' milk.) The company *contracts* with the Eccards (for the milk but not for the price), and cheese from this milk must compete on the *global* market. (There may be a similar situation at the farm supply end, in the purchase of seed and feed, where the farmer may also face consolidated, integrated, globalized corporations.) How much freedom and leverage does a dairy farmer have in this situation?

Consider a nameless apple wholesaler in Washington State: he can buy up the orchards that supply him, then raise the apples at a loss if necessary (though he may have federally subsidized water for irrigation and state-subsidized housing for his pickers), contract out the apple picking, and profit on the storage, processing, and transportation, so as finally to compete with the heavy supply of apples from China and Chile arriving on the market in New York City. This drastically affects the market for apples and the fate of apple farming in New Hampshire (and elsewhere), and it tells us why there is now a housing development on the former apple farm. Is there something wrong with this picture? There are hundreds of such pictures. Shall we call the sum of all gains and losses a success? For whom?

If indeed there is something wrong, if we don't like parts of this picture, can't something be done about it? This is not rocket science. Of course there are points in this system of processes that could be brought under restraining legislative control. And of course there are points where tax policy could reward socially responsible behavior and penalize the other kind.

But is there sufficient political wit or will to do so? Doubtful. Easier for the legislator to turn up at a local parade and make a warm speech about the importance of the family farm. Easier for the Farm Bureau official to tell us about the glories of free enterprise.

## (2) The Logic of Farm Technology

Technology itself, when brought to the farm and given time and opportunity, may express its own callous and bitter logic. To be sure, many technological innovations make life better for farmers, since they ease physical labor and often make it safer and less onerous; but just as surely technology in the aggregate is also a farmer's seducer and his punisher. The logic of farm technology is so simple that its core can be described in a few steps, and it is so cruel and powerful that many past and present family farmers can hardly believe that American capitalism (which most farmers revere) is doing this to them. It is astonishing how much of the last half century of the American family farm experience can be illuminated by putting it in a simple abstract outline.

*Step One*: Suppose a farmer has a certain standard of living, then acquires a new piece of technology (threshing machine, milking machine, computer) that increases his efficiency and thus lowers the unit cost of producing his commodity. The farmer now has a slightly larger profit—to pay for the technology and perhaps provide a margin. This is called progress.

*Step Two*: Other farmers see the advantage of the new technology, and they acquire it too. These farmers' combined efficiencies in production will invariably put more of the commodity on the market.

*Step Three*: The market adjusts to increases in the commodity and the corresponding need for more sales by lowering the price, both at the consumer end and at the production end. (The intervening processors, shippers, distributors may, but need not, be much affected by this—except that they will have more business.) Thus the farmers' income per unit of production falls.

*Step Four*: To maintain his standard of living the farmer expands his operation, as his new technology permits, to produce more units at the now lower price per unit.

*Step Five*: The reduced price per unit squeezes the smaller and less efficient farms, which eventually fade or disappear.

*Result*: Fewer farms, larger farms, all with larger investments and more at risk. And (persuading us that the system is benign), lower prices at the consumer end. Success?

Of course, there are many other results of this logic as well. Fewer farms and larger ones—this has multitudes of social implications for the health of communities, for the economies of small towns, for the ecology of rural areas, for choices available to citizens, and on and on. But whatever personal or policy or political decisions are made about these matters they rarely reach—and are not designed to reach—to the underlying logic at work here, which is in fact *a largely unrestrained and unseen force*, and which almost no modern farmer can evade. The force of this logic results directly from *the combined effect of each individual farmer making perfectly rational decisions* about his own farm's welfare. Because this collective force is so crucial and so powerful, while not at all conspicuous or even visible to all, it deserves its own name, so let us call it simply the *logic of farm technology*. We have to understand that this thing is a ruthless and devouring beast.

It is useful to think of the logic of farm technology, as outlined above, even more abstractly for a moment, as itself a kind of system, machinelike, with nameable inputs and fixed processes and outputs. At the front end of the system, the farmers' end, is any new farm technology—which is the input. Imagine that the "system" runs its course, powered by the logic of farm technology; then speculate for a moment about what morally *ought* to emerge at the other end. In a just and fair world, one might think that the output deriving from the farmer's new technology and his increased productivity *might be* increased profit for the farmer. But one would probably be wrong. Although it is the farmer who has assumed the risk of borrowing capital to invest in the new technology, and also the risk of testing its effectiveness on his farm, the reward for this input does not automatically come back to him. Rather, the logic of farm technology drives the benefit of the input of technology down to the end of the line, where it emerges in lower prices at the grocery store. In short, the logic of farm technology *assures* that the output is not larger profits for the farmer but rather cheaper groceries for the consumer. Is this success? Or cruel irony?

The logic of farm technology has been with us for a long time—ever since serious technology came to the farm. But only in recent decades was it let loose into a world already dominated by the growing power and reach of the logic of the farm-food industry (with all its consolidations and integrations). The logic of technology and the logic of the farm-food industry work hand in glove, now an inseparable combination. And nothing successfully resists it.

### (3) The Vicious Cycles of Farm Economy

What has just been said from the point of view of farm technology is more generally (and even more importantly) true from the point of view of the farm economy as a whole—when viewed in terms of other efficiencies besides technology.

The vicious cycles revolve around an *efficiency-production-price axis*. Simplified, the cycle looks like this: increased farming efficiencies lead to higher production, which often leads to oversupply and lower commodity prices, which drives farmers to higher efficiencies, which lead to higher production, which leads to lower commodity prices, which drives farmers to higher efficiencies . . . and so the cycle goes. This is why farmers get bigger or get out.

You can describe this situation more accurately by enlarging the described cycle to take in more concrete elements, but you cannot thereby reduce the viciousness of the cycle. Here is a slightly elaborated version: Typically, low commodity prices oblige most farmers—seeking the path of survival—to find ways to increase production. Usually they do, often by specializing, by consolidating operations, by working longer hours, or investing in new technology or larger acreage to achieve economies of scale, thus becoming more efficient. In short, they learn somehow to produce more units at a smaller cost per unit. Higher individual volumes, however, when multiplied by the other farmers seeking to do the very same thing, have usually led, sooner or later, to overproduction and thus directly to lower prices for farm commodities. (Which, in the case of many commodities, is the rationale for government subsidies.) A farmer, then, will tend to concentrate ever more intensively on greater efficiencies and higher production—per acre, per animal, per hour, per dollar expended. And almost all other farmers will reasonably do the same.

Often, however, it is precisely this narrowed concentration upon needed efficiencies that will tend to suppress or postpone other long-term concerns, such as sustainability, health of the soil, the energy source, waste by-products, the landscape, the community, the environment. Farmers as a group may get caught in a narrow cycle of low prices, increased efficiency, and overproduction, and, alas, still lower prices—precisely because of their productive effectiveness, their "success." And if one looks carefully at the larger version of this vicious cycle it becomes apparent that it is not only the American farmer who is caught. In an important sense, American society is caught in the same vicious circle as well.

The reason is that many of the true costs of the elements that enable the farmer to achieve production efficiency are in fact borne not only by the farmer but also by the larger society. These elements may include much more than just technology: they may include tangibles, such as cheap and subsidized energy, mostly from foreign sources, also cheap and subsidized transportation on public highways, both to and from the farm and throughout the economy as a whole to create and supply the seed, fertilizer, livestock, machinery, and so on; also direct farm crop subsidies, now running to dozens of billions per year; also hosts of intangibles, such as costs to the landscape and environment, to the air, water, and community; also costs extending eventually to such things as chemical and toxic cleanup, and even to health and insurance costs. It is a widening circle of unmeasured and hidden costs of farm productivity. The bottom line is simply that society at large—that's us, the people—pays the bill in a multitude of ways for many kinds of efficient farming "success."

In the scenarios described in the previous paragraphs there is very little that has not been said before, nothing new or original—except perhaps in brevity and explicitness. Moreover, in this cycle, whether narrowly defined in terms of the farmers' cycle of efficiency, production, and price, or broadly conceived in terms of society's silent complicity in the farmers' efficiencies (by accepting the externalized costs), there is nothing, no strategy or decision, that is, as such, irrational or unreasonable. There is no obvious villain in the story. But it is the story of a system so structured that the rewards of technology and scale go not to those who produce but to those who market and those who buy. And the total result is clearly not what our country has always wanted from and for the family farm.

As a society, we have not desired a system where small farmers struggle with commodity prices about double what they were fifty years ago, with their costs up to ten times as high; small farmers going out of business left and right, in the shadow of massive government subsidies paid largely to industrial agriculture. Nor have we asked for a system that heavily subsidizes overproduction of U.S. commodities, which then enter the world market below the cost of their local production in poor countries—so that these nations lose their rural economic base. We have not even asked for a system that subsidizes dairy farms with tax dollars so that the people who pay the taxes can have cheap ice cream at the grocery! So we have a system of food and agriculture made up of many rational components and many rational farmers' decisions, but combining into many unreasonable results, for farmers and for society and the world at large—

indeed, leading to results that are often ironic or unwanted and some-times plainly absurd.

American farming is fraught with ironies and even vicious cycles, and the fate of family farming is bound up with them. And that is hardly news. But certain mistaken notions obscure the ironies and encourage us to swallow it all as acceptable. I shall name two of these deeply misleading ideas.

One is a philosophical idea to the effect that the agriculture system (even as described above) is composed of reasonable steps taken by reasonable people, mostly farmers, trying to make a living within severe constraints. Such a system, it may be supposed, is *not* absurd (contrary to what is implied above); it may be painful, require getting used to, but it is, like it or not, the modern result of a series of modern rational strategies, and is therefore reasonable. . . . So it may be said—mistakenly, I suggest.

A second thing that masks the absurdity is even more seductive, and it too easily silences a serious critique. It is the simple and potent fact that food is cheap at the grocery store. Indeed, as a percentage of the average family budget it has never been lower. Consequently, the glib rhetorical question is this: how can anyone argue that a system is broken or absurd when it supplies us with such an abundance of cheap food? Is this not suc-cess? Or at least "success"? . . . So it may be said—mistakenly, I suggest.

These are both bad arguments—but bad for complex reasons (see above) that most people have not the patience to look into. Both tend to mute criticism of our agriculture system. And both views are dangerously partial and shortsighted. Briefly: sequences of rational steps by different individual farmers can very well lead to undesired, even absurd, outcomes for society as a whole: that is the irony to come to terms with, not to deny. (Stupid wars are sometimes entered into, step by reasonable step.) More-over, cheaper food is surely among the least of the needs of this rich society. And we should know by now that the grocery store price is not in fact the true measure of its ultimate cost. As to *why* grocery prices are as low as they are, that is exactly what this chapter has been explaining. Return to the beginning.

# Chapter 9

# Biotechnology and the Future

A good part of agriculture is to learn how to adapt one's work to nature. . . . To live in right relation with his natural conditions is one of the first lessons that a wise farmer or any other wise man learns.　　　　　　　　—LIBERTY HYDE BAILEY, *The Holy Earth* (1915)

Biotechnology represents the most recent, the most explicit, and potentially the most far-reaching arm of industrial agriculture. Its program for agriculture is extremely ambitious and at the same time extremely vulnerable—to scientific miscalculation, to economic vested interest, and to world politics. Consequently, its ultimate impact upon small farms throughout the world, and upon American family farming, though still uncertain, does not now appear to be favorable. Although biotechnology is the professional pursuit of individual scientists in hundreds of laboratories, so far as the farm-food nexus is concerned it is the special economic dominion of a small handful of extremely powerful multibillion-dollar global seed and chemical corporations. That is why it is a matter of interest for those who reflect on the fate of family farming. (It should also be of interest to those who eat food purchased in grocery stores.)

*A Seductive Story*

Farmers are forever at war with plant pests and diseases, a war never won and never wholly lost, and they are also forever on the lookout for ways to improve their methods of production, through use of fertilizers, hybrids, superior seeds, timely cultivation, whatever. These two aims are always up front: better weapons against the enemy, better production of crops. Today, on both sides of this double quest the hottest news maker is biotechnology, a general term sometimes used loosely for the more particular *transgenic technology*, whereby the gene structure of crop seeds is modified ("genetic engineering"). In this context it has become convenient to use *GM* as an adjective, meaning *genetically modified*, and *GMO* for the results of this process, namely, a *genetically modified organism*.

Biotechnology and in particular genetic modification and the production of GMOs may be approached against the background of certain events a few generations ago, namely, the development and widespread dissemination of hybrids. Plants naturally mutate and develop new strains, and they also naturally hybridize by cross-pollinating, and develop new strains that way. Hybrids have long been created deliberately, in order eventually to create plants and fruits strong in certain desirable characteristics. That is an old and familiar story, and it is impossible to imagine twentieth-century farming without it. Indeed, in the middle of the century, just after World War II, new hybrids for most commodity crops were the big news in the farming community—new hybrids and new pesticides, such as DDT. Indeed, especially DDT. Farmers had a new weapon against pests and a new hybrid strategy to enhance quality. At last farming would be scientific and so much easier—quality bumper crops and no pests! Within decades the DDT saga came to a bad end, and hybrid seeds became a standard thing.

Genetic modification takes the ever losing battle against pests to an entirely new front. Its chemistry, biology, molecular genetics, and technology are extremely sophisticated, but its basic idea is quite simple. To understand it, we start with the familiar fact that most plants are unhealthy for most eaters (because indigestible), whether humans, animals, or insects. We plant-eating humans are very fastidious about what our stomachs can handle; the stomachs of most pests are even more fussy. Corn borers, for example, perfectly nasty little creatures, need corn plants; they cannot live on potato plants, or maple leaves, cannot digest those particular proteins. (Neither can we.) Potato bugs need potato plants and cannot live on corn, because they cannot digest those particular proteins. Monarch butterfly larvae can digest milkweed leaves, and not much else. Human beings cannot live on silage; for all its wonderful protein, which cows thrive on, we cannot digest that stuff. We and the bugs and our stomachs have our very fussy limitations.

That is the boring part. The interesting part is this: if you could develop a strain of corn that was unhealthy for corn borers (that is, with a protein that their highly specific stomach could not handle), you might save your corn from attack by that pest. Genetic engineering refers to the technique of inducing certain perfectly healthy plants (corn in this case) to make themselves unhealthy to certain specific insects. The plants do it simply by accepting into their genetic makeup a gene whose business is to produce a protein that is indigestible by the chosen insect. *Bacillus thuringiensis,* usually known on the farm by its nickname Bt, is a naturally occurring soil bacterium, and it contains such a protein, generally indigestible for corn borers *and* for potato bugs. Accordingly, corn has been tampered with (that's the engineering) at the genetic level—in effect, a new gene was spliced in among the other 250,000 genes already resident in corn. This one will generally produce the Bt in all its successor cornstalks, and that simply means death by indigestion to the corn borer larva that tries to dine on that corn. Potatoes have been developed that will reliably produce this Bt protein in their leaves, and that means . . . well, it means the bugs (some of them anyway, the smart ones in my garden, for instance) have figured out (I don't know how) that they ought (if they want a family) to lay their eggs on the other, old-fashioned potatoes in the garden. (It gets complicated.)

But it is such a neat and seductive idea: plants that will prudently kill off just the predators that love to dine on them.

And it gets better. Call to mind the farmer's immemorial war against weeds. Some herbicide sprays have very desirable features, such as effective weed killing in crop fields and very rapid breakdown of the herbicide itself, minimizing residues. But the best of them (Roundup is a famous example) would damage the crop as well. Genetic engineering rides triumphantly to the rescue and develops crops—soybeans and corn are spectacular cases—unable to absorb, and thus be damaged or killed by, the particular toxins in that particular herbicide, and so they remain unharmed by it. And that's not science fiction but recent history. Today, more than two-thirds of American soybean crops—millions of acres—are sprayed with an herbicide that kills the weeds but leaves the (genetically modified) soybean plants unaffected. Presumably, the beans themselves are unaffected by this: it's just the *leaves* that are modified not to absorb the toxin. It gets still better. Just over the horizon—if we can believe the major seed and chemical companies—are genetically modified crops that may deliver into our diets much larger quantities of selected vitamins and minerals. A much touted example is a GM rice strain that might significantly reduce iron deficiencies of millions of people in rice-eating developing countries. Another is a rice aimed at widespread vitamin A deficiencies, another is a corn or canola oil low in saturated fat. The long-term promise (it is only promise) is that GM foods will eventually prove an important bulwark in keeping malnutrition at bay throughout the entire world. Who would not applaud such prospects?

### Doing Just One Thing

That is an attractive but one-sided story. Whether all this is as nifty a breakthrough as it may seem is a wide-open question, but there are certainly problems: some known from the beginning, others just cropping up, so to speak. Insect pests, for example, have an awesomely impressive record of developing resistance to poisons; we know now that what works against them today may not work for long. (The pesticide kills off the most susceptible individuals first, leaving the toughest ones to breed; same for the next generation, and the next. A pesticide is a rigorous device for developing insects immune to it.) Consider the record of DDT, the Second World War miracle pesticide that saved hundreds of thousands of soldiers and maybe as many civilians from mosquito-borne malaria and from louse-borne typhus. By 1950 it was known that 137 species of insects had developed resistance to it, and by the time it was banned in the United States in the 1970s there were over 500 resistant insects. And then there was the melancholy message of Rachel Carson's *Silent Spring*, that our insecticides were laying waste to many species of birds. DDT had performed miracles, and it promised more. But it did too much. Its unintended consequences obliged us to kill it off instead. While it is certainly true that GMOs in the short term have enabled some farmers to reduce pesticides on some crops, and to avoid them on others, it is simply not knowable what this will amount to in the long term. Today's confident predictions may be no more reliable than predictions about DDT in 1945.

Is that relevant to the boring corn borer? If tomorrow's corn borers are resistant to Bt (if, for example, they can eventually digest the Bt incorporated into the new corn), then the organic farmers and gardeners, those who stuck with the old-fashioned miscellany of pest control methods, will be dealing with tomorrow's resistant borer too. And organic farmers have long used Bt, because its chief insecticidal ingredient is a naturally occurring bacterium. So the scientific farmer with his Bt corn may be inadvertently creating new problems for his organic neighbor, by rendering ineffective that organic neighbor's most potent natural insecticide. Success is a splendid breeder of defeat: the more effective Bt corn is, the more farmers will want to plant it, and the more rapidly the pests will develop resistance to it. The prospect of such unintended (unpredicted, unwelcome, unknown, uncontrollable) consequences of genetic engineering has stimulated predictable (unfriendly, uncompromising) resistance to the whole program by some critics.

The Indians who taught the Pilgrims the technique of inserting a fish in the corn hill were good on the *technology*, but they understood little of the soil *science* supporting the practice. Similarly with GMOs: splicing in the foreign genes is a reasonably well-mastered technology, but the underlying science of molecular genetics (which includes understanding and predicting the dynamics of altering organisms in these unnatural ways) is still very primitive. We are about where the Indians were with the fish. That is why there remain underlying questions, crucial but easy to put aside, questions generalizable to every example of genetic engineering: when we splice that clever gene in among the resident 250,000 corn genes, the one whose sole mission is to stimulate the production of the Bt protein, do we also thereby stimulate *anything else* within that organism—something with possible results that we may not like? Usually, we simply do not know. Unexpected things are often initiated by the splicing in of an alien gene, for each gene works not alone but—somehow, mysteriously—in concert with its companions. Undoubtedly, we should care that we do not know. And by now it should be recognized as the first principle of ecology, perhaps of science and wisdom itself: *you can seldom do just one thing.*

*How We Got Here*

It is a most disconcerting fact that genetic engineering came upon us extraordinarily quickly. A legitimate and important scientific research program was commercialized almost immediately, aided and abetted by the U.S. government through the Department of Agriculture, and facilitated (it is now almost universally admitted) much too readily by the Food and Drug Administration and the Environmental Protection Agency. As a result, it was very quickly almost out of the control of reasonable scientific, regulatory, and public relations protocols. Before most of us had heard about the technique in the late 1990s, there were already millions of acres of food crops sown with GM seeds. By the beginning of the twenty-first century a large percentage (more than half) of the products in almost all American grocery stores contained ingredients from GM plants, and throughout the world there were over a hundred million acres of GM crops planted each year, chiefly corn, soybeans, rice, other grains, and cotton.

There is now a belated but widespread consensus that very few of these GM crops had been sufficiently tested or regulated, and almost none of them are labeled in American grocery stores. The average reader of these lines will have unwittingly consumed some of these GM products within the last couple of days. They had been genetically modified for various purposes: for resistance to herbicides, so crops could be sprayed with weed killers; for built-in resistance to insect pests; also for cold and heat and drought resistance, and so on. This widespread and rapidly expanding use of GM seeds did not derive from the expressed needs of farmers, nor was there any consumer demand for food from GMOs. The techniques were developed not because they were required but because they were *possible* (making them attractive to scientists), and because they would be *profitable* (making them attractive to giant seed and chemical companies).

This headlong rush produced a string of scientific blunders and public relations disasters, and consequently in recent years a worldwide storm of opposition to GMOs has blown up. Initially, some of the opposition was poorly informed—critics caught off guard by the sheer magnitude of the corporate commitment to the project—and some of it borne on winds of ideology. But this changed rapidly as it became ever more apparent that a major agricultural revolution is well under way. Each year brings good news and bad news. There was good news from Hawaii when a GM papaya proved resistant to ringspot virus, and maybe an African GM sweet potato will prove resistant to the feathery mottle virus. In a more celebrated case, it was discovered in 1999 at Cornell and in Iowa that pollen from Bt corn appears to be toxic to monarch butterfly larvae—apparently bad news for monarchs feeding where the milkweed loves best to grow, along the margins of cornfields. As it happens, this kind of bad news was "good bad news" for GMO critics, namely, a disaster made to order for negative campaigning against GMOs. Subsequent research suggests there may not be serious long-range worries about monarchs and Bt. But sober critics wonder: Is this to be a global experiment with the health of the planet and with the world's food supply? Who authorized that? Who supervises it? And who benefits from GMOs? And they answer: not the consumer, not the world's poor, occasionally the agribusinessman; but it is very certain that many corporations benefit enormously, those that produce and patent and sell the seeds and the herbicides, such as Monsanto, Novartis, DuPont, Syngenta, Dow, and others.

At the root of the matter was an initial corporate obtuseness that some critics believe is endemic to industrial agriculture. Instead of starting modestly with items where the public could easily see the immediate benefits (if any)—food products that were healthier, or richer in certain vitamins, or looked better, tasted better, had a longer shelf life—the industry initially concentrated upon pesticide resistant corn, soybeans, and cotton, where they could patent and sell both the GM seed and the pesticides it was resistant to, reaping billions in profits. (There was one famous exception to this: Calgene's much promoted GM Flavr Savr tomato, introduced in 1994 and withdrawn as an embarrassing flop in 1996.) Meanwhile, the corn and soy were smoothly and massively slipped into the public food chain virtually without regulation. It was hardly a conspiracy—just morally blind corporate power with nothing to restrain it. Indeed, the U.S. Department of Agriculture and the American Farm Bureau facilitated it. In 1996, 3 million American acres were planted with GM seed; in 1999, 71 million; in 2001, 88 million acres.

*What's the Problem?*

Three ranges of concerns about the rapid, widespread use of GMOs have arisen, and are very far from being resolved. One has to do with (1) *world ecology*, the effects of GMOs upon the environment; another has to do with matters of (2) *food safety*; and another has to do with the (3) *corporate policy* of leading GMO companies. With all these issues very much in play the European Parliament in 2002 imposed very strict labeling requirements on food imports that contain genetically modified ingredients. This concerns U.S. exporters, since 75 percent of the world's GMOs are grown in this country. In this and many other ways GMOs become deeply implicated in international politics.

(1) As to GMOs and the world ecology: There are local issues as well as concerns for farming communities around the world. Some examples: (a) *Gene flow*, or GM genes contaminating other crops. Spliced genes are hyperactive and so tend to spread; how readily is unknown, but it happens: in Minnesota, GMOs spread to and ruined a neighboring organic crop. (b) *Escaping GMOs*: undesirable GM species might even escape human control and grow like kudzu or worse; how likely is unknown, but it happens: vigorous GM canola has invaded wheat fields in Canada, and the seeds were withdrawn from the market, so it's not a kudzu case yet. (c) *Super pests*: a natural pesticide, Bt or some such, when introduced into the plant will indirectly encourage resistant pest species, with the prospect

of inadvertently developing much more resistant pests; how dangerous or likely this is, is unknown. (d) *Ecological disruption*: a GMO planted near one of its wild relatives could cross naturally with it, making a species that was far more naturally competitive, and so alter the entire ecosystem. How likely this is, is unknown: at last report there was no known wildly thriving bastard that has become a dangerous outlaw. Many potential ecological side effects of genetic engineering are completely unknown, and cannot in any way be reliably predicted. Moreover, the huge variety of genes that might theoretically be spliced into even the standard repertoire of crops suggests that reliably predicting even the principal ecological side effects of many GMOs, whether good or bad, may not be possible.

(2) As to food safety: Most of us are now probably eating lots of food products containing GMOs, and for the most part we do not know it, because they are not labeled. The long-term effects of this are unknown, but there are significant immediate concerns. A few examples: (a) *Allergies*: if you are allergic to peanuts and a peanut gene has been spliced into your corn, you may get a reaction from the tacos and not know its origin. Similarly for many other allergies. Indeed, an allergy-causing protein from Brazil nuts was unwittingly spliced into soybeans, and caught just before the seed went to market. The real danger of allergens is perhaps from genes spliced into food from plants or animals that haven't traditionally been used as food—but this is not known. Indeed, generalizing is precarious precisely because the gene splicing technology is so crude, and the underlying science so primitive. (b) *Nutritional value*: few studies have been done on GM foods, but an early and isolated one showed that at least one set of GM soybeans was less nutritious than normal ones. Whether this is likely to be generally true is still unknown. (c) *Health effects* of food made from sprayed crops: plants engineered to be herbicide tolerant may be heavily sprayed with a weed killer such as Roundup, which contains glyphosate (possibly carcinogenic), and the effects of this kind of massive exposure have not been thoroughly studied. (d) *Antibiotic resistance*: for highly technical reasons genetic engineering often employs bacterial genes in such a way that the resulting product is sometimes antibiotic resistant; if consumed by humans it is likely to pass this resistance on, not only to administered antibiotics but also to naturally occurring bacteria in the human body. While many such food safety questions may be raised, few or none of them now have definitive answers. Extensive scientific testing combined with strict labeling requirements may eventually corral the relevant questions and answer some of them. But we are not yet there.

(3) As to corporate policies: For many observers a matter at least as disturbing as the foregoing is the extraordinary manner in which the major seed and chemical companies seem intent upon securing a legal and economic hold on the world's seed supply. They have employed two striking techniques, one political, one scientific. The first is by (a) *securing patents* on GMOs. The patenting of life-forms is an entirely new development— made possible by a Supreme Court decision of 1980, and suddenly put into widespread practice during the 1990s. Now the farmer who buys patented GM seed really is only leasing it for that one year, as it is illegal to save seed for next year. In the eyes of many critics the economic prospects of monopoly patents on whole groups of farmers' seeds and chemicals more than anything else explains the very rapid appearance of GMOs. A similarly aggressive strategy is (b) *terminator technology*, involving GMOs that kill their own seeds, rendering them sterile, a process also patented for many crops. The aim is to forcefully prevent purchasers from saving seeds, leaving these farmers wholly dependent upon the seed company.

Of course, these two strategies set off alarm bells all over the world. Indeed, many ecologists believe that widening use of GM seeds, sterile or patented or both, may ultimately lead to extinction of many traditional, non-GM seed varieties and hence loss of the world's genetic diversity, and also the dependence of many third-world farmers (already happening) on multinational companies for their seed. Add the dangers of wind-borne pollen drift from terminator crops killing off the seed in neighboring crops; add the fact that creating terminator seed requires the use of antibiotics, which could well undermine the medical usefulness of those antibiotics. The list goes on. Indeed, fully implementing the potential of "patenting and terminating" could well become a major cultural disaster, but we may be spared that because it is already such a public relations disaster. Opposition to terminator technology from many world organizations (including the Council for Responsible Genetics and the Consultative Group on International Agriculture Research) has persuaded some companies to declare that they will not use it for the present.

*Now What?*

Different observers will rate the importance of these questions, and others like them, differently. Outside the United States, many nations appear convinced that, altogether, the outstanding questions are reason enough for them to declare a moratorium on the use of GM seeds or, in many cases, require the labeling of GM food products or prohibit the importation of them. No one expects such actions in the United States in the near future, but many urge at least a radical redirection of research focus: away from new GM products for sale and toward assessment of GMO risks. Most observers are now persuaded that the U.S. government must develop far more regulation and public review of GMOs. Hitherto, there has been virtually a revolving-door policy between the U.S. government and the corporate structure: in effect, biotech agribusiness has been regulating itself. Recently, even the (American) National Research Council emphatically recommended stronger supervision of GMOs, though it remains to be seen if there is political will to do so. Many ordinary citizens, impressed with the sheer weight and number and variety of the unanswered questions, may wonder how we got so far into this thing and how it spread so widely and so quickly with so little supervision and scientific testing. But they know the answer: there was money to be made.

To the ardent proponents of GMOs, none of this seems to suggest caution. The American Farm Bureau has been from the beginning, and is to this day, an ardent GM proponent, and the press reports that the Farm Bureau Foundation will launch a campaign at the middle school level to spread the acceptance of GM products, and that Philip Morris will assist by financing the production of a video and learning kit to be distributed through the Agriculture in the Classroom program and also through the National Science Teachers Association. There is also planned a CD-ROM-based project especially for teachers, explaining to them the many benefits of GMOs. Thus the issue—or at least one well-financed side of it—is headed into American classrooms. This concerns some critics on the other side, who see this initiative as corporate propaganda disguised as education.

A few generations ago, it is possible that some alarmist might have wondered if food derived from hybrid seed was safe to eat and if the widespread use of hybrids might unfavorably affect the environment. So it is relevant to recall that hybrids occur commonly in nature, and that new varieties have occurred by precisely that means for millions of years. But GMOs do not and could not come about in that natural way. Nature cannot splice its genes. Indeed, it is in the very nature of genes and genetic structure itself to prevent that kind of genetic modification. To do it, a boundary has to be breached among the building blocks of life. In the case of hybrids, therefore, the maxim *innocent until proven guilty* seemed to point out the right path. Inasmuch as nobody now has reasonable doubts about eating hybrids, it may be declared that they are proven innocent. (Moreover, the chief ecological effect of their success is that thousands of people have joined seed saver organizations to ensure natural-world genetic diversity.) A different guiding maxim is needed for something so contrary to natural phenomena as genetic engineering, so unpredictable in its potential effects, whether for good or ill. It might be wise to shift the burden of proof and to treat each new GMO as *guilty until proven innocent.* Such a maxim would then require careful protocols to determine exactly what is required for proof of innocence.

However, this is not the policy that the Food and Drug Administration adopted. It did the exact opposite: in 1992 it issued a "Statement of Policy" declaring that GMOs were "substantially similar" to other crops and therefore required no labeling or special testing. As was to be expected, this opened the gates, and within a few years more than fifty different GMO products had marched into American grocery stores. Nor should we expect cautions to be spearheaded by the U.S. Department of Agriculture, which, for the most part, has been a full-scale supporter of GMOs. In recent years less than 5 percent of its research budget on biotechnology has gone for assessing the risks of GMOs. A recent major policy document issued by the department contains not one hint that anyone could have any reasonable qualms about GMOs. As with the American Farm Bureau, the USDA propaganda horns are going full blast whenever the subject comes up: GMOs are an unmixed good. "Biotechnology has introduced new options to farmers, increased profits, and made farming more environmentally friendly. It promises advances in combating hunger and malnutrition. . . ."[69] And so on.

Outside the United States, however, the situation is very different. Winds opposing GMOs sweep around the globe: many European, Asian, and African countries have outlawed the planting of GM seed, or forbidden the importation of GM products, or have imposed strict labeling requirements. The agriculture press recently reported that the European Union had issued a "manifesto in favor of biotechnology and calling for the highest standards of governance of the science to win over a skeptical public." The same press report speculated that "opposition to biotechnology is expected to continue to be intense in Europe for the foreseeable future." As if to confirm that, the European Parliament then passed its GMO labeling restrictions. Different countries regulate GMOs differently; the United States least of all. Thus global trade rules involving GM products are an inevitable bone of contention. In 2000 an international treaty under the

Biosafety Protocol of the United Nations—in opposition to the U.S. Food and Drug Administration's "substantially similar" declaration—recognized that GM foods were different and needed to be regulated differently from conventional foods. The controversy swells and swirls.

## On Family Farms

Like most people, I come as an outsider to this sudden controversy, and to the large and rapidly growing literature in the science, the economics, and the politics of GMOs. My investigations tell me, as of 2003, that at least one thing is clear, though too seldom acknowledged in the literature, namely, that there is at present simply not enough firm evidence to make any blanket statement to the effect that GM food is safe, or that it is not; or to say that, on the whole, its long-range ecological effects will be benign, or that they will not be. Therefore a prudent policy would seem to call for at least two things: being extremely wary of dogmatic propaganda on all sides, and reining in and severely regulating the present American-led headlong rush into GM crops. It is a matter of concern that deeply rooted bureaucracies, plus extensive corporate economic interests and the power of their press, may overpower any sense of restraint.

Undoubtedly genetic engineering has potential more exciting than we might have imagined, and its ultimate consequences are more complex and unknowable than we like to admit. That is important but not an entirely new circumstance. Genetic engineering is to agriculture what splitting the atom was to physics: that was a watershed, and it opened entirely new vistas with new moral and political challenges. But when we are told that with GMOs we will feed the starving and ease the farmer's life, some of us will be reminded that when we were young we were told that nuclear energy was entirely safe and would make electricity too cheap to meter.

Meanwhile, it is important to reflect that without the American system of large corporate farms the world would probably not be in the midst of this global controversy over GMOs: there would not have been the market incentive for large industries to impose these products and this technology upon us. For the same reason, the principal issues surrounding GMOs pertain directly to agribusiness—but indirectly also to the fate of smaller family farming. For in the long run you can seldom do just one thing: whatever affects the conditions of farming will affect family farms. Indeed, it is precisely the way in which the techniques and economies of GMOs extend the grip of narrow corporate values upon American farming generally that constitutes their threat to family-size farms. The four commodity farms considered in this book appear to be still reasonably uninvolved with issues of biotechnology, but to whatever degree biotechnology invades smaller farms it will increase the corporate hold on agriculture generally. Thus, to some certain but unknown degree the fate of family farming is also tied to the future of biotechnology.

We can be a little more specific, starting with *Bascom Maple Farms.* We know that research by traditional methods on maple trees with sweeter sap has been under way for some time, so we may be reasonably sure that someone has already imagined a GM maple tree, perhaps with a sugarcane gene, that has supersweet sap. Once fully imagined it will eventually be attempted. Will that new sweet GM maple tree be more, or less, susceptible to the pests and diseases that plague nature's own maples? And will it be healthy and long-lived? In any case, when and if it is accomplished it will, of course, take a generation or two before the results can be harvested, and by that time we should know if its sap and syrup are safe to consume, and if its seeds are safe to plant. All in all, it may be a good thing that this GM maple is, in a manner of speaking, still a long shot.

At *Eccardt Farm,* where the Eccards annually raise sixty acres of corn, they do not find it cost-effective to use Roundup Ready (the tag for corn genetically modified to withstand the weed killer Roundup): instead they use, though only occasionally, a cheaper weed spray and can therefore also buy seed corn that is cheaper than Roundup Ready. As for Bt corn that is resistant to corn borers, they find that their borer problem is small enough so that it would not be cost-effective to fight it with more expensive seed. Although many dairy farms give their cows BST, a growth hormone (which involves biotechnology but is not transgenic) to increase milk production, the Eccards do not use it. Indeed, right now, the use of BST may be declining on dairy farms, since opposition to it means that BST-free milk now frequently commands a premium price. Meanwhile, a transgenic heifer presumed to carry a mastitis-resistant gene has been produced in Vermont, and other designer cows are in prospect. Eccardt Farm may now be outside the reach of most biotechnology—but for how long?

At the *Coll Farm and Farm Stand,* where sweet corn, chickens, and eggs are principal commodities, the Colls do not directly confront GM issues. Corn, of course, has been altered genetically in a variety of ways, to make it immune to corn borers, to weed killer spray, and so on. That would be of concern to them if there were more such field corn grown in their vicinity, where its pollen could contaminate their sweet corn. They are fortunate in their comparative isolation. And from the corporate perspective, sweet corn is a small crop, and its seed is a small market, and precisely for that reason GM scientists have not significantly experimented with it. Chickens and eggs are a bigger crop, and they are already targeted by biotechnology scientists. "Designer eggs," for example, are in the making—not GM, but researchers are experimenting drastically with hens' diet and metabolism so they produce eggs with yolks very high in healthy omega-3 fatty acids. (The Colls are already, in a sense, into a version of designer eggs with their organic eggs and fertilized eggs.) And we may be reasonably certain that the genes of hens will not long remain unmodified.

Finally, at *Gould Hill Orchards*, a GM apple tree? Not yet, but it may be in the offing. Apple trees and maple trees have almost opposite natural lifestyles. Unlike maples, apples are so notoriously prolific in producing new varieties, crosses, sports, hybrids, mutants, all with slightly different characteristics, that it might appear that tampering with its genes is not expedient. But some apple varieties are naturally more resistant than others to pests and disease, and this is to some extent genetically based. And so the hunt is on to locate the responsible genes—if they exist—and already field tests are under way. An apple that the worms wouldn't eat? That scab and fungus won't hurt? Or perhaps an apple tree with a gene from a turnip?

It would appear that GMOs are not yet a pressing issue for many small and medium-size family farms. But in ten years?

At the root of the GMO controversies there may be a fundamental difference of philosophical and moral perception. To transport genes, building blocks of life, from one organism to another, across species and genera and even families, and so create organisms impossible in nature and of wholly unpredictable character—surely, this is an awesome undertaking. It may be even more awesome to spread the results over the globe with only the slightest scientific testing. The technology attempts, not to draw upon, but to short-circuit the biological wisdom accumulated by ages of natural reproductive trial and error; to bypass also all the diversity and balance and ecological integration and individuation of nature as established over millions of years; to short-circuit also the accumulated results of thousands of years of farmers' selective breeding and seed saving and natural crossing. Small wonder that many should perceive such an enterprise in moral and mythic terms. Well may they ask: Is this an effort to storm the heavens and to steal fire from the gods, impelled by man's age-old sin of hubris? Or, on the other hand, is this simply another and new frontier of business—to manufacture new life-forms and to patent and sell them as commodities? Should we enter these foundational precincts of life and disturb the delicate economies of the earth with strut and swagger? Or only with extreme care and humility?

In the Book of Genesis, when the first family, who were gardeners, had tasted the forbidden fruit, they were sentenced to become sweaty farmers and driven from the Garden, and an angel with a sword warned them about approaching the Tree of Life.

# Chapter 10

# The Soul of Agriculture

The dominant model of agriculture includes astonishing levels of production, intense concentration of ownership, mechanization of the relationships among humans, animals, and the products of the soil, and alienation of food producers from consumers. It generates great wealth from the countryside but often returns poverty to farmers and workers, harm to nature, and depopulation and disintegration to its communities, churches, and civic organizations. It is industrial agriculture.

— SOUL OF AGRICULTURE PROJECT, *Charter for a Shared Farming Ethic,* 1997

One would like to steer a book toward a closing that breathes an air of optimism. That can hardly be done by counting up the traditional family farms, recording the rate of their disappearance, and restating the harsh reasons for it. In fact, however, there is much more going on and much more resistance to present trends among farm and food communities than might appear on the troubling statistical surface. We need to raise our gaze from the field to the horizon and consider what is really astir.

*Two Glasses*

True, family farms are ever fewer, and many of those remaining are ever larger, more industrialized, more technology driven, moving in steady if often reluctant lockstep with and within a gargantuan food industry that is ever more globalized, consolidated, integrated, monopoly powered. On this reading one discerns a relentless one-dimensional farm/food juggernaut: it can swallow up entire midwestern family farm communities in a single gulp, it is energized by bottom-line economics and the eternal quest for greater efficiencies, it measures crops only in quantity, it treats food as but a commodity, and its ruthless economy sweeps everything in its path.

It gains the world and loses its soul. Hence the sense of inevitability, and a corresponding sense of powerlessness of many a farmer and farm observer. The glass is already half empty.

On a further reading, beneath the surface of this scene appear an astonishing number of vital and restless *countervailing* movements: agencies, associations, organizations, advocates, committees, foundations, conferences, alliances, projects, centers, working groups, co-ops, councils, institutes, webs, programs, networks—all alive and alert and growing, addressing every aspect of the farm and food system with spirit and conviction, usually in direct opposition to the major farm, market, and global food trends. They are composed of individuals with convictions, first of all, but secondly they are organized and active and prepared to be heard in hundreds of ways. In short, there are powerful and subversive forms of aggressive *resistance* stirring almost everywhere within American agriculture, with goals and aspirations alien to industrialized agriculture and entirely unimagined a generation ago. For many of these miscellaneous and far-flung efforts, "saving the family farm" would be much too imprecise a designation, too narrow a rallying call, maybe even too backward looking, even though "the family farm" can and often does serve as working shorthand for the many and various traditional ideals embodied in these movements. The glass is still half full.

The chief impulse of this agrarian resistance is twofold: first, the search for viable and forward-looking *alternatives* to the bleak portrait of a large-scale industrialized chemicalized globalized agriculture of monocultures and feedlots and a consolidated food industry dominated by corporate economic power; and, second, a practical and *valid response* to broader social concerns, such as the fate of small farms and farm communities, social justice for farmers and farm laborers here and abroad, and issues of food quality and security. Everywhere, the crucial linkage is that between farm and food, in all their literal and their powerful symbolic meanings and connections. But it becomes ever clearer that this vital intersection needs to be understood, and can be illuminated, not just from the standpoint of the traditional family farm, but with other terms of reference as well—health, food safety and security, way of life, ecology, morality, history, economics, biodiversity, and the like. For some individuals this twofold quest, for viable alternatives and for valid response, is a deeply spiritual impulse, arising from a moral or religious commitment to live in healthy and honorable ecological harmony with the earth and with the rest of humankind. For them, reflecting on the fate of farming is anything but a one-dimensional economic matter, but rather a heavily values-driven and yet very practical quest for new forms of sound husbandry and good stewardship in their best and ancient senses.

Stewardship and husbandry—one is a biblical concept, and the other is an Old English concept. If there is such a thing as the soul of agriculture, these must be two of its attributes.

## The Soul of Agriculture

Such is the name of a project initiated in the Midwest in 1996, under the sponsorship of the Center for Respect for Life and Environment (Washington, D.C.). The project, inspired by ideas of philosopher Paul Thompson and put into working shape by farmer Frederick Kirschenmann, is focused on agriculture and ethics. One of its initial ambitions was to formulate and publicize a consensus on the fundamental values and ethics of farming, and to project a hopeful vision for the future of farming. Several conferences were held under the project title, and one of the documents hammered out, "Charter for a Shared Farming Ethic," began with the sentences quoted at the head of this chapter. Thereafter, the initial project resolved itself into various more regional efforts. In 2001, and in each of the ensuing years, a faculty group at the University of New Hampshire sponsored a Northeastern Soul of Agriculture conference at the university's campus in Durham, New Hampshire. It is from the original project and from its more recent staging in New Hampshire that I have boldly borrowed the title for this chapter. The meaning I wish to associate with that evocative and undefinable term, "soul of agriculture," will gradually become clearer. It will have to do, of course, with husbandry and stewardship, and with how the glass remains half full.

At the Durham conference in 2002 I joined more than a hundred persons in attendance, representing almost every conceivable ideological standpoint, or none at all. A third were farmers (many who had found or created a particular niche for a specialty farm product), the rest of us a varied group of activists, scholars, academics, educators, writers, seers, and seekers—all of us eaters, but most also committed, some abstractly and some concretely, to a sustainable agriculture. Such gatherings, under varying titles, all of them pondering the shape and fate of American farming and the source and processing of our food, are increasingly common throughout the country, and under a variety of auspices: some are mainly academic or intellectual sessions, clean fingernail groups, some are closer to the grass roots or to activist politics, some are farmer gatherings, most are a mixture. Within such diverse groups, one hears recurring ideals evoked: local is better, fresh is better, organic is better, small is better, healthy is better, family operated is better, community is better, knowing the farmer is better, fair return for the farm is better, hands-on is better, fewer chemicals are better, GMO-free is better, community involvement is better, earth-friendly is better, sustainable is better. It is to be remembered that all such earthy ideas and their kin were born and raised on American family farms and dwell today somewhere near the soul of agriculture, and that none of them is notably fostered by agribusiness.

Alternative agriculture movements have various origins and offspring, and many of them collect under one or another larger rubric, each with its own history and trajectory. I shall sketch profiles of some examples that have become conspicuous in the last quarter century, the same quarter century during which industrial agriculture has appeared to consolidate its hold on food, farms, and markets. They are therefore rendered all the more subversive by their presence and influence and success. It is appropriate that organic agriculture should head the list and that sustainable agriculture—the underlying theme of many other movements—should be the summary example.

### Representative Movements

*Organic Farming* is a very old thing, and also a big new thing, in farming. By definition it is a traditional form of agriculture, since among its core ideas is the rejection of synthetic additives—pesticides, fertilizers, hormones, preservatives, and the like—in the raising and processing of food, which are options our founding farmers did not have. It is a twentieth-century phenomenon, since its motive is to restore and improve traditional methods of healthy and sustainable farming and to make them economically viable in the face of chemically dependent industrialized agriculture. Organic farming was born on the fringes of agricultural practice, but as its central ideas matured it steadily moved into the mainstream. In an important sense, organics came of age in October 2002, when new national standards for USDA-certified organic labeling came into effect—this at a time when purchases of organic food were increasing at about 20 percent per year. So this old thing is the newest big thing.

In 1995 the National Organics Standards Board offered this declaration of principles:

Organic agriculture is an ecological production management system that promotes and enhances biodiversity, biological cycles, and soil biological activity. It is based on minimal use of off-farm inputs and on management practices that restore, maintain and enhance ecological harmony. . . . The principal guidelines for organic production are to use materials and practices that enhance the ecological balance of natural systems and that integrate the parts of the farming system into an ecological whole. . . . The primary goal of organic agriculture is to optimize the health and productivity of interdependent communities of soil life, plants, animals, and people.

Noble in sentiment but abstract in statement, such a paragraph suggests the difficulty of saying briefly just what organic agriculture *is*. For that matter, it was not even easy to agree on what the above statements indicate that organic *is not*. At present, the principal things excluded from the production and processing of organic food are synthetic fertilizers, chemical pesticides, chemical herbicides, antibiotics, growth hormones, GMOs, sewage sludge, and irradiation. Does that make organic food better? In many cases, probably so. Keep the environment healthier? In most cases, undoubtedly so.

The organic movement has founding texts and gurus. The first text appeared after synthetic fertilizer had been under fairly wide use for about fifty years on many American and European farms. Former U.S. Department of Agriculture official F. H. King traveled to China and on his return wrote *Farmers of Forty Centuries* (1911), an exposition of sustainable farming through organic methods as practiced in Asia for thousands of years. The next benchmark text came from an Englishman, Sir Albert Howard, who had also studied Asian farming, especially in India, and in 1940 published *An Agricultural Testament*. Howard's book is full of soil science, much practical observation and wisdom concerning erosion control and soil texture, and its recurring theme is working with nature to retain fertility and erosion control rather than trying to overpower nature by synthetic means.

It fell to J. I. Rodale to lend voice and conviction to the organic idea. "In the reading of *An Agricultural Testament*, I was affected so profoundly that I could not rest until I purchased a farm," he wrote. "This great book showed me how simple the practice of the organic method could be." Soon Rodale began publishing the periodical *Organic Farming and Gardening*, and for decades this was the vehicle and he the spokesman who kept organic ideas in circulation. In the late 1940s, Louis Bromfield (chapter 3) read and greatly admired King's and Howard's books, but regarded Rodale and some of his disciples as extremists. Successful organic farming, he concluded fifty years ago, included valuable ideas, but it was not "simple."

For decades after its inception in the 1940s organic farming languished on the fringes of the field, the serious interest of a very small minority, the religion of a still smaller minority, and widely dismissed as a cult. That began to change in the 1970s. The sober message of such books as Rachel Carson's *Silent Spring*, and in particular its indictment of the agricultural use of pesticides, began to seep into the public consciousness, and concerns about the environment began to grow on every side. Meanwhile, with the passing of the elder Rodale some organic spokesmen (including his son Robert, who inherited the mantle) moderated the more spectacular claims, just as the strategies of industrial agriculture became more chemically dependent. Rather suddenly, growing or consuming organic food came to seem no longer like joining a cult but like a healthy and responsible option, supportive of a more ecologically sensitive and sustainable agriculture. A Maine organic farmers organization was formed in 1971, and in the same year another was formed in Vermont and New Hampshire, and a similar one in California two years later. In 1976 the U.S. Department of Agriculture published a report favorable to organic farming and recommended a modest research agenda. In 1977 Wendell Berry (chapter 3) wrote very favorably about organic farming in his classic work, *The Unsettling of America*. By the end of the decade there was state legislation in California defining certain organic standards.

Although the politics of the 1980s were not helpful to the organic movement in an official way, on the grassroots level it had begun an inexorable process of growth: public interest expanded, organic certifying agencies multiplied, many state agriculture departments authorized and supported organic farming and certifying. By the early 1990s organic foods, under varying standards of certification and enforcement, were being consumed and transported across the nation and around the world. Indeed, a luxuriant organic chaos came to prevail, with thirty or forty different organic certifying bodies, public and private, the most conspicuous being California's. In 1990 Senator Patrick Leahy of Vermont introduced the Organic Foods Production Act, which created a process for developing uniform national standards for organics. That work took more than a decade; it took many versions and powerful lobbying; it took immense struggle and controversy; but eventually new regulations came into effect in 2002. Organic farmers and processors have until April of 2004 to bring all their labeling and practices into full compliance.

Organics are now a multibillion dollar endeavor and growing, and are clearly here to stay. What is not clear is what the ultimate place and shape of organic farming will be, whether, for example, it is to grow naturally as a newer version of small-scale farming in the family farm tradition or is to be dominated by corporate organic agribusiness. Or both. A number of small-scale organic growers find that the new rules require so much paperwork that they are planning to continue farming in the same way but to relinquish the official organic label and use another, such as "naturally grown" or some variant of this. There is also the concern that if corporate organic interests become dominant in organic production then the organic watchword—farming in harmony with nature—may be pushed aside. An additional concern is that corporate organic interests will neglect issues of food flavor and nutrition, which may taint the reputation of organics. These qualities are, after all, not an official part of the organic program, but have always been understood to be important by-products. It is not now clear where growers and consumers will be on these matters a decade or two hence.

*Community Supported Agriculture* (CSA) represents a form of farming that is genuinely new within the last quarter century. Transplanted here from abroad, it has now put down strong roots in American soil and grows vigorously in this climate, a delicate flower of dissatisfaction with industrial agriculture and of the search for alternatives. A Community Supported Agriculture farm is structured so as to involve members (sometimes up to a hundred or more) as, effectively, shareholders in a working farm. The members own or lease a farm and/or a farmer; they pay for their share before the growing season ($500 or so); and each member then receives a regular, typically weekly, share of the farm's diversified products, often mainly vegetables and fruit, but sometimes including meat, eggs, milk as well. Members come to the farm approximately weekly to pick up produce and sometimes to contribute farmwork.

Among CSAs (of which there are now about a thousand throughout the country) there is much variation in structure, arrangements, costs, ground rules, and even in underlying philosophy. In the more ideological version the farm may be collectively owned, thus implying a statement against the principle of private ownership of the things that sustain life. But the idea in nearly every case is that all members participate directly in the costs, successes, failures, and produce of the farm, that they receive fresh and wholesome food, often organic or nearly so, and (for some this is the most important) that they are part of a visible community trying to model a safer, healthier agriculture that is both communal and locally based. Thus are certain traditional family farm ideals elaborated into larger community ideals. Some CSAs are year-round operations complete with root cellars and other storage facilities, but most of those in northern zones are seasonal. From one beginning experimental effort in Wilton, New Hampshire, in the early 1980s, the CSA concept has sprouted and spread and hybridized widely across the United States and Canada.

The CSA concept is still in its infancy. Two decades of moderate success is too short a run of experience on which to base a serious projection into an uncertain future. Often it is the sheer unvarnished idealism of the idea, and the relative simplicity of the practice, that attracts and eventually holds people. Some enthusiasts see CSAs as a wave of the future: they envision a time, a generation hence, when cities are embraced by and suburbs interwoven with thriving community farms, and a local and regional accent returns to urban dining tables. Others regard CSAs as an inevitably small but nevertheless durable and powerful symbol, not only a tangible way for ordinary citizens, city dwellers included, to be significantly involved in their own food production but, just as important, a way to keep ourselves ever alert to questions of food origins and security and to its real costs.

*Farmers' Markets* are perhaps the most ancient and honored means of distributing fresh farm products to consumers. They have assumed a multitude of historical forms, and in some manner or other have been present since the dawn of agriculture and the beginning of human communities. Hard to imagine a social transaction more fundamental than farmers selling food to nonfarm neighbors, an idea almost as old as organic agriculture itself.

In ancient Rome the famous Forum was originally a farmers' market, open daily during the third century B.C., according to the Roman historian Livy; and in ancient Greece, references to farmers' markets go back to the eighth century B.C., the very beginning of Greek literature. Later, it was in the marketplace of Athens that Socrates walked and talked, striving as he said to acquaint Athens with her own soul. In almost all ancient cities of which we have record the market seems to have been the primary gathering place, and the principal items exchanged there were always conversation and food. Politics itself was born there. Farmers' markets have thrived and faded and been revived and superseded and returned in endless permutations for thousands of years, and the animating idea appears to be much too simple and obvious ever to go away. Yet our modern streamlined profit-driven efficiency-driven food system in America had almost succeeded in driving farmers' markets into obscurity. In recent decades, however, and especially in recent years, there has been a remarkably sharp resurgence of interest in and development of farmers' markets in all areas of the country, and especially in New England. In New Hampshire their numbers have tripled within recent years. It is possible that this rather abrupt change is, among other things, an expression of a deeper and more pervasive discontent with some aspects of our food system. From the central square in small or medium-size towns, to the edges of larger cities, to Copley Square in the heart of Boston and Union Square in downtown Manhattan, farmers' markets are thriving as they have not in many decades. Whatever the significance of this phenomenon, it is clearly a vivid part of the larger simmering of ideas within the soul of agriculture.

Farmers' markets, like CSAs, now respond to a huge variety of needs and desires—concerns for taste and health and convenience, certainly, but also for meaning and morality. For some the main reward is simply quality produce, fresh and local fruits and vegetables; for others it is the opportunity to have a relationship with the grower, and perhaps a place in some sort of community of growers and consumers. Some are on the lookout for exotic or unusual products, or for ethnic foods, or for certain varieties, or for foods grown in a certain way, or without pesticides. Other patrons of farmers' markets are doing convenience shopping, and some are using food stamps. One factor contributing to the resurgence of farmers' markets has been the Women, Infants, and Children (WIC) program administered by the U.S. Department of Agriculture, whereby qualifying low-income persons can obtain certificates for purchases at farmers' markets.

Significantly, farmers' markets often speak directly to the outlook of those who increasingly see food as much more than commodity, and see the choices they make about it as more than utilitarian decisions. Many of this persuasion are eager to withdraw support so far as possible from what they may call "the global food system" and engage with local alternatives. For them, sustainable farming is the staff of life, and eating is a moral act. Such citizens are attracted to both the ideals and the practice of Community Supported Agriculture programs and farmers' markets, as well as other alternatives. Farmers' markets normally employ clearly articulated and monitored standards to ensure authenticity as genuine *farmers'* markets: typical criteria require that vendors be the farmers themselves, that a high percentage of their products be from their own land, that nonfood items be handmade and employ local materials, and so on. These markets have become significant sources of income for some farmers, and they often open the way to other forms of direct retail, from the farm door or through the mail or web—meaning that farmers' markets sometimes extend the life of family farms.

*Beginning Farmer Networks* are among the newest rural initiatives. They respond to the idea that a key to maintaining vital farm communities is creating the next generation of farmers. Typically supported by a state department of agriculture or some other state agency, Beginning Farmer programs provide practical channels for turning inexperienced farming interests into direct practice. Some beginning farmers have grown up on a farm and always intended to farm but need help getting started. But these programs also assist men and women who may not have grown up on a farm, who may be young and idealistic, who genuinely wish to farm, not just to join the back-to-the-landers or a commune, but to raise crops and sell products. Such beginners may have little cash and no land, many ideas but little experience—but they wish to farm.

These beginning farmers represent the other side of that more familiar coin, namely, the family farmer driven from the land by debt or agribusiness or crop failure, the farmer who goes bankrupt, or sells out to a developer, or just slowly closes down—that story we know. But the other story, that of the young and the adventurous, is there too; and Beginning Farmer programs offer assistance on all manner of practical matters: getting started, finding land, acquiring credit, locating funding, developing networks for buying supplies, workshops for particular farm skills, networks for selling and delivering products, relationships with helping agencies. New Hampshire, like many other states, has a number of county-based Beginning Farmer organizations. Such programs not only assist budding careers but salvage a certain amount of practical idealism with which to fertilize American soil.

*Women in Agriculture Networks,* under the acronym WAgNs, are one of the newest things in the land, and there are now several of them in New England. These networks assist women in all phases and forms of agriculture, including organic farming, CSAs, beginning agriculture, farmers' markets, and other vehicles. The striking fact is that women are entering agriculture in surprising numbers at present; as it happens, New Hampshire, with 17 percent of its farms headed by women, leads the nation in this respect. According to Otho Wells of the University of New Hampshire, at a recent Massachusetts meeting of New England Small Fruit and

Vegetable Growers, nearly half the attendees were women, something he says was entirely unimaginable just twenty years ago.

Indeed, the feminine accent in agriculture—what it has been historically and what it might mean for now and tomorrow—is a far-reaching topic only recently beginning to get the attention it deserves. All along, of course, women have been the indispensable enablers, far too often unacknowledged, for much of what may count as success in American agriculture. We speak casually of the *family* farm, thereby both affirming and easily overlooking the fact that, traditionally, at the head of that family was a husband-wife team, with an understood division of labor, which typically occupied them both full time. Although a woman's role in running a complex household, nurturing children, preparing food, being a gardener, and being a standby extra hand for the barn or fields was labor no less arduous or important than a man's labors in managing the barn and fields, it often happened that she was taken for granted while he was applauded. Fortunately, it is now a cliché to say that farm women's role and work has historically been disvalued, and scholarship of recent decades is reminding us of that and, indeed, obliging us to view agriculture history now with more gender-sensitive eyes. Certainly, our inherited mythos is one of farming as essentially an aggressive masculine undertaking. Today women are entering agriculture in their own right in greater numbers than ever before, whether as partners, or leaders, or singly, or in company with others.

*Niche Farming* represents a growing dimension of agriculture, prompted by a variety of untraditional motives. Niche farmers are attracted to the challenge of producing a specialty product and carefully targeting a market for it; they like the planning and craft involved, or the exhilaration of working directly with nature, or managing a natural resource, or perhaps involving children in a farming effort. But these farmers don't want to be commodity farmers, or completely dependent upon farming for their livelihood. They do what they love and farm in the niches, filling in the many market interstices between the major commodity farm crops.

Niche farmers may not be moved primarily by a vision of farming as way of life, or desire to be part of a community devoted to farming. Their interest may be more restricted than that and their options more sharply focused; they may produce just one commodity, often retailed or delivered to local outlets. Theirs may be a part-time effort, dependent on off-farm income. Their primary farming community may not be their immediate neighbors but a statewide scattering of farmers who are producing a similar niche product and belong to the same associations. The product may be any one of many: shiitake mushrooms, angora rabbits, organic peaches, Thanksgiving turkeys, apple blossom honey, Easter lambs, elk horn powder, greenhouse flowers, rainbow trout, alpaca wool, black raspberries, goat cheese, sweet corn, red deer venison, day lilies, beef cattle, bison steak. In New England the prototype of niche farm commodities, now and for the past three hundred years, is maple syrup. A very recent addition to the list is a Vermont farm that specializes in fresh mozzarella cheese made with the water buffalo milk from their newly established dairy.

*Sustainable Agriculture*, perhaps the most important movement on this short list, has gained a great deal of currency within the last decade. To some extent it is the implicit theme of all the movements discussed above. There are various and overlapping definitions of sustainability, but at a minimum it is this: a socially responsible and economically viable agriculture so designed and implemented that it can be continued indefinitely, without exhausting its resources, corrupting its environment, or impoverishing its practitioners. The term occupies some of the space in the universe of values once occupied by the ideas of stewardship and husbandry. A good steward cares for resources in the name of the true owner, and a good husbandman employs the productivity of resources so as not to waste or contaminate them. It seems clear that the first immigrants did not originally bring these values to these shores, and they were not a notable part of the original American ideal of the family farm. In some regions the very opposite idea held sway: not stewards of creation, but expropriators of a resource. With land and other resources in such abundance, they were often perceived not as a gift to be husbanded and renewed for future generations but as part of a bottomless supply, to be mined, exploited, and abandoned when exhausted. The very word "husbandry" became obsolete in early America.

Sustainable agriculture is an idea that crystalized only late in the twentieth century, but it reaches back to older traditions of European husbandry and past them to ancient, even biblical, traditions of stewardship, and often points forward to a postagribusiness vision—to an agriculture that is economically viable and durable but is also socially and ecologically responsible. The idea of sustainable agriculture has concrete implications, some obvious, some debatable. It implies at least that farming is not mining, not extractive, must not degrade its resources of soil, air, water, minerals, trees, animals, people, communities, economies, neighborhoods. It implies that soils themselves are restored or improved at least as fast as they are exhausted, that they are not poisoned or polluted with chemicals or waste, or otherwise rendered unusable; that water resources are not corrupted or exhausted faster than they naturally replenish themselves; that communities are not undermined by the sudden intrusion of farm economies of gross scale. And much more—an endless but important discussion of its implications.

The energizing impulse of agricultural sustainability is direct and powerful, namely, that a pattern of agriculture that is not sustainable is pernicious, injurious to ourselves and a form of thievery from our descendants, who will be saddled with our failures. Accordingly, once the idea of sustainability is fully appreciated, it becomes a moral imperative. Indeed, it may be said that sustainability is at once the strategy and the tool for inserting the Golden Rule into the soul of agriculture, applying it across time and generations.

Such ideas and their implications are organizationally expressed through the Sustainable Agriculture Research and Education (SARE) program of the U.S. Department of Agriculture and its outreach arm, the Sustainable Agriculture Network (SAN); also through the independent National Campaign for Sustainable Agriculture. The latter, in its own words, is "a network of diverse groups whose mission is to shape national policies to foster a sustainable food and agriculture system—one that is economically viable, environmentally sound, socially just, and humane." The National Campaign and its subgroups are active in research, publication, public relations, and legislative debates. Across the country there are five regional Sustainable Agriculture Working Groups affiliated with the National Campaign, and each has numerous member organizations; that in the Northeast, for example, has over sixty member organizations. (In 2002 this working group published an unusually lucid and informative book, decorated with tables and statistics, *Northeast Farms to Food*.)

The sustainable agriculture movement is significant in and of itself at the grassroots level but is also significant for an external and structural reason. This derives from the fact that the food industry itself, as presently constituted (with exceptions, of course), tugs strongly in precisely the opposite direction. The food industry is a collection of business structures each expertly designed (not to seek sustainability, but rather) to seek competitive advantage through scale and efficiency. Sustainable agriculture at the supply end complicates, and thereby restrains, the built-in narrow impulses of the food industry. There is a larger dynamic at work here, and this example invites us to consider such restraints in larger terms.

*System and Resistance*

The many endeavors profiled and alluded to in the foregoing pages, together with the scores of organizations and coalitions, the projects and
alliances, the co-ops and networks linked with them, have profoundly
affected the choices and outlook of millions of Americans. Hundreds of
local and national organizations now focus specifically upon some particular, often local, aspect of the farm-food nexus, each a separate consumer or
farm-oriented endeavor, each with a particular affirmative goal or mission.
These purposes range all over the map: from savoring Slow Food to slowing soil erosion to promoting coffee from Guatemalan shade-grown beans.
Many of these organizations have little in common with each other—
*except* for the crucially important fact that their goals and ideals are invariably perceived to be incompatible with the principal strategies of globalized
industrial agribusiness. In just that sense they are—some by design, some
by implication—one and all "resistance movements." By their differing
affirmative efforts they form an implicit alliance: directly or indirectly
resisting the influence and strategies and values of global agribusiness, its
consolidations and integrations and monopolies, resisting its increasing
economic control of crucial entities, from fertilizer and seed to chain stores
and shelf space. They are resisting soulless totalitarian tendencies.

There is a certain utility, I suggest, in thinking of all these farm/food
issues collectively, as one vast and scattered drama, a single complicated narrative with two principal contestants. Dozens and dozens of different issues,
involving hundreds of organizations, may be regarded as different facets of
one big issue, a single contest waged on many fronts for the soul of agriculture—to give it at last a conveniently dramatic name. Seen in this way,
American farmers, and not farmers only, are involved in a contest between
the united pressures of an industrial farm/food *System* on the one hand and
a large and amorphous farm/food *Resistance* movement on the other. Each
contestant is made up of innumerable strands, individual causes and cam-
paigns, whose goals, strategies, and clientele overlap, run parallel, reinforce
each other, and sometimes collide. To see the matter as one melodramatic
contest rather than many, and the opposed forces as just two, System and
Resistance, rather than hundreds, is a conceptual maneuver at once distort-
ing and clarifying, and doing so has a limited but valuable advantage.

It is possible to be somewhat more precise about the shape of the Resistance by thinking of it as a subversive effort with two distinct components,
a Farmer wing and a Consumer wing.

The *Farmer wing* of the Resistance includes all the alliances and initiatives profiled above—organic farmers, CSA farms, farmers' markets, most niche farmers, farmers who supply food co-ops, most beginning farmers and women in farming, and their allied regional and national organizations. It includes those affiliated with sustainable agriculture movements, with natural systems agriculture efforts; and it involves many centers such as the Alternative Farming Systems Information Center, and members of organizations such as American Farmland Trust, National Family Farm Coalition, National Catholic Rural Life Conference, National Farmers Union, Institute for Agriculture and Trade Policy, and similar organizations (some associated with state departments of agriculture or with land grant universities), almost all of them also committed to the spirit and aims of the National Campaign for Sustainable Agriculture and to the perseverance of American family farms. It includes the work of a variety of research and action centers such as the Center for Rural Affairs, the Leopold Center, the Land Institute, Small Farm Institute, Henry Wallace Center, Heifer International, and a few dozen others, and most of their members. And it includes many individual farmer-spokesmen: some of long-standing influence (Wendell Berry, Frederick Kirschenmann, Wes Jackson) and others who both farm and write about it in ways that cut against the grain of industrial models (Gene Logsdon, Eliot Coleman, Joel Salatin, and many others). Those in the Farmer wing of the Resistance have, collectively, by their ideals and actions and public relations, an enormous amount of influence, and sometimes considerable direct political power.

The *Consumer wing* of the Resistance has even broader contours, and intersects the Farmer wing at hundreds of points. Indeed, it is so vast and diffused that it cannot be defined, but its presence and effects can be indicated. It is responsible for the increase in natural food stores, organic stores, organic aisles in chain groceries, and for the fact that an increasingly common way for purchasers to learn about the kind of stewardship practiced by the grower is the use of ecolabeling—"Fair Trade," "Free Farmed" "Protected Harvest," and so on. The Consumer wing has spun dozens of local food webs and fosters a host of farm-restaurant, farm–co-op, farm-school relationships and, generally, may be said to be responsible for raising the consciousness of Americans about their food, its sources, its safety, its connection with social justice issues. Those in the Consumer wing sometimes have extraordinary direct leverage, as, for example, with product boycotts. The Consumer wing includes many thousands, undoubtedly millions, of individuals, and dozens of organizations outside the government, some of them networks of numerous other agencies, many with an explicit mission to resist the economic interests of a globalized and industrialized agriculture. Random examples among dozens are the Center for Food Safety, Consumers Choice Council, Community Food Security Coalition, Food Alliance, International Forum on Food and Agriculture, Thoreau Center for Sustainability, Organic Consumers Association, Greenpeace, Institute for Food and Development Policy.

It is important to realize that the Resistance has its own powerful and subversive logic, a quiet guerrilla war waged upon the soft underbelly of the System of industrial agriculture. If System farmers inject growth hormones into cows to force out more milk, then Resistance farmers identify their milk as hormone-free and secure a premium price. If System farmers feed livestock antibiotics, then Resistance farmers sell products free of antibiotics and command a better price. If System farmers use GMOs, then Resistance farmers avoid them and put a GMO-free label on their products. If System farmers put their chickens in cages, then Resistance farmers uncage theirs and highlight the fact that their birds are free range or organic or natural or whatever. Organics are a major Resistance weapon but by no means the only one. If System farmers fatten beef on corn in huge polluting feedlots, then Resistance farmers fatten theirs on open grass and tell the public about it. And so on, with dozens of issues—alternatives sprouting like mushrooms, and all playing directly upon the identifiable extravagances of the System. Indeed, it is precisely the System's favorite business strategies of scale and efficiency that create the openings for subversive alternatives.

*Prospects*

What I call the Resistance—which is not an organization but a vast community of interest and a visible presence with many faces, all of them family farm–friendly—may still seem to have but slim prospects in the struggle for the soul of agriculture. It may be said that the numbers and the economics are against it. The momentum and the massive economic and political power of industrial agriculture, of global food production, processing, and transportation is breathtaking; and all the agencies of resistance can seem to be but minor irritants in its side. By the numbers it might seem that resistance to the trampling march of industrial agriculture is a lost cause, that the clock does not run backward. On the other hand, many within the Resistance do see the industrial farm/food System—its infra-structure of borrowed capital, cheap labor, externalized costs, global cartels, increasing pollution, subsidized transportation and irrigation, its chemically dependent and mass-production factory farms—as danger-ously vulnerable to breakdowns, social dislocation, economic collapse, and even terrorism. An ordinary New Hampshire farmer can pose a devastating rhetorical question: Hans Eccard is alarmed that through consolidation just two milk processors will soon handle 90 percent of the milk in the Northeast. He asks: "What if one of those companies collapses like Enron or Worldcom?—think of the utter disaster for all us farmers if our milk checks suddenly bounced!"

Less dramatically, some see the 1970s as a prophetic moment: that was when organics were a fringe cult, CSAs unknown, the environment was hardly an issue, and an ever more chemically dependent agriculture be-strode the world unresisted. No more. Whatever the pattern of the future is to be, hardly any of those consciously linked to the Resistance believe the current global trends in corporate farming, production, processing, and transportation of food are sustainable. Moreover, the resisters note that their own numbers, their organizations, issues, memberships, sympathiz-ers, and general influence are flourishing, expanding every year; no longer mere voices in a wilderness, they now represent collections of genuine and growing and sustainable alternatives.

The historic question is whether the collective influence of the Resis-tance, which is growing, will eventually exceed the steady momentum of the System. Such a thing probably cannot be measured, but it can be sampled. Two recent events, I suggest, are especially revelatory—in them-selves, and especially as metaphors for the entire contest itself, and for its present undecidedness. Both of these events reach to the soul of the strug-gle, and both illustrate circumstances that cut across the deepest interests of literally hundreds of organizations, thousands and probably millions of people. Both events may contain important portents for the future. More-over, these two both deal with frontier issues, both were definitely win-lose events, and they suggest that to this point, in 2003, the score is tied. Of these representative contests, each side won one event.

(1) Despite the immense and growing body of scientific opinion offering numerous reasons for proceeding slowly and cautiously with GMOs, in most American grocery stores today 60 to 70 percent of the processed foods have some unidentified GMO ingredients—any one of approxi-mately a hundred, but probably mostly corn, soy, and rice. This is a truly

astounding fact. And it came about with equally astounding rapidity—about seven years. It is also obvious that this fact would make a potential requirement to label GM foods in the United States, as is mandated in scores of countries around the globe, extremely difficult. Without being able to track GMOs through the food chain, it is hard to determine their health effects. We may be very certain that this particular triumph in the grocery store did not come about through normal and natural growth of the market. The penetration of the entire processed food chain with unlabeled GMOs is manifestly a well-structured achievement of the highly integrated industrial farm/food System, nicely designed to render a battle over GM food obsolete before it could fully begin—and done with profits aforethought. It was probably achieved not through the conspiracies of a few, but by the coinciding vested interests of the relevant elements of the whole System. Moreover, it happened under the open but unseeing eyes of the active and growing Resistance movement, both of whose wings, in this test case, were supinely folded. Although this fight is not over, this extremely shrewd opening maneuver completely rearranged that part of the battlefield. The Resistance movement not only lost this round to the industrial System; it was a rout.

(2) There now exist, under the authority of the U.S. Department of Agriculture (USDA), organic standards that are more or less acceptable (save for the paperwork) to the organic community. They became effective October 2002, more than twelve years from the date of the initial enabling legislation. During the politically charged development of these standards an extremely revealing crisis erupted. A draft of proposed organic standards was published in 1997 by the USDA: they would have allowed food labeled as organic to include GM foods, allowed sewage sludge to be used in their production, and allowed organic foods to be irradiated—all of this to be unlabeled. The proposed rules would also have prevented producers from identifying store products based on production practices, which would have effectively ended "ecolabeling," making it illegal, for example, to put a "no antibiotics used" on meat, or "raised without pesticides" on produce, and so on. In short, in proposing these rules the USDA had completely capitulated to the crudest lobbying and power plays of the System. This time Resistance sentinels were fully awake, and set off the alarm. The USDA was soon buried in an avalanche of protest letters, over 275,000 of them during the prescribed public comment period. The secretary of agriculture, Dan Glickman, called it "an absolute firestorm." Eventually the USDA had to retreat completely. Ultimately, none of these offending

permissions and proscriptions survived into the final version of the rules. The System not only lost this round to the Resistance; it was a rout.

Both stories are political, and either might have turned out differently.

## The Fate of Family Farming

A hundred years ago Teddy Roosevelt could allude to what was universally cherished in our agricultural traditions by gesturing toward the family farm, achieving simple and automatic consensus. But today what is most valuable within our national agriculture is contested; and a gesture toward the family farm is not an automatic consensus builder, and in any case does not have the same clear meaning it would have had a century ago. Time was, when the family farm stood alone as custodian of the soul of agriculture. And, indeed, for most of our history, "family farm" has been a term of value as well as a specific designation, and historically we have used it almost as much to convey approval as to describe.

Yet when we have tried to be precise, we have thought of family farms as those exhibiting a treasured way of life, small enough to be essentially operated by a family, farms that provide a decent living and are economically viable, that are ecologically and environmentally healthy and sustainable, that are community oriented, and also, it must now be added, farms that are not in economic thrall to a remote corporate entity over which the farmer has no control. In short, we have honored farms that are small, viable, sustainable, communal, independent, wholesome places to live, and that exhibit good husbandry and stewardship. Such a family farm we have been willing to associate with the soul of agriculture; and such a family farm, because of its historical resonance and beleaguered condition at present, also stands as a potent symbol of Resistance to the industrial farming System.

But only a symbol and only ambiguously so. What I have called the System and the Resistance are certainly conceptually distinct, and they reflect two outlooks, two different worlds of values and ideals. But ultimately those are just terms of art: convenient for summary and analysis, yes, but not names of real-world entities with a street address and a phone number. Down on the family farm the messy matters of fact cannot always be so cleanly distinguished; there the system and the resistance to it are both lowercase and fatefully intermingled. Farmers and consumers as well participate in both worlds, willy-nilly, and many family farms throughout the country belong to both worlds, participating in and facilitating a mode of agriculture that they often would rather not endorse.

And simultaneously, the development of the global industrial farm/food system in the last quarter of the twentieth century has quite transformed many issues traditionally associated with family farms, and in many ways has incorporated the fate of family farming inextricably into a network of broader and more complex issues. So much so, that it may be a question whether the idea of family farming, associated with certain traditional ideals, will or should prevail as the leading symbol of value for the eternally important linkages between culture and agriculture. Of course, like Humpty-Dumpty, who paid his words extra and made them mean just what he wanted them to mean, we can make "family farming" mean what we want it to mean. In a way, we are always engaged in that process, by implicitly rearranging the hierarchy of ideas and values we collect under that term. For example, environmental health and ecological sustainability are newly prominent values that we, more ardently than our predecessors, would prefer to enlist high among family farm ideals. Indeed, such shifting of values and meanings is inevitable if we wish to retain the *idea* of the family farm as a major repository of social value.

Although the four family farms profiled in this book are, in differing degrees, small, viable, sustainable, and communal, they are scarcely independent. In fact, they all participate, like it or not, in some aspect of what I have called the system of industrial agriculture. They could not survive without it, for they are commodity farms, and most farm commodities are now processed by very large corporate entities. These farmers, like almost all family farmers, are concerned about their role within a system they cannot escape and cannot wholly approve, and all of them sometimes cringe in the face of that system's raw economic power. They know only too well that over the decades as the system has extended its reach and power it has contrived to return to the farmer—that is, to themselves and their neighbors—an ever shrinking portion of the public's food dollar, while an ever larger portion of that dollar is soaked up by the intervening marketing, processing, and distribution system. They feel powerless and at times furious in the face of this brutal fact. These farmers did not choose to be part of a national cheap food policy, certainly did not choose to pay for it themselves with low commodity prices, do not desire to be complicitous in a system that ruthlessly squeezes out small farmers.

But there they stand—together with hundreds and thousands of others. The Coll family farm depends upon the system, not only for its grocery chains large and integrated enough to handle the Colls' thousands of dozens of eggs, but also for its distant large corporate farms and transportation systems to supply produce at a cost and quality that enables Archie Coll to buy it, always selectively, in Boston and haul it back to the New Hampshire countryside. The system gives, and the system takes away: it lowers the unit price of the item—eggs, apples, whatever—and at the same time clears the way for marketing it in large quantities. Likewise, the Leadbeaters depend upon the system to market their apples, knowing it is the same system that obliges their apples to compete with those brought to New England from worldwide sources, including apples grown under government subsidies from Washington State and New Zealand and China. Eccardt Farm milk too, when it leaves the premises, enters the liquid embrace of a two-billion-dollar-a-year milk conglomerate that markets milk products under a dozen brand names, belonging to its once lively but now cannibalized competition. The Bascoms also completely depend upon the system for nationwide retail chains and other worldwide wholesale avenues to market their syrup and sugar. It may be ironic that, of these four, the Bascoms' maple operation, just because it is the most completely integrated into the larger system, has the most leverage in negotiating the price of its products and, as it happens, is also the farm most comfortable with its positioning in both worlds: though it lives and breathes in a world of agribusiness, the Bascoms' maple enterprise is also securely tied to the farm's ancestral acreage with ten thousand individual tap lines.

On these family farms themselves, as on so many others all across the country, no clean line can be drawn, except abstractly, between System and Resistance; for the farmers live and move and farm in both worlds. Thus for most family farmers it would be an indulgence they could hardly afford to see themselves as resisting Davids doing battle with a giant Goliath. Because they cannot survive by selling milk, eggs, maple syrup, and apples locally, they are swept into the enveloping agribusiness system, even as they would resist its embraces in a variety of ways, including their family-size scale. It is but one of their many challenges to find ways to be viable while they remain commodity farms and remain small enough to continue as family farms. Only rarely, perhaps, in reflective moments or in intense times of triumph or disaster, would they see themselves as also ambiguously engaged in a larger struggle for the soul of agriculture. But so they are. So, in effect, are we all.

# Notes

Sources listed here document quotations of two lines or more in the text.

1. Henry David Thoreau, "The Bean-Field," in *Walden; or, Life in the Woods* (Boston: Ticknor and Fields, 1854). There are many editions; my citations will be by chapter title.

2. Verrazano and Champlain quoted in Howard S. Russell, *A Long Deep Furrow* (Hanover, N.H.: University Press of New England, 1976), pp. 9, 5. See G. P. Winship, ed., *Sailors' Narratives of Voyages along the New England Coast, 1524–1624* (Boston, 1905).

3. Richard Hakluyt, "Discourse Concerning Western Planting," quoted in David S. Muzzey, *Readings in American History* (Boston: Ginn and Company, 1915), p. 22.

4. Quoted in Samuel Eliot Morison, *Builders of the Bay Colony* (Boston: Houghton Mifflin, 1930), p. 10.

5. Alan Taylor, *American Colonies* (New York: Penguin Putnam, 2001), p. 130, and chapter 6, passim.

6. William Bradford, *Of Plymouth Plantation*, written between 1630 and 1650, and published since 1856 in many editions, chapter IX. I follow an edition that retains the original spelling, and citations are by chapter.

7. Ibid., chapter XI.

8. Ibid., chapter XV.

9. "Letter of Thomas Dudley to Bridget, Countess of Lincoln," reprinted in John A. Scott, ed., *Living Documents in American History* (New York: Washington Square Press, 1964), pp. 39–54, passim.

10. Jacob Van Hinte, *Netherlanders in America* (Grand Rapids, Mich.: Baker Book House, 1985), chapter 1, passim.

11. Walter Ebeling, *The Fruited Plain* (Berkeley: University of California Press, 1979), pp. 74–75.

12. Cicero, "The Joys of Farming," *On Old Age*, in *Cicero: Selected Works*, tr. Michael Grant (Harmondsworth, England: Penguin Books, 1960), pp. 233–34, 236.

13. Thomas Jefferson, *Notes on the State of Virginia*, 1785 (New York: Harper Torchbook, 1964), p. 157.

14. Thomas Jefferson, Letter to John Jay, 1785, in *The Life and Selected Writings of Thomas Jefferson* (New York: The Modern Library, 1944), p. 377. See also Carl J. Richard, *The Founders and the Classics* (Cambridge, Mass.: Harvard University Press, 1994).

15. J. Hector St. John de Crèvecoeur, *Letters from an American Farmer*, 1782 (Harmondsworth, England: Penguin Books, 1986), Letter II, p. 54.

16. Ibid., Letter I, p. 43.

17. Ibid., Letter II, p. 65.

18. Ibid., Letter II, pp. 89–90.

19. Daniel Webster, *Report of the Agricultural Meeting, Held in Boston, January 13, 1840* (Salem, Mass.: Salem Power Press, 1840), p. 29.

20. Thoreau, "Economy," in *Walden*.

21. Ibid., "The Bean-Field."

22. H. D. Thoreau, "Chesuncook," in *The Maine Woods* (New York: Thomas Crowell Company, 1961), p. 203.

23. Odell Shepard, ed., *The Heart of Thoreau's Journals* (New York: Dover Publications, 1961), p. 125.

24. Ibid., p. 81.

25. Ibid. pp., 187–88.

26. The speech was published under the title "Farming" as a chapter in Emerson's *Society and Solitude*. This and subsequent quotations are from the essay as it appears in Brooks Atkinson, ed., *The Complete Works of Ralph Waldo Emerson* (New York: The Modern Library, 1940), pp. 749–58, passim.

27. Ronald Jager, *Eighty Acres: Elegy for a Family Farm* (Boston: Beacon Press, 1990), pp. 13–14.

28. Ibid., p. 16.

29. Ibid., p. 14.

30. John Gerarde, *The Herball; or, Generall Historie of Plantes*, 1597, quoted in Betty Fussell, *The Story of Corn* (New York: North Point Press, 1992), p. 19.

31. Quoted in Harold Fisher Wilson, *The Hill Country of Northern New England* (New York: Columbia University Press, 1936), p. 16.

32. Quoted ibid., p. 19.

33. Levi Bartlett (of Warner, N.H.), *First Annual Report of the New Hampshire Board of Agriculture* (Nashua: New Hampshire State Printer, 1871), p. 316.

34. Kate Sanborn, *Abandoning an Adopted Farm* (New York: D. Appleton and Company, 1894), p. 72.

35. New England Agriculture Statistics Service (Concord, N.H.), a field office

of the National Agriculture Statistics Service. (Source of many of the annual statistics in this book.)

36. Louis Bromfield, *Pleasant Valley* (New York: Harper & Row, 1945), p. 54.

37. Louis Bromfield, *Malabar Farm* (New York: Harper & Row, 1947), p. 4.

38. Ibid., pp. 4–5.

39. Louis Bromfield, *From My Experience* (New York: Harper & Row, Publishers, 1955), p. 231.

40. Victor Davis Hanson, *Fields without Dreams* (New York: Free Press Paperbacks, 1997), p. xi.

41. Ibid., p. 268.

42. Ibid., p. 269.

43. Ibid.

44. Ibid., p. 270.

45. Victor Davis Hanson, *The Land Was Everything* (New York: The Free Press, 2000), p. 1.

46. Ibid., p. 251.

47. Ibid., p. 252.

48. Hanson, *Fields*, p. 271.

49. Ibid.

50. Wendell Berry, *Clearing* (New York: Harcourt Brace Jovanich, 1977), p. 5. Unless otherwise noted, quotations on the next several pages are all from this book.

51. Wendell Berry, *The Unsettling of America* (New York: Avon Books, 1978), pp. 54–55.

52. Ibid., p. 43.

53. Wendell Berry, *A Timbered Choir* (Washington, D.C.: Counterpoint, 1998), p. 7.

54. Eric T. Freyfogle, ed., *The New Agrarianism* (Washington, D.C.: Island Press, 2001), p. xiii.

55. James Lawrence and Rex Martin, *Sweet Maple* (Shelburne, Vt.: Chapters Publishing, 1993), p. 9.

56. Quoted ibid., p. 61.

57. Ibid., p. 91

58. Douglas Harper, *Changing Works* (Chicago: University of Chicago Press, 2001), p. 261.

59. Ibid., p. 276.

60. Ibid., p. 277.

61. Edward Sewall Guthrie, *The Book of Butter* (New York: The MacMillan Company, 1923), pp. 164–65.

62. *Northeast Farms to Food* (Belchertown, Mass.: Northeast Sustainable Agriculture Working Group, 2002), passim.

63. John Gerarde, *The Herball; or, Generall History of Plantes* (London: John

Norton, 1597), quoted in Peter Wynne, *Apples* (New York: Hawthorn Books, 1975), pp. 13–14.

64. John Josselyn, quoted in Peter Bidwell and John Falconer, *History of Agriculture in Northern United States, 1620–1860* (New York: Peter Smith, 1941), p. 16.

65. James Thacher, *The American Orchardist* (Boston: Collier, 1825), p. 14.

66. Quoted in Anne Mendelson, "The Decline of the Apple," in Eric Freyfogle, ed., *The New Agrarianism* (Washington, D.C.: Island Press, 2001), p. 117.

67. Ibid., p. 118.

68. Liberty Hyde Bailey, *The Principles of Fruit-Growing* (New York: The Macmillan Company, 1915), p. 35.

69. *Food and Agriculture Policy: Taking Stock for the New Century* (Washington, D.C.: United States Department of Agriculture, 2001), p. 31.